THE LOST CITY OF FRUITVALE MICHIGAN

Volume 1

100th Anniversary Edition

1911 - *2011*

It is with great pleasure, that on the 100th anniversary of the founding of the "City of Fruitvale Michigan," that I can offer this printing. This anniversary limited edition of the original book has the same exciting history as the first, with only changes being made to correct errors and to add color that was not available during the first printing.

William P. Hansen
Author, Historical Researcher

Author: William P. Hansen

Rochdale Publishing Company
250 Castleair Dr. NE
Kennesaw, GA 30144

signed copy # __________

TABLE OF CONTENTS

Harrison M. Parker

Lost City Of Fruitvale

"On To Fruitvale, Mich." Tent camping to house the overflow crowd.

FRUITVALE

It was in the late 1850s when in an area of virgin white pine, clear waters and peaceful Indians that the first saw mill, in what was to become Blue Lake Township, was built. The original mill was constructed by Isaac M. Norton and located in an area described as: commencing at a pine stump on the North bank of the White River, Southeast of the East Stable at the place known as Nortons Mill, then running 990 feet North, 792 feet East, by 1089 feet South, bounded to the river, thence by the river back to the first mentioned bound, being 20 acres, more or less. Isaac operated the mill for a few years before moving on into Oceana County in pursuit of the bigger trees. Purchased from the State of Michigan for back taxes on December 6, 1862, Henry L. Brown and his partner Orvis French of Milwaukee, Wisconsin, paid 17 cents an acre for 234 acres bounded by Big Blue Lake on the east, the White River on the south and Sand Creek to the west.

Logging roll-a-way on the White River near Fruitvale

With the help of his mill hands, and starting near where Fruitvale road is today, a channel was dug between Sand creek and the White River. This new creek bed allowed Henry to dam the old one which was about 200' wide with the creek in the center, and construct his mill over the new site. The dams that were constructed created a small pond on the creek and the water-powered saw mill was put into full operation. Just to the North of the mill was the house for Henry, his wife Ann and their daughter Annie, along with another house for the workers and a barn for the livestock. On October 19, 1865, Orvis French sold his 1/2 interest in the mill property to Samuel Mena of Greenwood Michigan, for the sum of $2,500 or 500,000 feet of lumber, "while reserving whatever logs would be cut in Sections 9 and 10 and the right and privilege of drawing and banking into the pond or White River all the timber he may have on Section 32 in Oceana County, Otto Township. Also reserving the use of two small houses and a barn while cutting and hauling the timber." Even though work was hard and the hours long, the land was good to Henry, until April 14, 1871 when his wife Ann died three weeks before her 50th birthday. Shortly thereafter, Henry moved near Montague and on March 27, 1873, he sold his 1/2 interest in the lands to Samuel Mena for $2,000.

Little activity occurred at the old mill site, but the area surrounding it was far from quiet. Thousands of acres of land to the North were purchased or leased by the lumber families of Staples and Covell from the Whitehall - Montague area, where their mills where located on White Lake near the mouth of the White River. To move the thousands of giant pine logs that were being cut each' winter, a narrow gauge railroad was built from Otto Township to the North, around Fogg Lake and past the old mill site, and to the rollaway on the high bank of the White River. Even today, a hundred years later, the bed of the railroad is still visible, and some of the old rail spikes, as reminders of a lost time, can still be found. Then, as in most of Michigan, when the trees were gone so were the people and the desire to "harvest" the land. What was left was a waste land of shrub trees, millions of pine stumps and brush. After a few years of drying in the hot summer sun, the pine branches and tree tops, often caught fire and burnt, destroying any thing in its path.

Next, came the farmers who tried to work the land. Faced with all of the tree stumps in their fields, it would require months of back breaking work, just to clear the land for planting. While waiting for the crops to come in, these pioneers would cut most of the remaining smaller trees on their property for extra income. Having inadequate irrigation, and no means of enriching the sandy soil, most gave up and let the land revert to the State for nonpayment of taxes.

In 1889 George F. Sibley and his wife Sadie A. Sibley purchased several hundred acres of this land in Blue Lake and Otto Township from the State for $22.82. This purchase also included the old mill site for Henry Brown and what was known as Brown's Pond, the back waters of the dam from the mill site. Even with several hundred acres of land, George's land was not the most productive for crops or cattle, so in 1902 George and Sadie sold their lands for $7600. It

wasn't until the summer of 1910 while on vacation in Western Michigan, that a young 33 year old newspaper executive from Chicago had an idea, and started purchasing property in the area. Harrison M. Parker, born July 9, 1877 in San Bernardino, California, the son of Thomas G. and Mary (Owings) Parker. Harrison married Edith Stubbs of San Francisco on October 23, 1901, and by 1910 they had two children, Harrison M. Jr. and Mary Stubbs Parker.

The first land he purchased was in Muskegon County, near where the current Waste Water System is located and also 40 acres in Muskegon Township. But setting his sight on bigger and better things, in 1911 he optioned up several thousand acres of land, including the old Sibley farm, Brown's Pond and mill property, and large tracts from the Covell holdings. Surveyors were hired, subdivisions platted, and streets named.

The whole idea was based on the ROCHDALE COOPERATIVE system, used widely in England in the 1800s. A simple principal: "The voluntary union of individuals in production and distribution, apart from government, and in which the burdens and the benefits are equitably shared and the profits and management divided among the consumers" as outlined in a Master's dissertation at the University of Chicago, by Carl D. Thompson in 1902. The first lands included the Original Town of Fruitvale, a subdivision with 2,035 lots, the Riverside Addition to Fruitvale with 2,053 lots, the Rochdale Inn and Club House on Brown's Pond, and many five acre 'Fruit and Poultry Garden' parcels. Each lot was 25' x 100' in size and fronted a street, such as Harrison Boulevard and Marydale Avenue. The surveys were accurately done, with concrete monuments set in the center of each road intersection and wooden stakes marking the comers of the individual lots. Many of the monuments that were set still can be found today and are off very little when checked with modern laser transits used by surveyors today. It should be made clear at this time that the land called 'Fruitvale' or the 'Original Town of Fruitvale,' being one and the same, consisted entirely of these small lots. There was no city planned as we may think of a city; large stores, banks, hospitals, lumber companies, etc., but when needed, these services could be obtained in Whitehall or Montague, about eight miles down stream by river or dirt road.

In October of 1911, with work rogressing smoothly with the developing of Fruitvale, Harrison and Edith started purchasing the needed property. Their first purchase, 120 acres on the White River for $1,200, was the land used for the "Original Town of Fruitvale." With partners Harry R. Gibbons and William M. Gibbons, the Fruitvale Land Development Company was formed. Next, back in Chicago a large land show, called the United States Land and Irrigation Exposition was being held at the 'Coliseum' on Wabash near 16th Street. It was an ideal place for Harrison to promote his 'City of Fruitvale,' as the ads in the Chicago Tribune proclaimed, "one free lot with each admission ticket to the Land Show, "The Greatest Exposition in Chicago Since the World's Fair." The show

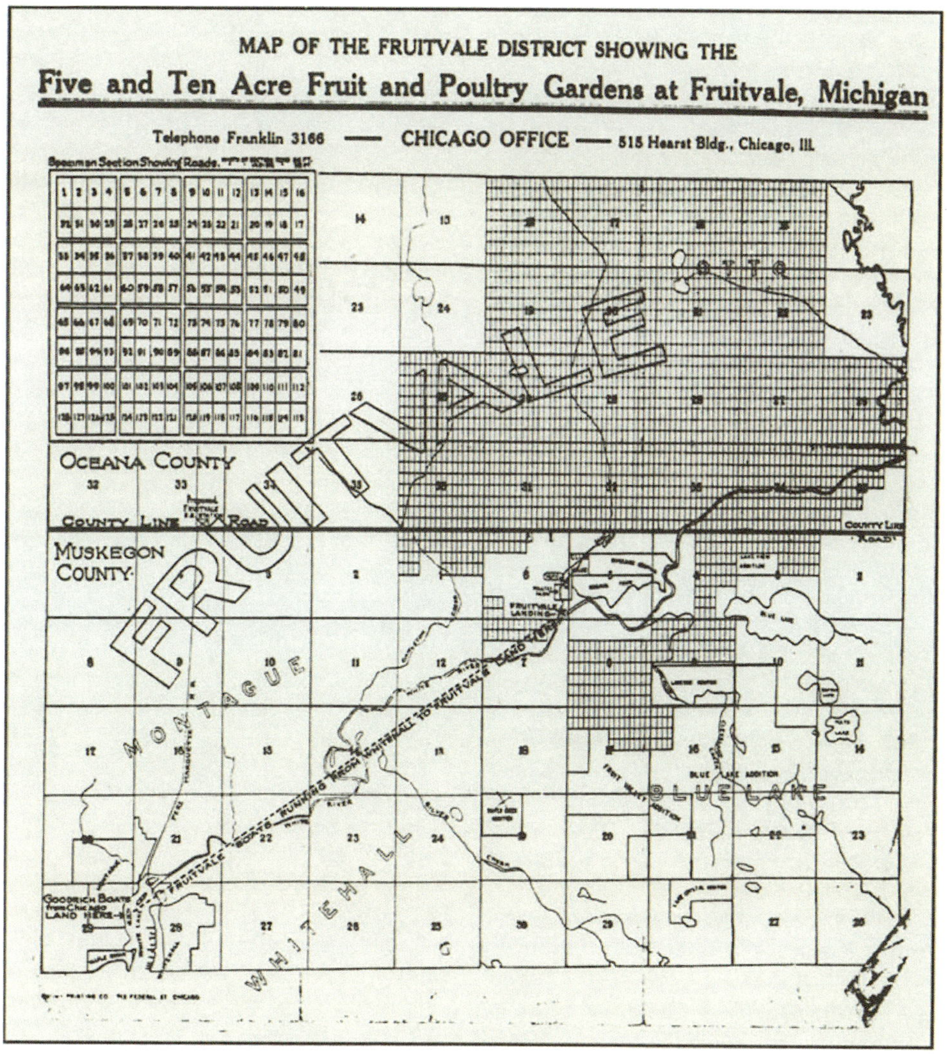

opened each morning at 11 o'clock with admission of 50 cents for adults and only 25 cents for children, "with all Moving Picture Shows FREE." But as thousands of Chicagoans stood in line for a certificate for a free lot in the beautiful City of Fruitvale, the controversy surrounding Harrison's plans were building equally as fast in Michigan and to this day, Fruitvale still appears in the news occasionally.

The following article appeared in the November 29, 1911 issue of the MICHIGAN TRADESMAN, a Grand Rapids, Michigan publication.

ANOTHER LAND SWINDLE

"The Chicago Tribune is a great newspaper - the greatest newspaper in the world, in the estimation of the Tradesman - and it is entitled to much credit for the manner in which it has planned and is conducting the Land Show open to the public in the Coliseum at Chicago. The exhibit is a remarkable one and cannot fail to result in great benefit to the country at large. Unfortunately, Michigan is not represented at the Land Show, except by a small but very interesting and attractive exhibit from the Upper Peninsula. While the Lower Peninsula is not represented in a creditable way, it is represented in a very discreditable way by a gang of swindlers who claim to own the "City" is represented to be located on White River, in Muskegon County, and every person who attends the Show is handed a certificate entitling him to a lot in the "City of Fruitvale'" on payment of $3 for recording the deed and securing the abstract. Herein is the milk in the coconut. The undertaking to build on at a summer resort where land is cheap and air and sunshine are the chief essentials. The $2 which purports to pay for the abstract is practically all profit, because the abstracts can be printed in quantities at a cost of a fraction of a cent. The Tradesman has no means of knowing how much of the land is devoted to streets and parks, but it looks as though the schemers would get about fifteen lots out of an acre of land. The land probably cost them $1 an acre-perhaps only a few cents an acre-and they are selling it out to the gullible people who visit the Land Show at the rate of about $45 an acre.

The whole scheme bears the impress of fraud because Fruitvale is represented to be a city, whereas there is no city by that name in Muskegon County - not even an incorporated village. It looks very much like some of the swindles that have been worked on the public around Houghton Lake and Higgins Lake and the Tradesman will be very much mistaken

if any purchaser of a free lot at $3 per is ever able to obtain his money back. The worst feature of the affair is that these lots will, undoubtedly, all be sold for taxes, which will cost the State of Michigan forty cents a description for seven consecutive years. Such being the case, the cost to the State of selling these lots for taxes from the year to year until the State acquires a title, will be from $10,000 to $20,000. Appearances indicate that thousands of people are availing themselves of this "great offer" to acquire a free lot in the "City of Fruitvale." At the office on Wabash Avenue, where the certificates are being exchanged for cash and a receipt for $3, hundreds are in line and a glance at their faces leads to the thought that if they were offered a free lot on Mars or a free seat in Heaven, they would be just as greedy to avail themselves of the opportunity. The Tradesman is very much surprised that a paper of the character and standing of the Chicago Tribune should permit such an arrant swindle to be worked in connection with a worthy enterprise.

Undaunted, Harrison fights back with a $100,000 Libel suit against the editor of the Tradesman, E. A. Stowe, while Clifford S. Gamble, the surveyor for the 'Plat of Fruitvale' and former Muskegon County surveyor is reported in the local paper as saying, "I personally have been over every foot of the land laid out for Fruitvale," he said, "and there is no more beautiful spot in the state. Instead of it being a sand dune, the trees and shrubbery at Fruitvale are so dense as to interfere with and delay the surveying. "The entire town site was laid out, surveyed, and staked in compliance with the laws of Michigan, the plats were filed" with and approved by the auditor general of the state, and are recorded in the court house at Muskegon."

Since the opening of the exposition at the Coliseum 13,000 lots in Fruitvale have been placed at the disposal of the patrons of the land show. Certificates have been given to every visitor at the Coliseum. On payment of a fee of $3, for recording and the purchasing of an abstract of title, the holder is entitled to one lot 25 x 100 feet in Fruitvale. The Michigan publisher attacked the scheme, which was started for the purpose of stimulating attendance at the show, and the suit was the result."

SAYS SUIT WILL BE PUSHED

"The suit will be pushed to the finish," asserts William Gibbons, treasurer of the exposition, "Before the United States Land and Irrigation exposition accepted the Fruitvale lots for distribution at the show, we investigated the proposition thoroughly. The directors personally visited the property and found it lay on both sides of the White River, seven miles from Whitehall. It is beautifully situated, and in the surveying not a lot was staked that is not on high ground, removed from all danger of overflow." State and county officials in Michigan are now criticizing the venture. The Auditor General of Michigan says "Fruitvale" was extensively advertised at the Chicago land show. Pamphlets, describing in glowing words the beauty of Blue Lake and the Fruitvale district, were circulated. Hundreds eagerly accepted the offer of a free lot in Fruitvale. Auditor General Fuller is frank in his condemnation of the scheme because in his opinion within a year or so the buyers of these "abstracts" will begin to cease paying the taxes and the descriptions will commence to come in with the delinquent tax lists. That is where the expense for the state starts. It cost 40 cents for every advertisement of every description and there is an endless chain of expenses until the land is finally deeded to the land department where it is placed on the market and may be put through the same course again."

As we look back, apparently most people did not know who the officers of the Fruitvale Company were. This article stated that William Gibbons, from the land show, had checked and approved the Fruitvale development and its properties, but as noted earlier, he was also an officer of the Fruitvale Company.

Most of the opposition to Fruitvale was coming from people outside of the immediate area. State officials, county commissioners, newspapers, and a variety of trade journals. But, back in Blue Lake Township, and the nearby cities of Whitehall and Montague, the feelings were different. The local communities had experienced a loss of income and people since the forests were stripped of trees, and were thus eager for local development and dollars. In support of the project, a banquet was given by local businessmen .

"A banquet was given at the Mears Hotel last Tuesday evening by the Whitehall Board of Trade in honor of Harrison Parker, H. R. and W. M. Gibbons, promoters of the famous Fruitvale tract of lands eight miles northeast of this Village. A large number of Montague businessmen were invited and present. A delicious chicken dinner was served in the spacious and beautifully decorated dining room of the hotel. T. B. Widoe , village president, acted as toastmaster and those called upon responded with booster speeches. Mr. Parker was the first one to speak and his remarks were liberally applauded. He gave a brief history of his Fruitvale project which was listened to with great interest. He said he was a newspaper man and by hard work and perseverance managed to accumulate a little money. In looking around for a safe investment, he said, on a visit to White Lake, he hit upon the idea of investing in the lands now known as Fruitvale. He expressed great confidence in the future

of Fruitvale as he said it would soon be a city of 40,000 people, 18,000 lots having already been sold. As he lived in California 21 years he asserted that the Fruitvale lands were just as good as the greatly advertised and much exaggerated California lands. He laid special stress upon the damage and loss Michigan, and especially White Lake people, had sustained by chronic knocking. The west, he said, were deluding us to stop knocking' but boost along the same lines. The western lands, he said, selling up to as high as $1000 are not a bit better than the fertile soils around White Lake. His straight from the shoulder talk made those present sit up and take notice and at the close of the banquet every one present pledged himself to be a loyal booster. Mr. Parker said there would be about 40,000 people over from Chicago next summer.

Other out of town guests present were D. M. Cockrane and H. W. Thorpe, officials of the Goodrich Transit Company, State Senator John Vanderwerp of Muskegon and Clarence McConnell, president of the Eagle Tannery Works."

CITY OF FRUITVALE

"Chicago capitalists, who are expanding Fruitvale, are preparing to go into the matter still deeper and plans are being made for a power dam on the White River and an electric railway to run from Fremont to Whitehall.

About 40,000 lots have been given in connection with the Chicago land show, and there are about 4,000 acres still to be platted.

Seven surveying parties will reach Muskegon some time this week to begin the work of laying out the unplatted land. There are about 14,000 acres altogether to be handled. Five thousand acres will be cut up into lots and the remainder will be cut up into five and ten acre farms.

The project which has been started for a dam to supply power for an interurban line, is well underway, it is said, it being the plan to select a site on the river where a 50-foot dam might be built.

While in Chicago the other day Mr. John S. Walker met the gentlemen who are interested in the Fruitvale project and received assurances from them which caused them to sit up and take notice. They said:

"Fruitvale will be a good sized city in two years. We have the money to put the project through and we intend to do it. Included in the enterprise now is a water power proposition which means that we shall develop it for power purposes. Our city will thus have power and lights, together with a water works system second to none.

Of course we shall need transportation facilities and we propose to build an electric railway to give us communication with the outside world. Ultimately this may run to Muskegon and may develop into quite a system. "One thing is certain. We shall make a thriving city at Fruitvale and those who are now doubting Thomases will be obliged to "see the cat" whether they will or not."

As the Land Show continues, more land is purchased for the City, 687 acres from Mary H. Wickes and Caroline Wickes, both unmarried and living in Los Angles, California, for a sum of $957.36 in gold coin, or $1.39 per acre. The next purchase was report in the paper as follows:

BIG DEAL Is CLOSED

Harrison M. Parker, secretary and treasurer of the Fruitvale Land Development Company, was in the county last week to close the deal concerning the land which he had recently secured by option from C. E. & M. B. Covell. The deal was a big one and he turned over a check for $22,528.45 for his deed of the property. (This purchase was for 2878 acres at a cost of $7.83 per acre.) Mr. Parker is very enthusiastic over

River Side Inn, Fruit Vale, Mich.

River Side Inn; Fruit Vale, Mich. Earliest known picture of the Riverside Inn (Rochdale Inn) while under construction in 1911 .

View of the Riverside Inn (L) and the Annex (R) taken from Harrison (Fruitvale) Road.

the prospects of this venture and is sparing neither time, expense nor effort to make this proposition go. He appeared before tile Muskegon Chamber of Commerce and endeavored to show them the advantage of boosting rather than scoring the undertaking. The newest phase of the lot distribution is that several large Chicago firms like Montgomery Ward & Co., have arranged for parcels of land where a colony of their employees can find a good healthy outing place at the lowest cost. Twenty thousand people is the number Mr. Parker says he hopes will be brought to this county in this way. They will either build summer homes on the lots they have acquired, he declares, or buy farms. This latter is the ultimate aim of the Fruitvale Land Development Company - to get people to buy these five and ten acre tracts and thus develop the country, he says. "The only trouble with the country north of Muskegon, " declares Mr. Parker, "is that it never had people. All this country north of Muskegon and to Fruitvale is good. All it needs is to be worked right and it will produce good crops. We are just beginning our development. We gave away 20,000 lots to people. It is a mistaken idea that the lots were only 25 by 100 feet. People who wanted lots 100 feet square got them (four lots together). The lots are all on or near White River or on Big Blue Lake. They were given away for these people to build their summer homes. It marks the beginning of the development of this country. The land we just paid for is in sections 4, 5, 6 and partly in 7, 8 and 9 in the northwestern part of Blue Lake township, between Big Blue Lake and White River. We also own about 4,000 acres in the southern part of Oceana County. Most of it is in Otto township. We expect to own about 14,000 acres altogether, which we will split up into small farms. Michigan is the most knocked state in the union. The big Western Railroads paid men to be at the land show and say that all of Western Michigan was one long stretch of sand dunes. We are getting the people to disbelieve this. We are getting them acquainted with Muskegon County. We want them to come here and look, and get a good impression when they get here. We want the people here to boost. I have received over 1,000 letters already since the land show from people who acquired lots and who want to know where they can buy lumber to erect bungalows and summer homes. Doesn't that mean something for this county? We are for the proposed trolley line north. We are going to spend money to get good roads into that country and want the board of county road commissioners to work with us."

1912

It was the hope of the promoters of Fruitvale, that with a new year, the controversy over the land development would cease, but this would not be the case. The Muskegon County Board of Commissioners continued their assault on the 'City' and those connected with it. In the forefront leading the crusade were Supervisors Thomas J. G. Bolt and Lee H. Trott. It was their feeling that the citizens of Chicago would look unfavorably towards Western Michigan with its land swindlers, and that when they discovered the reported worthlessness of their lots, the property would revert back to the state for back taxes, costing not only the State, but the County of Muskegon and Blue Lake Township thousands of dollars.

Fruitvale Land Exploitation May Bankrupt Townships
Countless Dupes of Chicago Promoters
Protest Loudly At Swindle

River Side Inn as opened in the spring of 1912.

Hurts Whole County

Thousands of Dollars Paid By Hundreds Who Find They Have Bought Land Useless For Any Purpose...

"THROUGH THE ACTION OF THE FRUITVALE LAND COMPANY IN SELLING THOUSANDS OF WORTHLESS LOTS TO GULLIBLE PEOPLE OF THE WEST, THE LATTER ARE NOT ONLY OUT THOUSANDS OF DOLLARS, BUT THE STATE OF MICHIGAN, MUSKEGON COUNTY AND THE TOWNSHIPS IN WHICH THE PROPERTY IS LOCATED, WILL PROBABLY BE OUT THOUSANDS OF DOLLARS ALSO. IN FACT, IT IS PREDICTED BY COUNTY OFFICIALS CONVERSANT WITH THE CONDITION'S, THAT THERE IS A STRONG POSSIBILITY THAT THE TOWNSHIP IN WHICH THE LAND IS LOCATED, MAY EVENTUALLY BECOME BANKRUPT THROUGH THE GIGANTIC LOT SALE WHICH IS NOW CAUSING PROTEST FROM COUNTLESS DUPES WHO WERE GULLED INTO PURCHASING PROPERTY IN THE MUCH ADVERTISED RESORT."

The United States Land and Irrigation Company, whether willingly or innocently, caused many persons to invest in the Fruitvale proposition and the scandal which has resulted from the gigantic boom may result in the wrecking of that Chicago institution.

Those incorporating the Fruitvale Land Company are three Chicago men, Harrison M. Parker William M. Gibbons and Harry R. Gibbons. The articles of Association show that they capitalized for $6,000 and paid that amount in.

Obtained Worthless Land.

The company then secured several thousand acres of worthless land a few miles from Whitehall and proceeded to do business. Obtaining quarters, at the United States Land and Irrigation Exposition, when the latter held forth at Chicago last fall, the corporation controlling such a vast amount of Muskegon county sandhill property advertised extensively in Chicago papers. Their advertisements were coached in the most alluring language of a past master in the art of land booming. It was set forth in the most glowing manner that the Fruitvale lots were ideal plats for summer cottages, easily accessible from Chicago. If disposed of in consecutive numbers, communications from protesting purchasers that have poured into the office of County Clerk Barlow showing that over 10,000 have already been sold. Complaint is now being made that the buyers have been unable to get their deeds.

Fruitvale Waste Land.

Instead of being an ideal location for a summer resort, Fruitvale is declared to be nothing but a lot of waste sandhills, adorned by a shrub growth of timber. The only way to get water there is by carrying it. At the present time, there are no summer cottages there and the indications are that there never will be. No interurban or other railway line runs to Fruitvale. The only way of reaching it is through heavy sand roads which would spoil an automobile and ruin the temper of any individual who erroneously attempted the trip for pleasure. Whitehall and Montague are several long, deep and weary miles away. Led by the tempting offer of the Fruitvale Company, which made many of them believe that it was part of the United States Land and Irrigation Company, the thousands of purchasers of lots have never seen their property. In fact the major portion of it is still unplatted, although it is said that this will be done, for the purpose of complying with the law.

May Be Fraud

Should the land be all platted, and abstracts and warranty deeds be furnished purchasers, selling company will be within the pale of the law, so far as that part of the booming scheme is concerned. Whether the advertisements can be construed as a fraud for which the promoters may be criminally liable, is a question for the Illinois authorities to wrestle with. Even though the actions of the Fruitvale Company are within the law, the fact remains the purchasers have been induced to part with their money for lots which are of no value to them. There is also the strong probability that many, if not all of the lots will eventually be sold for the non-payment of taxes.

Costly to State. If this is done, the advertisement of the sale of each of the many thousands of lots will cost the state forth cents. Should the tax roll containing them, through any mistake in the description, such as frequently happens, be rejected, they would be turned back to the county. In this event, each lot description would cost the county a dollar. This would eventually be charged against the Township in which the property is located. It is thus possible that the latter will finally face bills aggregating thousands of dollars, and which probably will bankrupt them, if they were compelled to liquidate. "Not only have investors been stung to the extent of thousands of dollars," said a prominent county official yesterday, but it is extremely probable that the state, county and townships will also suffer thousands of dollars through the sale of these worthless lots by the Chicago land boomers. "Besides costing the community a vast amount in that way, the black eye which this part of the state will receive as a result of this scheme, will cost us an inestimable loss. People who have been defrauded will hold the impression that the entire county is as worthless as the property they have been induced to purchase, and it will take years to overcome this impression. Practically all of the thousands of people who have been inveigled into purchasing lots, are residents of the west who went to Chicago to attend the United States Land and Irrigation Exposition. None of them reside in West Michigan.

$100,000 Paid. It is estimated by the American Real Estate Advisor, a Chicago real estate publication, that 28,000 lots have been sold, and that fully $100,000 has been secured from purchasers. It states that the promoters of the United States Land and Irrigation Exposition are taking steps to prevent it from being used in the future by land boomers to exploit their fake lot schemes for the purpose of defrauding a gullible public. Fearful lest the exposure of the manner in which the public were led into investing in Fruitvale sand hills, should wreck it, the Secretary of the United States Land and Irrigation Company was recently here for the purpose of ascertaining the value of the Fruitvale lots.

He was frankly told that they were no good for summer resort or any other purpose, and that the property was probably not worth anymore, if as much per acre, is each lot has been sold for.

Supervisors Trott and Bolt Active in Placing True Conditions Before Officials.

GIVES COUNTY A BAD NAME

Lakewood, Fruitvale and Other Schemes Similar to Higgins Lake Imposition; Illegality Suspected in Operations of Boomers Who Have Duped Public.

Unless prompt action is taken by the legislature to prevent it, grafting land boomers will soon be exploiting fake summer resorts, and over half of the counties in the state, similar to the scheme of the Fruitvale fraud which was exposed in the Times yesterday. The foregoing declaration was made by Chairman, Tom Bolt, and Lee Trott, of the board of supervisors last night. Those two officials have already had conferences with Gov. Osborn, Auditor General Fuller and Sen. Vanderwerp on the matter, and were the investigators of the bill now pending before the legislature to put a curb on such schemes in the future. Supervisor Trott is the official who first commenced the investigation of the summer resort lot frauds. He was promptly joined by Chairman Bolt, and they are now waging a vigorous campaign to put a stop to the evil which has already caused gullible purchasers in other states to lose thousands of dollars.

Discussed by Supervisors. At the last session of the state association of supervisors, the fraudulent practices of the land sharks were forcibly brought to the attention of the delegates. It was shown that worthless lands had been subdivided and sold to victims, not only Muskegon County, and in other communities as well. The notorious Higgins Lake scheme was exposed, and other nefarious transactions in which hundreds of people were victimized, were brought to light. With prompt action the state association of supervisors passed a resolution introduced by supervisor Trott, referring the matter to the executive committee and recommending that the later body confer with the governor, supervisors Bolt and Trott decided upon a bill such as the one introduced by Sen. Vanderwerp yesterday, and asked the later member of the legislature to take charge of it. Under the existing law, any township plat outside of an incorporated village can be approved by the supervisor for that district. Should the Vanderwerp bill go through, the approval of the entire board of supervisors will be necessary before such a subdivision can become legal.

Present Method Wrong.

"Not only can people be defrauded under the present method of approving plats, they have been to the extent of hundreds of thousands of dollars," said supervisor Bolt last night. These schemes, although in their infancy, have already been worked in many places an unless promptly stopped, 50 out of the 83 counties of the state are liable to suffer from the effects of them. Every fake summer resort lot sale is not only a fraud upon the purchasers, but the state, counties and townships where the lands are located, will also suffer great financial losses through the cost attended upon the delinquent tax sales where no buyers can be found for the land offered for purchase under such proceedings. There is no finer summer resort locality anywhere than to be found in Muskegon County. Every sale of a fake lot gives the reputation this locality was received, as a summer residence place, a black eye. The entire western and northern part of the state should unite in the effort to efficiently stop these schemes. Plat over 17,153. Figures secured from the record by supervisor Trott showed that within the past few months, a total of 1753 acres have been platted a Muskegon county. Approximately, 17,153 summer resort lots have been thereby created. Of this latter number, only a small fraction of over 2,000 are included in the thousands of lots sold by the Fruitvale Land Company. It is estimated that the latter concern has disposed of somewhere in the neighborhood of 30,000 lots. Everyone of this number sold, or the number already platted, is declared by supervisor Bolt to be absolutely illegal. "Practically all of this land is sandy," said Supervisor Trott, "with proper treatment and cultivated under scientific methods, it could undoubtedly be made productive. No man should undertake to farm it unless he has capital enough to carry him for two or three years. Worth $3 an acre. Placing it at the maximum figure I should say that three dollars an acre is

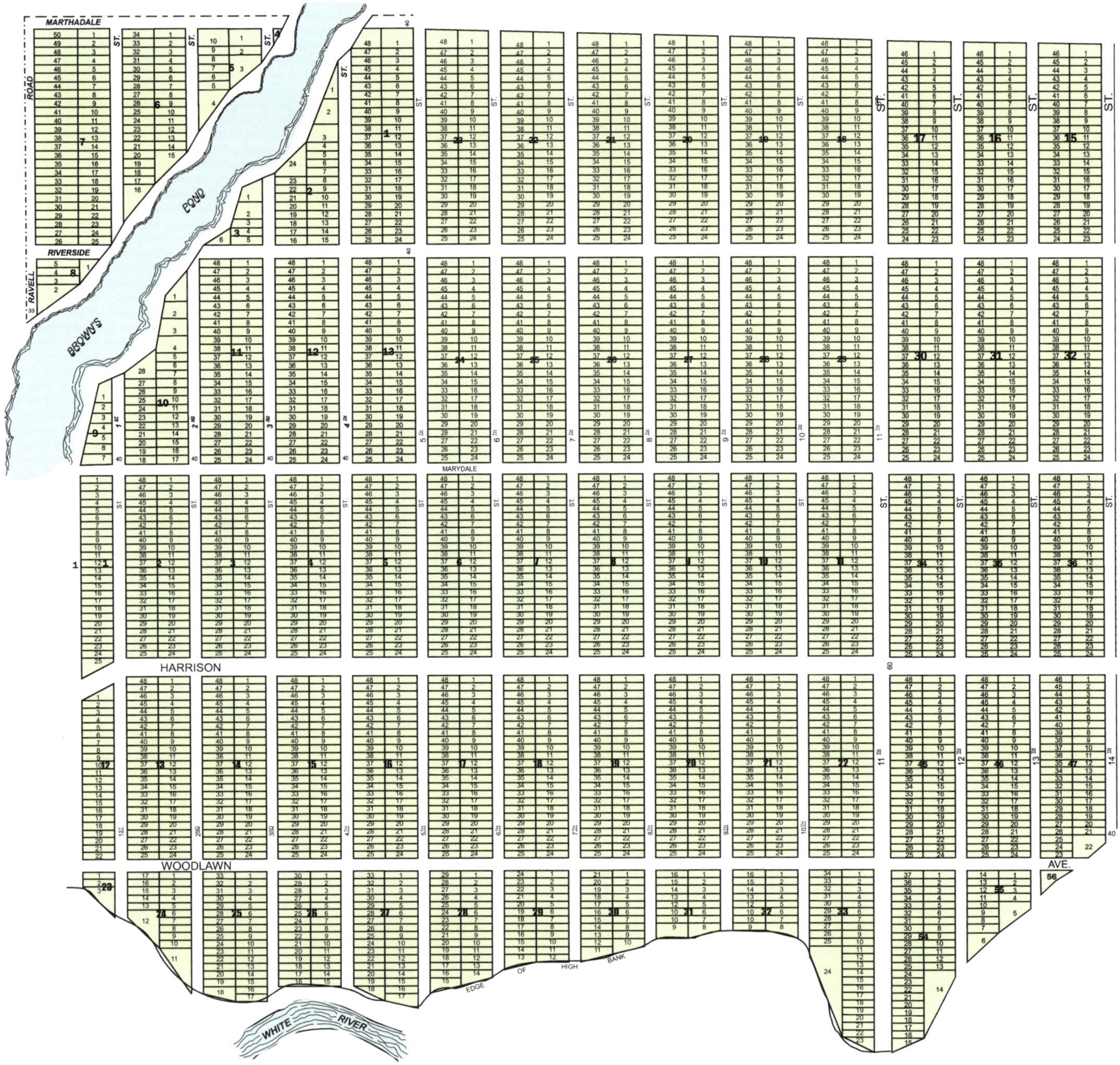
MARTHADALE
RIVERSIDE
RAVELL
ROAD
BROWN'S
POND
MARYDALE
HARRISON
WOODLAWN
AVE.
EDGE OF HIGH BANK
WHITE RIVER

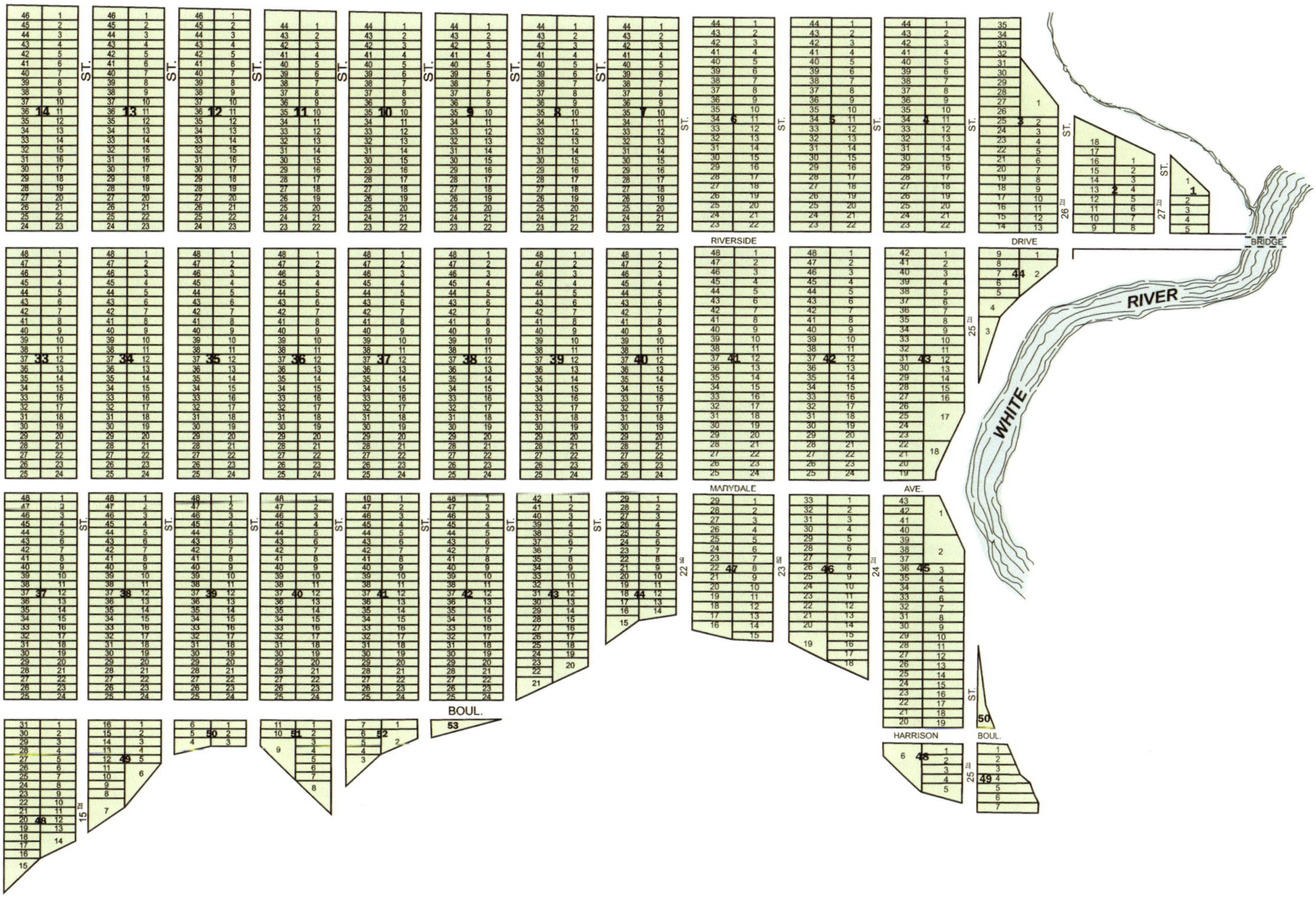

PLAT

OF THE ORIGINAL TOWN OF

FRUITVALE

COUNTY CLUB ADDITION AND

RIVERSIDE ADDITION

ALL IN

MUSKEGON COUNTY - MICHIGAN

all the land is worth. It has been subdivided on an average, into fourteen lots to the acre. For summer resort purposes, it is valueless." "Practically all of the subdivided land is without water frontage," said Supervisor Bolt." It is composed principally of sand hills on which scrub timber grows, and for summer resort purposes it is no good. The sale of it for such purposes is a fraud upon the purchaser, and a black eye to the good name of Muskegon County as a summer resort." The effort to stop such lot sales is meeting with strong endorsement of Auditor General Fuller, as well as Gov. Osborn.

The Fruitvale Land Development Company continued with the platting of additional lands as part of their holdings, in the beginning of 1912. Adding to the plats of Fruitvale and Riverside, where the Lakeview Addition to Fruitvale - 881 lots, Silver Creek Addition to Fruitvale - 2,202 lots, Lake Crystal Addition to Fruitvale - 1,732 lots, Lakeside Addition to Fruitvale - 2,765 lots, Blue Lake Addition to Fruitvale - 21,027 lots, Fruit Valley Addition to Fruitvale - 9,326 lots, and the Countryside Addition, (latter changed to the Country Club Addition) - 351 lots. The total of the eight subdivisions was spread over an area greater than 2,400 acres, with more than 33,000, 25' x 100' lots."

Just how many people came to the land show to obtained a lot in Fruitvale may never be known. The only clue that we have today is located in a basement vault of the Muskegon County Register of Deeds in Muskegon. Within this seldom used room, contains county records dating back to 1856, and of great importance to this research, the Fruitvale books. As deeds are received at the registers office for recording, copies are made and placed into books called Libers. Due to the huge amount of Fruitvale deeds from the land show, and for the only time in county history, special books were created just for Fruitvale. All of the books were called Liber 158 and comprised 34 volumes. From the numbering sequence used in recording the deeds, a total of 33,696 where recorded using the date of May 17, 1912. The index to these Libers in itself is quite large, and thus it is beyond the scope of this research to list the original land owners in Fruitvale. But due to the reports as to how the lots where given out, I will list the first 18 recorded owners and their lots obtained.

THE FIRST LOT OWNERS IN FRUITVALE

Name	Block	Lot	
Josephine Baring	45	34	Riverside Addition
William J. Rinehart	48	6	"
Anna R. Guthman	45	38	"
Sol A. Guthman	45	37	"
Arthur Charles Rinehart	48	1	"
Clara M. Knight	45	36	"
Bertha Guthman	48	35	"
Edwin I. Guthman	45	34	"
Francis G. Bloom	45	33	"
H. M. Bloom	45	32	"
Mildred I. Bloom	45	31	"
Dorothy H. Bloom (H. M. Bloom Guardian)	45	30	"
Mary Neil Kruger	45	24	"
Henry M. Kruger	45	28	"
Wm. Conner Kruger	45	27	"
Neil Lowe Kruger	45	25	"
George Wm. Brady	45	20 & 21	"
Henry Fischer	390	4&5	Blue Lake Addition

As was told in all of the news articles, and by Harrison, each person attending the land show was entitled to one free lot in the City of Fruitvale. For reasons unknown, other than perhaps as close friends, there were a few people who received more than one lot. The eight people listed below not only received one or more full blocks (50 lots), but these where often the closest to the Rochdale Inn and the pond, or nearer to the White River.

Original Town of Fruitvale

Name:	Block	Date
Henry Mackeben	47& 56	8 April
Ernst W. Reuber	13	17 April
Alfred Charbonnean	50	17 April
George Maier	12	23 April
A. J. Schmid	1 & 23	23 April
John & Joseph Schmid	2	23 April
Anna Pool	3	25 April

Riverside Addition

Name:	Block	Date
Gertrude Gane	1 & 2	29 April

VERY TAXING

As is the case today, when a deed is recorded the new owner will receive all further tax bills. In the case of Fruitvale, much criticism was received by Harrison and Fruitvale's tax collecting method. As the above deeds were recorded, none of them contained any owner's addresses. All property taxes were paid by Fruitvale. This would seem like a good deal for the county, as they would save a large amount of money in administrative cost for the collection of these taxes. But again, not everyone agreed with Fruitvale's method and fees received. For example, in 1916 the plat of Silver Creek Addition contained 2,202 lots and comprised 160 acres. For that year, Muskegon County set the True Cash Value of the 160 acres at $800, with the total property tax of $21.72. During this time, Fruitvale assessed each lot owner 10¢ per lot for their share of the tax bill. Computing this out, Fruitvale paid .000986 cents per lot in taxes, figuring in the land used for roads that they also paid tax on. If paying the same tax amount on all lots, their tax would be $325.80, while they collected $3,303. One must consider though, that Fruitvale needed to send out reminders each year, and pay the full tax whether or not the individual lot owners paid their bills. After about a year, the fervor died down and the practice continued to some extent into the 1950s. The Fruitvale Improvement Club was later setup to handle the tax collecting procedure, and as taxes increased, bills for "dues" based on "12 months at 5¢ per month or .60¢ with a cash discount of 10¢ were mailed out. From" these 'dues' collected, the taxes were paid by the Club.

Fruitvale Is Big Swindle
That is the Opinion of Supervisors Bolt and Trott, Special Committee.
Promoters Working Tax Dodge Which In Itself Will Yield the Promoters Several Thousand Per Cent Profit.

(Special to The Times)

Declaring that the Fruitvale summer resort scheme in Blue Lake Township is the most gigantic land booming fraud ever perpetrated in West Michigan, Supervisors Lee Trott and Tom Bolt, of the special investigating committee, stated last evening that they would probably call a special meeting of the board of supervisors for the purpose of devising ways to stop the deal. Not only have the Chicago land boomers who engineered the scheme sold about 35,000 lots, most of which are utterly worthless for summer resort purposes, to gullible people at $3 apiece, but also they are said to have originated a supplemental scheme through which they are mulcting each purchaser out of fifty cents additional on every lot disposed of. This is done, it is asserted, through a tax scheme. The property embraced in the big summer resort deal is assessed as acreage. The assessment, which amounts to about ten cents an acre is paid by the promoters. They have levied an assessment of sixty cents on each lot sold, with a discount of ten cents to those who pay within a month.

<u>Getting Easy Money</u>. Each acre has been subdivided into 16 lots. To pay the taxes on these, the boomers assess the purchasers an aggregate of at least $8. After paying the real tax, which amounts to ten cents, they have $7.90 left. As the property originally cost them but $8 an acre, this levy against the lot purchasers almost pays the original purchase price. In addition to learning this, the investigating committee of the board of supervisors ascertained yesterday that the original plat had never been approved at a meeting of the township board of Blue Lake. Instead, each member of that body signed it, and no record of the transaction was ever made by O. E. Yeoman, the clerk. Several additional plats which have been recorded were never submitted to the township at all for approval, according to the statements of Supervisor Aaron Baker and Clerk Yeoman, of Blue Lake. These facts will be laid before Prosecuting Attorney Alex Sutherland by Supervisors Trott and Bolt.

<u>Ignorant of Plats.</u>

"I signed the original plat last fall," said Clerk Baker yesterday. "Since then, I have not seen the promoters, and have not looked at the additional plats. Had I known as much about the scheme last fall as I do now, I would never have endorsed the lot surveys. I have never seen any of the additional plats that have been filed this spring, and they were never presented to the township board for approval," declared Supervisor Baker.

"The whole deal looks pretty rotten." A trip through the vast tract of land which has been subdivided into 25 x 100 foot lots in "beautiful Fruitvale," failed to reveal any of the delightful summer residences, club house or hotels that have been so extensively advertised in Chicago by the boomers behind the scheme. The nearest point is six and a half miles to a railroad, while some parts are 10 miles away. There is only one way to reach the property.

<u>Hotel a Rambleshack Building</u>

The headquarters of the land exploiting syndicate is located in a dilapidated old farmhouse which has been designated as a magnificent club hotel. It is surrounded by sand hills covered with jack pine or rag weed. The nearest point with a water frontage is at White River, and there is but little of that in the subdivided section. On the river, another ramshackle old farm house has been secured by the company. This has been dubbed as a hotel and clubhouse. No pretence is made at either place to accommodate summer tourist. The price of many of those remaining lots have been boosted to more than double the original price of $3 each.

<u>Many Come: Few Remain.</u>

"An average of 25 people come here every day to look at their lots," said former treasurer Davis, of Blue Lake Township, "but mighty few remain. It is the biggest swindle that was ever sprung on the public. Eventually, all of the lots will probably be sold for delinquent taxes, and if this occurs, the township will be swamped by the expense." "How many people have located on lots bought by them?" was asked. "Three that I know of. They are located in tents close to my farm. When they first came they were delighted. When they learned that it was a couple of miles to the river over a heavy sand road, however, they became disgusted. "No water can be secured for drinking purposes, without sinking a hundred foot well. This will cost $100, and when lot purchasers learn of this, that fact alone disgusts them. They just take one look at their purchases and then start back for Chicago."

<u>Thousands of Lots.</u>

No streets have been cut through the property, and the only thing to designate the layout of the land are flimsy street signs stuck up at intervals. They are placed along the regular township roads and what are supposed to be boulevards and beautiful drives are nothing but jungle land, filled with a tangled mass of vegetation. "This swindle beats any land booming scheme that was ever perpetrated in the west during the palmy days of real estate sharks," declared Supervisor Lee Trott, after making a tour of the worthless land, far from water, which had been floated as beautiful summer resort property. "After skinning the people on the purchase price for lots, the boomers even have nerve enough to go after the gullible ones again, and entice them out of fifty cents on each lot, through a snide tax assessment." According to the statements of Supervisor Baker and Clerk Yeoman of Blue Lake township, the only plat approved by the township board contained but about 4,800 lots. This leaves thousands of parcels that have been recorded as subdivision property, which the investigating committee is wondering over. They will make a thorough examination to ascertain how it got on the records.

<u>Lakewood All Right.</u>

Before looking over the Fruitvale scheme, the investigating committee also made a trip through the Lakewood summer resort proposition, which is being exploited by the Chicago Evening Post. It was found to be a legitimate scheme, backed by responsible batsous, who are spending thousands of dollars in improving the property. The Lakewood Company has already built a splendid depot at the railroad point close by, and has also erected a really delightful club house, cafe and cottages at Fox Lake, where the subdivision has a water frontage. A large force of men have been at work improving the property since early last spring - the monthly payroll being $2,000. Among those interested in the venture, beside the Chicago Evening Post, are G. Daniels, owner of the Oakland, (Cal.) Inquirer, the leading newspaper of that city; former Governor Pardee of California, and B. C. Mayo, a Chicago and Oakland capitalist. Those three mentioned gentlemen are now at the resort personally supervising the work of improvement. "

Although the sister development of

'Lakewood' in Dalton and Southern Blue Lake Township started out on a much more upbeat scale, a larger number of lots in the Lakewood plats would come up for delinquent tax sale in the early years, than from Fruitvale.

As will be evident later on in 1912, most of the disgruntled lot owners were the ones who unfortunately obtained lots in the outlying subdivisions. Most notably those in the Blue Lake and Fruit Valley Additions to Fruitvale.

These lots were far from the Whitehall area and the center of activity at Brown's Pond where the Inn was located. While on the other hand the "Original Town of Fruitvale and the Riverside Addition" had much greater success as the news of the day suggests;

Montague Observer 1912

"W. W. Harmon of Chicago, who is foreman for the Fruitvale Development Company, has charge of 42 men and is making very rapid progress on the magnificent hotel. The new hostelry will have modem improvements including a ladies rest room and laundry room."

"H. M. Campbell of Chicago, spent Sunday on the Hurst tract of land near Brown's Pond last week. This tract of land consists of 4000 acres and is owned by W. R. Hurst, and will probably be cut up into 10 acre farms and put on the market in the near future."

"Fred Nordhof, who is caretaker of the Hurst property here, expects to go to New York next month in the interest of the Hurst property here."

"The Fruitvale Land Company has completed a new $3000 hotel at Brown's Pond and will have a grand opening dance Saturday night. The new hotel overlooks Brown's Pond and is picturesquely situated."

"Large numbers of people are arriving at Fruitvale every day. Several cottages are going up and others are living in tents. The Montague side of the river seems to be more in favor with the lot owners than on the other side of the river, and those possessing lots near the river are well pleased and satisfied. There are two launches running up White River daily and a third one will be put on soon. It is nine miles by land to Fruitvale, but owing to the winding conditions of the river it is 22 miles by boat."

"A. Westpelt, a contractor at Fruitvale recently fell and broke his leg."

In addition to the Inn that was built on Brown's Pond, the Fruitvale Development Company also constructed an annex, an ice house, barns, large sheds, a two story home with 12 small guest rooms in the back, a water tower, pump house, oil shed for fuel, a boat landing on the White River, and a long wooden walkway from the landing to higher ground, where the passengers would be brought the rest of the way to the Inn by horse carriage.

Even though more and more "Fruitvalers" were coming in every day, the political problems from Muskegon had not gone away. Following are excerpts from a Muskegon County Commission meeting dated July 29, 1912.

"The following report was read: To the Honorable Board of Supervisors of Muskegon County, Michigan: Gentleman-

Your committee appointed to investigate the matter of the unlawful platting of large tracts of heretofore considered wild and worthless lands, and the exploitation of such fraudulent schemes by unprincipled promoters and land sharks, beg leave to report progress and report the following as their findings to date. Our report is submitted on the two land schemes that by very virtue of their size are attracting the attention of the citizens of our county, namely, Fruitvale, situated in. Blue Lake Township, and Lakewood, situated in the northerly two tiers of sections in the township of Dalton and extending into the township of Fruitland. Our report deals with these two propositions in the order that your committee is convinced that the magnitude of the resultant evils to the public and to the County of Muskegon seem to them to warrant, therefore, pursuant to this idea we must of necessity take up first the plat of Fruitvale. A total of 3,570 acres, approximately, divided into a grand total of 40,800 lots, the prevailing size of all lots being 25 x 100 feet. This gigantic swindle comprises more acreage than there is in the entire City of Muskegon and is divided into more than four and a half times as many lots, there being about nine thousand descriptions of land in the City of Muskegon. The average size of a lot in the City of Muskegon is 66 x 132 feet, or about five lots to acre, while the lots in so-called Fruitvale are 25 x 100 feet, or about 14 lots to the acre. The streets in the City of Muskegon are uniformly four rods wide, while in so-called Fruitvale they are in nearly every instance but forty feet wide, according to their alleged plats. The so called City of Fruitvale is not platted in one piece, but on the contrary, is platted in three separate parts. The original plat of Fruitvale and Riverside Addition, being situated north of the White River and between it and one of its tributaries, a small stream called Sand Creek. This portion of the tract being about eight miles from the Village of Montague at its nearest point. By far the largest portion of the lands platted that lie contiguous are embraced in the Blue Lake Addition, Fruit Valley Addition, Lakeside Addition and Lake Crystal Addition, and situated in Sections 9, 10, 15, 17, 30, 21, 22, and 28 of Blue Lake Township. It is one-half mile from the White River to the nearest point in this vast tract, while to the farthest point is about four and one half miles, while the average distance to the Village of Whitehall or Montague is about eight and one half miles. The third piece of this city, so-called, is on the extreme west side of the township of Blue Lake, in Section 19, and it also is half a mile distance at its nearest point from any of the other lands platted. It is called Silver Creek Addition.

The lands included in the stupendous grafting scheme are covered, where found in their wild state, mostly by scrub oak, jack pine, sometimes called crocodile pine, sweet fern, whortleberry brush and other flora indigenous to a light and arid soil. The surface of the land in the main is from undulating and hilly to very broken, due to the fact that Cleveland Creek and its tributaries cut through the central and eastern half of by far the largest portions of the land platted. The soil generally is light, dry sandy and nonproductive, as is evidenced by the number of run-down and abandoned farms that are included in the platted area. Farms where the settlers of an early day lived, not on what they produced from the soil, but on the wages they earned and the money they acquired in the turning of a mighty forest into saw logs. We call your attention to a full page advertisement by the Fruitvale Land Development Company, printed in the Muskegon News-Chronicle on July 26, 1912, and which is attached hereto as a part of this report (see below). This advertisement is so misleading as to be sufficient proof to the average person of the kind of men back of the Fruitvale scheme and of the very character of the scheme itself. The phraseology of each statement and of the advertisement in its entirety give rise to the thought it is the product of a mind long used to writing advertisements that had for their purpose the easy gulling of an innocent public, and is the public expression of a man whose previous experience has taught him just how close he could go to the line, the crossing of which would bring down upon him the wrath of the United States postal authorities. Your committee is of the opinion, and in this opinion we are backed by the Prosecuting Attorney of the County, that in the interest of public policy, and to avoid expense such as would be entailed on the county should any large number of these worthless lots be returned as delinquent for taxes, that these plats of Fruitvale and all of its additions can be and should be vacated. From a careful review of all the records connected with the platting of these lands we believe that a suit to vacate the plats can be successfully brought on the grounds of fraud by the promoter, Harrison M. Parker, in obtaining the signatures of the Town Board of Blue Lake Township to the various plats and for intimidation in the same connection, and for failure generally to follow the lines laid down in the statute that provides for the making and recording of plats. In this connection we desire to say that no stigma attaches to the Town Board of Blue Lake Township for their part in the matter, as their actions were guided by what they believed to be for the best interest of their township. To sum it all up. Mr. Harrison M. Parker has attempted to have platted in Fruitvale and its many additions something over forty thousand lots, thirty-five thousand of which, we are informed, have been sold at an average price of three dollars each, netting the promoters one hundred, two thousand dollars gross, less their expense in buying the land, surveying, selling expenses, etc., etc., which is estimate at:

Cost of 3,775 acres at an average price of $8.00 per acre	$30,200.00
Surveying and platting	10,000.00
Advertising, selling and general expenses	25,000.00
Total	$65,200.00

Leaving an estimated profit for the promoters of nearly forty thousand dollars, to which should be added such sums as were received from his demand of sixty cents a lot for taxes and which is estimated at ten thousand dollars. And, further, we must add such moneys as will be grabbed by the promoters from the sale of the six or seven thousand lots which remain unsold and which are being advertised as having risen in price. It has been reported by your committee that a large number of purchasers of lots in Fruitvale have come over from Chicago for the purpose of looking up the property they have bought, and in a large number of cases they were unable to locate the lots they had bought and in other cases, after having seen the lots, they have tom up their deed and returned to their homes with a knowledge of having been victimized and with a profound disgust for Western Michigan in general and Muskegon County in particular. It is the opinion of your committee that from the forgoing facts it must be apparent to your honorable body that as the result of this vast fraud but two things can result, namely, an ‘ immeasurable damage to the County of Muskegon for the very reason that these victimized lot owners will return to their homes and advertise the fact that they have been dishonestly and fraudulently led into the purchase of land in Muskegon County that was not at all what it was represented to be and will advise their friends and neighbors to have nothing whatever to do with lands or land owners in Muskegon County, and secondly, it requires no great knowledge of mathematics to figure the financial loss to the County of Muskegon that will result when from thirty to forty thousand of these lots are returned as delinquent for taxes and the County is compelled to pay one dollar for each description, together with other expenses attenuate upon the advertising of these lots for sale. In thc furtherance of this vast scheme, which in the opinion of your committee, so riddled with fraud, Mr. Parker is said to have invested all of six thousand dollars of his own money.

In conclusion, your committee is of the opinion that this whole vast fraud, labeled Fruitvale, is so transcendentally great that were it not for the loss suffered by thousands of the promoter's victims and that large expense that it will eventually bring to the County of Muskegon, it would be sublimely ridiculous. Your committee now will take up the Lakewood proposition. This proposition embraces the original plat of Lakewood and six additions thereto, designated as the Lakewood Additions Nos. 1, 2, 3, 4, 5, and 6 respectively, comprising nineteen hundred thirty acres, situated in Sections 5, 6, 7, 8, and 9 of Dalton Township and Section 12 of Fruitland Township, divided into twenty-six thousand six hundred eighty-six lots, twenty five by one hundred feet in size. There are two vital points of difference, in the opinion of your committee, between this proposition and that of Fruitvale, namely, its accessibility from the railroad and the generally level land embraced in the tract platted. There are a number of matters of minor importance in connection with this plat that are better than Fruitvale, one of them being the width of the road as shown on the plat, a number of them being sixty-six feet wide, others forty feet wide, and a fewer number twenty-five feet in width. The drawing feature of this resort is Fox Lake, a body of water covering about one hundred acres, situated on the north side of the lands platted. It is nearly three miles from the depot on the Pere Marquette railroad to the nearest point on the lake and it is nearly three and one-quarter miles from the lake to the farthest point in the tract platted. The land around Fox Lake is owned by the promoters and no streets in the entire tract run to the lake. At this time the low (lot) owners posses no legal right of access to the lake, and any privilege they have in that respect is solely by the sufferance of the shore line owners, in other words, the promoting company, such privilege can be terminated by the owners of the property abutting on Fox Lake at any time and for any or no reason. Lakewood was platted by Mr. B. C. Mayo, and we are given to understand that the Chicago Evening Post, a reputable newspaper of that city, is back of the scheme, they using the lots in connection with a campaign to increase the circulation of the paper. By contracting to buy the paper at the regular rate of thirty cents a month for a period of four months one gains the right to purchase a lot in Lakewood on monthly installments of $2.90, extending over a period of four months, making the price of every lot platted the same, $11.60. These lots run about fourteen to the acre so that the return to the promoters will be about one hundred sixty-two dollars an acre, less the cost of the land, platting, selling and other necessary expenses. The Chicago Evening Post has contracts out at the present time for about twenty thousand of these lots. The promoting company has expended some considerable amount of money in cutting out roads on the property and has built a club house and dining hall and some other buildings on unplatted property owned by them on the shores of Fox Lake. Mr. B. C. Mayo, one of the promoters of Lakewood, and the man directly in charge, met your committee and assisted them in every way he could during their investigations at Lakewood. Our examination of the plats and records had disclosed nothing startling, a few minor defects in the records being all that we have found to date. In view of all the facts set forth above, your committee is of the opinion that there is no action called for at the present time as regards the platting of Lakewood and its additions, but in regard to the platting of Fruitvale and its additions your committee respectfully recommend the adoption of the following resolution:

Resolved, That the Prosecuting Attorney for this County be and is hereby directed and authorized to take such action as may be necessary in the Circuit Court for the County of Muskegon to vacate any or all of the town plats of Fruitvale and the additions thereto above described which have been recorded without having been properly executed or acknowledged or for any cause legal and valid assessments of taxes cannot be made upon the lots situated within the limits of such plats; be it further Resolved, That the Prosecuting Attorney of said County be and he is hereby directed to sue for the recovery in any court of competent jurisdiction for any penalty or forfeitures from the proprietor or proprietors of any lands laid out in Fruitvale or its additions above referred to because of the failure of the proprietor or proprietors of said lands to comply with the provisions of Chapter eighty-nine of the Compiled Laws of the State of Michigan for 1897 as amended; be it further Resolved, That the Prosecuting Attorney of this County be and he is hereby directed to investigate all the circumstances surrounding the preparing said plats of Fruitvale and the additions thereto for recording, to ascertain whether or not any of the criminal statutes of this state have been violated; be it further all of which report of progress is respectfully submitted. Lee H. Trott, Harry A. Rietdyk, Tom J. G. Bolt."

The above stated report seems to be somewhat bias, in that the commissioners complain as to Fruitvale 'selling' their lots for $3.00 each, while the approved Lakewood lots were being sold for $11.60 each!

This is the ad referred to in the commissioners report:

THAT FRUITVALE PROPOSITION

Do You MERCHANTS OF MUSKEGON KNOW WHAT Is HAPPENING To YOU?

$70,000, not marbles or chalk, but real silver dollars into which you could put your teeth - dollars such as they take for money over at the Muskegon Savings Bank or at the Hackley National Bank - have been put into Muskegon County by the Fruitvale Land Development Company within the last year.

This money has been absorbed in the regular course of business, and its beneficial effects have been felt by everybody from the president of the Lumberman's National Bank down to the poorest laborer who works on our lots.

Every dollar taken in by the Towner Hardware Co., and the People's Hardware Co., and by every other merchant in Muskegon County, with whom we do business, has been felt in every home in the City of Muskegon.

The development of the Fruitvale District is one of the greatest enterprises undertaken since Muskegon County was put on the map. It means the ultimate occupation by orchardists and truck farmers of that vast empire to the northeast, which was lain dormant for the last half century, simply because no man of enterprise and with sufficient money was interested.

Capital has been going West, and it has increased the value of the land in Washington and Idaho from fifty cents an acre to, in some cases, one thousand dollars an acre, And there isn't one acre of land in Washington or Oregon that is any better than the land to the northeast of Muskegon.

The development of the country around Seattle and Portland has made the population of those cities over 200,000. While Muskegon, with the country around it equally as good, comparatively speaking, has been growing but little in the past ten years.

The Bank of Whitehall and the National Bank of the Republic in Chicago will tell you that the Fruitvale Development Co., is as solid as the Rock of Gibraltar. At different times this company has owed as much as $20,000, and the banks did not hesitate at any time to take its paper. It's a business. And the men back of it are sound, substantial, hard-working men.

More than thirty-three thousand men, women and children, through owning a piece of its land, now have an interest in Muskegon County. They are tied to this county by the strongest tie known-ownership of land.

These people have their lots in fee simple. Nothing in this world, except their own act, can take this land from them. There isn't a grafting politician in Muskegon County who has "nerve" enough to dispossess these people of their land.

At a minimum, these thirty-three odd thousand people will spend one million dollars in Muskegon County within the next five years. If they merely come over to look at their lots, every person who comes over from Chicago will leave at least $10 in the county.

This $10 is divided among the hotel men, livery men, restaurants, soda fountains, etc., etc., and in the ordinary course of business is distributed so that every man and woman in this county gets his or her part. You merchants in Muskegon, never in all your lives, have had such a big enterprise at your doors, without any effort on your part.

Of these thirty-three odd thousand people, some will be disappointed. You couldn't give away lots on Western A venue in the City of Muskegon and not have some people disappointed.

You couldn't give away a lot with a house on it across the street from the Hackley Library and not have some people kick because the walls were not frescoed by Michael Angelo.

There are all classes and kinds of people in Fruitvale: weak and strong, dead ones and live ones, ne'er-do-wells, and everything else.

But Chicago has two million people. Some are good, some are bad, some are indifferent. But in the final analysis there are enough people in the city of Chicago to make it destined to become the greatest city in the United States.

So with the resort city of Fruitvale.

There are enough good people interested in it to make it one of the greatest summer resort cities on the western shore of Lake Michigan.

As in every other proposition started since the world began, the weak will drop away, leaving only the strong in control.

The court records of Chicago show that not more than fifty years ago, a man who sold a piece of property on State Street for $250 was arrested as a swindler. Yet that same piece of property within the last six months has sold for $625,000 in cash.

Every lot in Fruitvale is worth $3.00 of any man's money. There are over 6,000 lots facing on Cleveland Creek, some of which are worth over $100. And if you yourself went over and looked at them, you would gladly give $100 for many of them.

Some of the Fruitvale lots have $50 worth of timber on them. Some of them haven't a stick.

But you can't buy a Fruitvale lot in Chicago for less than $10.00, an increase in value of 250 percent in six months.

Blue Lake is the great underdeveloped township in this county. It's as good as any you have in your entire county. We're not children. We brought experts out here from Washington, who reported that so far as the soil is concerned, many parts of Blue Lake are superior to any land which you have right here in the City of Muskegon.

Yet there are men in this city with nerve enough to ask as much as. $2,000 for some of the acres in this township.

If there is a foot of land in the City of Muskegon worth $2,000 an acre, no man who got 25 x 100 for $3.00 within fourteen miles of Muskegon has been swindled.

When your politicians started the cry that anybody who bought land in Muskegon County was swindled, thousands of people came to our office. We told them frankly that we knew nothing about the county, except Blue Lake. We had our money invested there. We were selling our land and anybody who wanted his money back at any time could have it.

We told them that the politicians knew more about the rest of the county then we did, and if the politicians said it was a swindle, the politicians must be right.

It is our judgement that the politicians have hurt land values in Muskegon County by millions of dollars.

There is a county in Idaho that ten years ago had an assessed valuation of $180,000. Today its assessed valuation is $28,000,000.

A Chicago real estate man bought 100,000 acres of this land for 50 cents an acre and sold it for $60 an acre. He was called a swindler by everybody in the county and at times was threatened with the penitentiary. Yet this same land is now selling for $200 an acre. The real estate man made a fortune for himself, and made millions for the people who bought the land at $60 an acre.

The native son politician is no different in Muskegon than he is in Idaho or California. He's a "knocker." He can't develop his own land and he won't let anybody else do it. Land is developed, whether it be in Michigan or California, only when the developing company is stronger than the native son "knocker."

We thank our heavenly stars that at all time, having confidence in Blue Lake where we have invested our money, having confidence in ourselves and knowing that we had more brains than the grafting politicians who can't even keep a regular job, we have kept our property and developed it, and will continue to do so.

Real estate men in Chicago have about concluded that it is almost impossible to sell land in Muskegon County, simply because everybody who comes in talks with some of these knockers and is sure to be reminded that the land in Muskegon County is a swindle.

We have a saloon keeper in Chicago, out on Archer Road, named Dooley. He lives in a little flat above his saloon. One morning as he was eating his breakfast the bartender whistled up the tube and asked if Hennessey were good for a drink. The saloon keeper whistled back, "Has Hennessey had the drink?" The barkeep answered, "he has." Dooley said, "He is good for a drink."

So with Fruitvale. It is in your county and establishment. The whole county can't take it off the map. It is here to stay.

We have a hotel up at Fruitvale, with hot and cold water, modem toilet facilities, two cooks, five waitresses. The building and equipment have cost over $7,000 - the kitchen alone cost $800, equipped with a modem hotel range, sinks, etc.

There is a fleet of passenger, baggage and freight steamers plying the White River between Whitehall and Fruitvale. The river is opened up for traffic. This doesn't look as if we weren't here to stay.

Now, instead of "knocking" Fruitvale, why don't you merchants do everything that you possibly can to bring these people over from Chicago to live? There isn't any poison in the air here. No man owning 100 feet square, which cost him $12 is swindled.

The knockers passed out by your politicians hurts Muskegon County only, and everything in it. It can't hurt Fruitvale. We have sold our lots. If the knocking continues it will ultimately reach every lot owner in Fruitvale, and the only difference it will make is that they will not come over here to leave their $10.

Over In Chicago, when anybody moves into our neighborhood, we usually call on them. If they are no good, we leave them alone. If they are decent people, we send our children over to "mix it" up with their children.

Now, we are thoroughly decent people. We have a lot of money invested in this county. The politicians have certainly raised hell with us. But we are not the kind of fellows to drop. We have mixed up with politicians before.

Instead of taking a cheap politician's estimate of us, why don't you merchants come over and see us? Sit down and have dinner with us. Stay at our hotel over night. Ride in our boats. Look over our pay roll; we are spending right now $300 a week and have been for over a year.

If we are no good, we ought to be ridden out of town on a pole. On the other hand, if we are what we say we are, decent, respectable fellows, why don't you be neighborly with us? Give us a chance for our lives.

If we build a town up there, the business will ultimately come to . Muskegon. If we can put 30,000 people in Fruitvale, it will double the business in Muskegon, and double the profits of every merchant in the town.

The land was nothing before we started to develop it. It did not bring in a dollar to Muskegon or anywhere else. Now you couldn't be any worse off than you were. On the other hand, if we succeed, you succeed.

We are going to have an old-fashioned picnic and barbecue at Fruitvale on Saturday, August 3. We are going to bring people over from Chicago, and we have invited all the farmers to come over and spend the day with us. We are going to have races and we are going to have prizes. We are going to have an old fashioned day.

Why doesn't some enterprising merchant start a committee of your Chamber of Commerce to come over and see us? Watch us at work? We will entertain the committee Friday night and Saturday at our hotel. It won't cost them a cent.

We got in with an awful bunch of grafters over here, but our bank and our lawyer will tell you that we never gave up a cent: that every time we put our "dukes" and fought our weight in "wild cats."

But it is all over with now. We are here to stay, and we want to be neighbors and friends with everybody in the county. Our interest are your interest and your interest are our interest. We all ought to work together for the benefit of Muskegon County, for Blue Lake, Moorland, and every other township in the county. We ought not to fight. We ought not to knock each other.

Chicago people are crazy to have a summer resort city. The people over there want to own land in some cool, quiet place. There isn't any better place on Lake Michigan, than Muskegon County.

If they don't come to Muskegon they will go to Holland, South Haven or some other county. Why should not these people be brought right here to leave their money and build the business houses of this city?

Now let us all be friends and neighbors and work together to bring these people over here to increase the business of Muskegon, and to make the County of Muskegon the greatest in the state of Michigan.

Let's be good fellows with each other. Your "knocking" can't hurt us. Our lots are sold. Come on up to Brown's Point next Saturday night - all of you - break bread with us. We'll hand around pipes and we'll smoke with you the pipe of peace. Come on up - you politicians, too."

Fruitvale Land Development Company

The next step was for the Commissioner's who were unfamiliar with Fruitvale, those from the north that backed it, and those who were just as strongly opposed to the whole idea, to see first hand, just what was happening. So on July 31, the excursion was made.

"The board of supervisors accompanied by citizens of the towns made a trip to Fruitvale yesterday via White River on Fruitvale Land Company's boats at the expense of the promoters of the enterprise, and was for the purpose of giving the entire membership of the board an opportunity of learning the true conditions surrounding the proposition, so far as the actual improvements made there are concerned. The members of the board were taken up the river from the landing to the center of Fruitvale tract, thence to the shores of Blue Lake, where the proposition for the five and ten acre tract farms is to be worked out in the future. The members were then treated to one of the best dinners the Fruitvale hotel could serve, and in the afternoon, after looking over a portion of the tract, went back to Whitehall on the boat. After returning from Fruitvale the board was banqueted at the Mears hotel by the Fruitvale people, and a number of Whitehall and Montague business men were also present. Speeches were made by many of the banqueters praising the work already accomplished at Fruitvale and the bright prospects of the project."

At its next meeting on August 1, the supervisors acted as follows:

"By voting to adopt the report of the special investigating committee on the Fruitvale resort proposition, but refused to concur in that part of the report which called for action by the prosecuting attorney looking to the vacation of the plats of that resort.

THE FIGHT ON FRUITVALE

The struggle over the adoption of the report on the Fruitvale proposition was bitter, and at time became personal. The supervisor from Blue Lake Township, Mr. Baker, and his colleague from Whitehall, Mr. Haverkate, were earnest in their support of the contention that the report be not adopted. In the debate upon the matter it developed that the filing and approval of the plats of Fruitvale were not regular, as they had never been approved at a regularly called meeting of the township board. It was also admitted that the plat had not been signed on the date indicated on the paper. Supervisor Trott asserted that one of the plats filed last fall bears the signature of a justice of the peace of Blue Lake Township who did not become a member of the township board until last spring. For all of these reasons the committee asked that steps be taken to vacate the plats.

After debating the matter all morning, the better part of an hour was consumed in the afternoon session in discussing the report. Supervisor Bolt pointed out that there was a misapprehension on the part of the members as to the legality of these plats. He said that the committee had found that the plats were signed by the township board in piecemeal, and not at a regularly called meeting and that the question was not whether the board wanted to put a dollar in the pockets of the merchants of Whitehall and Montague, but whether or not the report of the committee is correct as to the lawful filing of these plats. "If the promoter sells a lot, in a plat not legitimately platted," said Mr. Bolt, "he becomes liable to a fine of $10 for each of such lots so sold. If all this be true, the promoters of this proposition are liable to a fine of over $300,000." After spilling considerable more words, the supervisors finally agreed to lay the matter of taking action to vacate the plats over until the October meeting, they having been advised by Prosecuting Attorney Sutherland that the board has power to legalize the plats if the board so desires."

As indicated from the last supervisor's report, nearly all the businessmen and local residents from the Whitehall and Montague area were strongly in favor of Fruitvale, as they could see a boost to the local economy. After sponsoring in part the supervisor's trip to the 'city,' they next turned to the same media that was giving Fruitvale a bad name, the newspapers.

The following article appeared in the August 31 addition of the Montague Observer:

BUSINESS MEN ALL UPHOLD FRUITVALE DECLARE THAT REPORTS PUBLISHED IN OUTSIDE PAPERS CONTRARY TO THE FACTS.

"Incensed over the unfair reports which have been published about Fruitvale and other parts of the county, in papers at Grand Rapids and Chicago, the Business Men's league of Montague have made a formal protest against the statements, and declares them to be unwarranted. In doing so, they declared that the report now passing before the board of supervisors was actuated by political malice, and will be over whelmingly condemned when it comes up before the board of supervisors again in October. They declare that the report is misleading and is foreign to the facts. Following is a portion of the statement issued by the Business Men's league:"

"We know from personal contact with many hundreds of people returning from Fruitvale that fully 90 percent of the lot owners are perfectly satisfied, which is just the reverse of the statement made in the report of the special committee. "An inspection will show that Fruitvale consists of about 4,300 acres of land, all of which is beautifully wooded except about 200 acres. The beautiful White River flows through Fruitvale and there is over ten miles of river frontage reserved for the use of the lot owners. There are five small spring lakes on the property besides the widely known Big Blue Lake, which is two and one-half miles long and one and one-half miles wide."

Has good soil.

"The surveyors have reported that there are 800 springs. The soil is mostly a good quality sandy loam, in a few places running into a sandy clay, especially adapted to orchard and small fruits. There is not to exceed five acres of blow sand in Fruitvale. "The western part consists mostly of oak, ash, pine and soft maple, and is exceptionally fine for camping purposes. The eastern part contains similar mixed timber and is hilly and rolling. "Fruitvale as a whole is a picturesque wild stretch of country particularly adapted for its purpose. "The Fruitvale Land Development Company, at its own expense, has cleaned out the logs, sand bars, and debris for 23 miles up White River and opened this beautiful stream for navigation. It owns two passenger boats a freight barge and two launches.

Haverkate Condemns Report.

Supervisor John Haverkate also denounces the report. His statement is as follows: The statement of John Haverkate, supervisor of Whitehall is: "Chairman of Finance Committee of Board of Supervisors, Muskegon County, Michigan: "The action on the report of this special committee consisting of Messrs, Bolt and Trott, which has been given recent publicity, has been deferred until regular October session of the Board of supervisors of Muskegon County, and will not be adopted as a majority of the supervisors have expressed themselves to that effect, and inasmuch as they visited Fruitvale and are satisfied that this report contains many erroneous and scurrilous statements.

Points to Things Omitted.

"Why didn't the report state that the Fruitvale Company has spent several thousand dollars in opening the White River for navigation, built a hotel, established bus lines all for the benefit of Fruitvale lot owners, also say that many Fruitvale lot owners after seeing their property have bought more, and that several new bungalows are now being erected. Also that a large construction crew is opening up roads, etc., preparatory to next season. "The citizens of Whitehall and Montague have publicly expressed themselves as believing in the honesty and integrity of Harrison M. Parker and consider him a public spirited and progressive citizen and will resent at the polls this political attack on Fruitvale which has been an injustice to him "John Haverkate"

In addition to the businessmen of the area, most local residents also looked favorably upon Fruitvale and its prosperity. In what was to become a tradition that would last several years, "Montague Days" were held at the Rochdale Inn at Fruitvale. This is the account of the first one held there.

MONTAGUE DAY

"The excursion to Fruitvale yesterday was an" event long to be remembered by those who participated. Nearly a half hundred Montagueites boarded the Fruitvale Company's boat at the pavilion yesterday morning for a trip up the river and a visit to Fruitvale. Much had been heard of the grandeur of White River, but one must make the trip to appreciate it to its fullest extent. The scenery on the river trip to Fruitvale brought forth many expressions of admiration from the party yesterday. Their isn't a dull moment on the entire trip as nature has lavished a great deal of natural beauty on White River. The banks of the river are densely wooded and many of the overhanging trees are festooned with wild grape vines and graceful ivy, while a variety of wild berries grow in clusters along the shores. There is also a marvelous variety of trees along the river, including even the cypress, a native of the south. The staunch craft bore its jolly crowd slowly but surely against the onrushing waters making the sharp turns in the river and avoiding the shoals, until it finally reached its destination at Fruitvale. The passengers disembarked and were escorted to Riverside Inn where a picnic dinner was enjoyed Montague ladies are second to none in the culinary art and on this occasion they simply out-did themselves. The management of Riverside Inn had the long tables prepared in the spacious dining room for the guest and served hot coffee. The courtesy of the Fruitvale people was greatly appreciated.

After dinner guests were shown through the grounds and the various buildings. The hotel building is a neat structure situated on a prominent point overlooking Brown's Pond. Besides the commodious hotel and an auxiliary rooming house the company has a number of comfortable tents for the accommodation of their guests. A number of private cottages are also going up. Before leaving the crowd posed before photographer Flood's camera for a number of pictures at Fruitvale. The homeward trip was made in about half the time it took to go up as the current of the river aidcd instead of retarding the motive power of the boat. It rained spasmodically but the party was well provided with umbrellas and did not suffer. Fruitvale has many features which commends it as a popular summer resort and Montague is greatly interested in its success and future development.

The only two incidents that marred the occasion in the least was the loss of Banker Mill's hat and the anxiety over Geo. Springer's absence. The latter was finally located up the pond on a prospecting tour. H. B. Carleton kept himself entertained on the trip by charming the turtles along the river banks and L. G. Ripley was so enamored with the beautiful scenery for post card views that he did not mind in the least the rain patting on his hat. W. E. Osmun and G. A. Whitback sat silent much of the time communing with nature while Simon Fehrenbach, Joe Potter and Grandpa Jager entertained the ladies and amused the only baby on board."

It is said that time heals all wounds, and by the October meeting of the Muskegon County Supervisors, the furry of Fruitvale had settled down to a murmur. The subdivision plats would stay as recorded. If any lot owner desired their money back or the exchange to a different lot, they could. Also, the Fruitvale Development Company was to start recording the deeds for the lots as sold. This would allow the county treasurer to tax each lot owner separately, eliminating Fruitvale from collecting the taxes, as reported, and making a profit from them. This turned out to be a slow process though, as it would not be until the 1930s when all the parcels would be listed. Just as much as the county wanted to make sure that Parker was not making a profit on the taxes collected, they did not look forward to having over 40,000 deeds dumped in their laps. Each one would need to be recorded, a process at that time required retyping or copying by hand, each deed, word for word, in the county's Liber books with the owners address. Needless to say, they would have had to devote all their resources to the project, and this they did not want to do. Thus not much more was said, as they allowed the deeds to trickle in, just enough to keep all parties contented. And so ended 1912, the first full year of Fruitvale.

1913

As a new year begins, the work behind the scenes become evident, the supervisors who opposed Fruitvale have convinced enough other members to vote against the plats.

FRUITVALE PLAT REJECTED

"A great deal of indignation is manifest in the northern end of the county over the action of the board of supervisors last Friday when they rejected the Fruitvale and Lakewood plats. They not only voted against allowing any more plats of these resorts to be recorded, but gave the Fruitvale resort project, which gave fair promise of becoming a large resort, a black eye. The board by a vote of 18 to 7 voted to accept the Bolt Trott Rietdyk report recommending to the board that the prosecuting attorney be instructed to take such action as is necessary before the circuit court to have the Fruitvale summer resort plats vacated.

It is true that many members of the board visited Fruitvale as guests of the Fruitvale Land and Development Company last summer and were in a position to investigate the proposition for themselves. The only legitimate reason the board could have for rejecting these resort plats is that they have reasonable grounds to believe that the taxes in the future will not be paid upon them, but allowed to become delinquent, in which case it would be a great expense to the county for advertising the delinquent tax sales.

The people of the north end of the county have great confidence in the future of its resort lands, which includes the great Fruitvale plat, and the fact that north end of the county raises no objection to having these plats accepted should have had some weight with our supervisors.

It is the belief, however, if Mr. Parker furnishes a bond for $20,000 to

"Montague Day" at Fruitvale, 1913

guarantee the taxes on Fruitvale for a ten year period, the proposed litigation will not be brought by the county."

Through a lack of legal grounds and the cooperation of Harrison Parker, supervisors were unable to have the plats abandoned, thus life in Fruitvale continued to prosper and grow during 1913.

So much activity was going on at Fruitvale, that starting this year, reports of the local happenings at the city were been reported in Montague and Whitehall newspapers:

April 3, 1913

"Harrison M. Parker and two friends were up to Fruitvale Sunday in his machine."

"Mr. and Mrs. Dan Gau were out to their farm home last week. Dan says Muskegon is okay in the winter but Brown's Pond is better in the summer. They expect to come back this week to live for the summer."

"While Chas. Weigand was returning from Whitehall Monday he lost a valuable horse at Carlton Creek bridge by caving in a washout that has been neglected for more than a year. Our mailman as well as myself have been fearful of that place and have been complaining without results. We think the people should get busy and fix that place before any more damage is done."

April 17, 1913

"Messrs. Jones and Brown of Chicago are at the hotel building Hogg and chicken houses."

"Tom Funnel of Whitehall has begun transporting passengers from the city to look at lots in Fruitvale which is going to be a big resort."

May 1, 1913

"Bert Sayers is hauling lumber for Fruitvale, the new hog and chicken houses are about complete."

"The resorters have begun coming to Fruitvale and expect to do business on a big scale the summer. Everything bids fair for a big resort time."

"A man from Chicago who have purchased one of the new five-acre tracts was misdirected by someone and lost his way. He followed wound up at the Riverside in it was put on the right road by John Nichols."

"Mr. Boyd, head manager of the bridge which is being completed on the county line, is among the Fruitvale passengers."

Open Local Office

Fruitvale Company Close Year's Contract for Office in Hotel Mears

"That the Fruitvale proposition will mean considerable to this locality before the present season is over is the confident believe of the men who have talked with Henry Frank, Jr., the new president of the Fruitvale Company. Mr. Frank is a keen businessman and has the local situation well lined up in his plans for the future are so logical as to give anyone confidence in the proposition under his management."

"The Fruitvale Land and Development Company has been reorganized and absorbed by the Fruitvale Company., With Mr. Frank as president, Geo. W. Brady as vice president and Mrs. K. F. Brady secretary and treasurer. The new company owns all of the holdings and property of both the Fruitvale Land and Development Company, and the Fruitvale Light and Water Co. Mr. Frank has been in Whitehall for the past two weeks and has just closed the contract with Alex Goleckner for the use of the West room on the first floor of Hotel Mears as the local office for the coming year. The office will be the Michigan headquarters of the firm and will be arranged to conform to the convenience of lot owners and prospective buyers. The plats and maps of the company's property may be found here as well as samples of timber and soil from various parts of their holdings. They will also continue to have an office in Chicago where Mr. Brady, the vice president, will look after the interest of the company. It is Mr. Frank's desire to get a gravel road built to the Fruitvale property this year and he stated to a representative of the Forum that if the townships of Whitehall an Blue Lake would give $1,000 a mile toward the construction that his company would pay the balance needed above that sum, and the county and state awards. He already has men at work placing buoys in the river to mark out the best course and to show the location of snags and deadheads and the boat service will start shortly. A construction department has been organized to assist the development and general improvement of the property. The department will aid and assist lot owners in clearing their lots and building cottages on their land. While the company still has numerous fine lots for sale, they will make a specialty from now on of the selling five-acre parcels adapted for fruit and poultry culture. They are now at work constructing poultry and hog colony houses and expect to raise about 3,000 chickens this year has a nucleus for larger operations next season.

Before next fall the company will have the old MacBeth farm devoted to an immense poultry farm, the equipment of which is estimated will cost in the neighborhood of $25,000. This ideal idea is not only to make a profitable investment for the company but to show to the people to whom they are selling small plats that poultry culture can be made to pay big returns and to demonstrate to them that the figures given in a pamphlet issued by the company, titled "Fruitvale Gardens," are not fanciful but are practical and possible to accomplish.

The buildings of Brown's pond are being remodeled and refitted and bathrooms and toilets are being installed. The name of the Riverside Inn has been changed to that of Brown's Pond Clubhouse and the other building at the same location will be known as Brown's Pond Inn. The opening day of the season will be on May 30, the full announcement of which will appear in these columns during the next two weeks.

Close Big Land Deal

Fruitvale Company makes another big by from C. E. & M. B. Covell

"What is probably the largest acreage land deal consummated in Western Michigan in recent years was completed by the M. B. Covell last Saturday where by C. E. & M. B. Covell sold to the Fruitvale company of Chicago about 6,000 acres of land, most of which is located in Oceana County. That the Fruitvale Co, is planning on big things for the future as evidenced by the fact of the additional heavy investments they are making in connection with their resort property at Fruitvale. All of the new property, as well as that lying at the edge of the resort plats, is to be sold in five and 10 acre tracts. About 30 of these plots have already been sold during the past two weeks."

May 22, 1913

"Mr. Bert Walker and family have moved to the Oak Grove Inn Fruitvale Hotel."

"Ms. Josephine Hersick who has been working in Chicago as stenographer as returned to her country home for the summer. A man and his family from Chicago have opened the Riverside Inn Hotel at Fruitvale. This man comes to is highly recommended as a number one hotel man."

"Everybody is busy in our vicinity planting corn."

" Miss. Simpson of Montague, who is teaching our spring term of school, will begin taking music lessons from Mrs. Bert Walker this week."

"Mr. Parker and Mr. Frank of Chicago were over Sunday. They have established quite a chicken ranch at the Riverside Inn Hotel. They have a large force of men hustling the work through to be ready for the summer."

Great Opening Day

Large Crowd of People Come From Chicago to Fruitvale

"Fully 100 people came to Whitehall by the special Goodrich boat last Friday morning to look over the Fruitvale Orchard plats and to locate lots of property they have purchased. It was a fine crowd and they were transported by boat to the Brown's Pond Clubhouse from where they were taken in buses to the several parts of the resort plat. Nearly everyone expressed themselves as being more than pleased with the proposition and several made plans for permanent improvements on their holdings while here. The Fruitvale Company also brought in 10 head of horses for use of their buses and expect to either purchase here or important a herd of extra good cows."

June 12, 1913

"Ms. Suria of Muskegon, who teaches our school, contemplates a visit to her home Friday."

"J. B. Nichols and Mr. Frank was over the camp Wednesday afternoon from River Side Inn. Their hotel has 40 boarders all the time and resorters are pouring in rapidly."

July 10, 1913

"J. B. Nichols is somewhat busy at the present time locating lots for Chicago people."

"The Fruitvale people have about 600 chicks at River Side Inn.

"The new boat for the Fruitvale Company has been named "Ankle-Deep." The other boat which is almost completed, is named Mary Parker after the daughter of Harrison M. Parker.

Record in metes and bounds.

"Fruitvale promoters unable to secure the approval of their two new plats, the Country Club addition and Lakeview subdivision of Fruitvale, by the board of supervisors at the present session, are going to record their deeds in these plats by metes and bounds descriptions. About 600 deeds, containing this type of description, will be filed with the register of deeds in the near future. Harrison M. Parker says: we are going to put on record deeds which will cost about 50 cents every time they are handled. Every description has to be handled at least once a year. Every time the county treasurer or the auditor general handles one of these descriptions it will cost the county and state about a dollar. We are going to continue this until the supervisors realize that they are in business for Muskegon County."

October 16, 1913 page 4

Another Fruitvale Plat

"The board of supervisors at their meeting Tuesday afternoon, refused to approve four new plats of the Fruitvale Company offhand and referred the matter to a special committee on plats for the investigation and report. Immediately upon supervisor Williams submitting two plats, Mr. Lawson expressed an opinion that as long as these companies sold lots through the medium of advertising some lake or river, that a part should be set aside for use by the general public or at least the purchasers of the lots. It appears that only those who buy right on the river are the only ones who have access to it."

Throughout 1913 Fruitvale had continued to grow and flourish, not only in population, but also construction of houses, some for full-time residents, most of summer cottages. While more and more Chicago residents purchased lots in the city of Fruitvale, those who have attained their lots in the outlying subdivisions, saw little activity, and were generally displeased with the location. During 1913 100 deeds were recorded at the Muskegon County register of

A Big Old Fashioned

BARBECUE

PICNIC

With DANCING in the Evening

will be held at the

RIVERSIDE INN
FRUITVALE, MICH.

JULY, 4th, 1913

FRUITVALE BOATS

Leave Sylvan Beach at 7:00 a. m. and 1:00 p. m.

Leave Whitehall City Dock at 8:00 a. m. and 2:00 p.m.

Come One and All!

Deeds office, consisting mainly of lots within the Original Town of Fruitvale, and the Riverside Addition to Fruitvale, while at the same time, 284 deeds were recorded showing the Fruitvale Company buying back lots from unhappy "Fruitvalers" in the Blue Addition and Fruit Valley Addition's.

Harrison, noticing the somewhat lack of major development taking place in the Fruitvale Plats as a whole, turned his attention to the remainder of the property he owned in Blue Lake Township, and the 6000 plus acres he purchased in May in Oceana County. On a scale that dwarfed the Fruitvale Plats, and using the Rochdale Co-op System, work started on the five acre Berry Patches and Poultry Gardens. Covering an area of some 10 miles East and West by nine miles North and South, it would contain 2,512 five acre parcels in Oceana County with options on another 1400, in addition to 444 more located in Blue Lake Township, Muskegon County. Included within this area was to be five 40 ·acre "Proposed Substation Canneries," a 20 acre "Central Poultry Substation Cannery" located across from the Inn at Brown's Pond, the site of the present day White River Campground, a 120 acre "Proposed Central Preserving and Canning Plant, and a 365 acre "Dairy Creamery - Cheese Factory Model - Stock Farm." Except from the main chicken farm across from the Inn, none of these facilities were ever constructed. Being that 1913 was just the beginning of the Fruit and Poultry Gardens, the idea behind this co-op will be covered in more detail later on.

1914

With the new year, news from Fruitvale that work is progressing with the development of the area and its resources continues.

It is Harrison's opinion that to sell the idea of raising fruit and poultry on the five acre tracts, that a display model must show success.

POULTRY AT FRUITVALE

"A hennery is being established at Fruitvale on a large scale under the management of Ed Raymond, an expert poultryman. Forty chicken houses are being built to accommodate the poultry which will consist of chickens, geese and ducks. Mr. Raymond will make a specialty of white leghorns and expects to raise 3000 the coming season. He has a brooder with a capacity of 5000. Poultry ought to thrive at Fruitvale under expert care, and no doubt it can be made a paying business, especially in connection with the resort business which is steadily developing in that locality. The Fruitvale Developing Company, which is going ahead making substantial improvements on their vast tracts of land, despite the opposition and obstacles they have met, are entitled too much credit. If Fruitvale is developed and populated to anywhere near the company's expectation, it will be a great benefit to Montague and Whitehall. The city people see things different than we do and often find value in what we consider worthless. Capital and pluck can do wonders and has made a success out of less promising places than the country around Fruitvale."

January 22, 1914

"August Krubeck returned from a trip to Chicago last Thursday. Mr. Keck started out on a trip to Milwaukee and it rumored that he will join the ranks of the benedicts before returning."

"Will Schneider was here last week from Chicago looking after his property here."

"Members of the Vjirs family here had a successful trapping season, capturing 130 muskrat and one mink so far this year."

"J. N. McLaughlin of Chicago visited Fruitvale last Tuesday."

January 29, 1914

More Detailed Deeds

Fruitvale Company Continue to Send in Transfers Described by Metes and Bounds

"Every day sees about ten or more deeds of Fruitvale lots described by metes and bounds arrive at the office of the register of deeds. Nearly 75 of this type of transfers have already been received and it is expected that they will continue to come for some time according to the statement of Harrison M. Parker, the Fruitvale promoter who declares that he must satisfy those who have purchased from him although he does not care to make any more work for himself or the county of Muskegon than necessary. The Fruitvale deeds are of a much different from than the ones usually employed in Michigan so it is necessary to record them in a special book used for irregular deeds. This entails considerable extra labor."

February 26, 1914

Getting Big Results

Poultry Farm at Fruitvale Making Spring Settings

"Scientific poultry raising is occupying the attention of Ed Raymond who has one of the finest poultry plants in the state of Michigan on the Fruitvale resort property. Mr. Raymond has 400 hens of choice varieties from which he is securing 200 eggs per day.

Since February 11 he has been setting eggs in his mammoth incubator at the rate of 200 every other day. Both the incubator and brooder buildings are heated by a hot water system of the most improved type automatically regulated with a thermostat so that there is no danger of the place becoming too hot or too cold if the fire boxes are kept full of fuel. It is his ambition to raise several thousand chickens this summer and have them ready for market during the early fall. The first hatching will come the first week in March and then the real busy season commences and lasts for several months, for every other day a batch of 200 eggs is due to hatch. All of the eggs which are placed in the incubators are tested as to their fertility and so some extra good hatches are anticipated. This is the first time in the history of the county that poultry raising has been carried on in such proportions and it is predicted that this will be but one of numerous undertakings of the nature which will be launched by owners of Fruitvale tracts."

February 26, 1914

Fruitvale

Ice harvest is now on at Brown's Pond and an excellent quality is being secured. About 850 tons had been packed away in the Fruitvale Co's ice houses on Tuesday night."

"C. T. Spicklemire has been busy building an addition to the company's barn at Fruitvale. The new part is 16x34 feet and will be used for extra horses which will be purchased or brought here from Chicago as soon as spring arrives."

"The next building to be constructed is a feed house near the barns."

"Four men who own a considerable portion of land in this section expect to clear 80 acres this spring and get it ready to set apple trees. This will probably be one of the first Fruitvale orchard plats."

"Preparations are being made to move one of the cottages which was built last summer on the street north from the landing over to the street where Riverside Inn is located."

"Chicken raising is to be among one of the greatest assets of Fruitvale. Already several of the finest and largest poultry farms in Western Michigan can be found there. One party has now over 3000 eggs in their incubators. J. H. Gerken of Chicago is now here to start a farm, with 2000 chickens, on section 9."

"Mr. Christian of the Blue Lake Club with Messrs McGinness and Gerken were all callers at The Forum office Saturday and all claim to have been very successful in fishing through the ice."

"Mr. Reubner is having a very chilly time. He is living in a tent with his son making improvements to his property."

"G. J. Helm agent for Fruitvale garden tracts was a pleasant caller at the Forum office with Mr. and Mrs. Toney. He expects to return to Chicago the end of this week."

August 6, 1914

Dam Goes Out At Fruitvale.

"The wooden dam at Fruitvale which was completed last week, broke away suddenly Tuesday night under the great pressure of the head-waters and the pent up waters of Brown's Pond went out with a great rush, caring out with it the new bridge and entailing a great loss. The dam was put in for the purpose of raising Brown's Pond five feet above its surface. Instead of five feet the water rose nine feet and the headwaters were extended back a mile and a half. This proved too much of a pressure on the retaining wall and the work of weeks has come to naught. The dam will no doubt be reconstructed."

December 3, 1914 Fruitvale Happenings

"Next year is expected to be the best year Fruitvale has ever seen. The Forum is receiving inquiries every week in regards to the outlook. They have now four distinct organizations at work, each doing a work to advance their interest at Fruitvale. First, they have the Fruitvale Improvement Club. This is in close connection with the Fruitvale Co., and looks after the taxation interest and improvements and much has been accomplished by its work. Second, is the Fruitvale Mutual Association of Chicago, made up mostly of lot owners and they have their regular meetings every month to talk over their interests. Third is the Tract Owners Association who now has Mr. McGinnis at Fruitvale looking after things for their interest. This association is made up mostly of parties who own tracts of five acres and upwards to 25 acres each. These meetings are attended by all who are interested in Fruitvale. Fourth, The Little Landers, a new organization which apparently will put new vigor and energy in the advancement of Fruitvale interest. The people of Whitehall and vicinity should boost as never before to further the cause of Fruitvale and let the people know that what is their interest in our interests and give them a square deal in everything. The Forum will be ready at all times to boost for Fruitvale."

December 24, 1914

"The bridge over Sand Creek is completed and the water which had been turned through a new channel some years ago is now running through the original channel again. The water has been raised in Fruitvale Lake and will furnish fine sport for fisherman and boating."

"Mrs. Robert Preston, assisted by Miss Barker, has assumed the management of the hotel. Mrs. Sullivan, the former manager, expects to spend the winter with her parents Mr. and Mrs. Blakeraly."

"Quite a number of surveyors are busy surveying the land recently purchased by the company."

"The pupils of the school are doing nicely with their work. The report for the month showed those neither absent or tardy were Helen Sullivan, Mary Stipe, Donald Walker and Agusta Stine. Average standing of examination 87 percent, and average attendance 99 percent."

1915

With the beginning of 1915, the thousands of different land owners started organizing into groups for the benefit of the community: the first being the Little Landers of Fruitvale, a group of lot owners.

March 25, 1915

"F. A. Ruebner and his nephew returned to Chicago in time for the meeting of The Little Landers of Fruitvale of which he is president. While here he built three houses under the most trying weather conditions. He was sorry to leave here so soon and is already wishing himself back at Fogg Lake Fruitvale."

"With the approach of spring the interest in Fruitvale is booming. New parties coming in to view the place report they are "tickled to death," as they express themselves. They also comment on the excellent treatment accorded them by all representatives of the Fruitvale Co. as well as the business people of Whitehall. "

"The Fruitvale Co. is now bringing lumber to Fruitvale in dozen car-load lots. This was made necessary by the increased demand for lumber for immediate building purposes."

"The tract owners meeting Thursday night was a lively affair, being addressed by a half dozen enthusiastic speakers, including Mr. McGinnis and Mr. Helm who had just returned from Fruitvale and near vicinity. All reports are highly flattering as to the progress now being made, which is going forward with leaps and bounds. Nothing left to stop it. Former drawbacks are practically removed. Everything is now going forward with a swing and the only conjecture now existing is as to when it will stop. Many of us are predicting never."

July 1, 1915

Local snapshots from the Fruitvale Messenger:

"The Fruitvale Company has some 8,000 chicks in plant." "Hundreds of tents and bungalows are going up this summer."

"The vegetable gardens are now in full blast and everything points to a good season."

"Thomas Lynch, of Section 31, had the most unique little home you ever saw. Don't forget to see it this summer when you are on your vacation."

"Numbers of reservations have been made with the Fruitvale Company for the months of July and August, and a great many for June. A capacity of two hundred a week will soon be reached for some of the trips.'

"Tom Brantford, the famous "Scotch comedian," who built in Fruitvale last summer, has returned this spring and is preparing to build a beautiful little home."

"0. Johnson Smith, of Pe-ta-ka, on the White River at Fruitvale, is erecting about 50 bungalows for his friends."

October 14, 1915

Fruitvale Land Owners Convention Owners Are Well Pleased With Purchases

"The first fall meeting of the Chicago Tract Owners' Association of Fruitvale was held on Thursday evening, October 7, at the Colonial Hall, State and Randolph Streets, Chicago. There were some 500 enthusiastic land owners present, all anxiously awaiting committee reports on the progress of land tracts and of the new town of Fruitvale, situated in the northern part of Blue Lake Township. The meeting was called to order promptly at 8 o'clock, and after the usual preliminaries Mr. Harrison M. Parker, founder of Fruitvale, was introduced. After describing the surroundings of the beautiful country up the White River, such as are to beheld particularly during the month of October "when the leaves of trees change color" and nature prepares to settle once more for winter's rest, Mr. Parker told the new hard surfaced road now under construction from Whitehall and Montague to the newly developed farm country. He also said a new road is being completed from the town of Fruitvale to the County line bridge, leading to Big Blue Lake. All this being but a starter and ere long he promises that the development company will finish other necessary highways as outlets to markets for farm and orchard products. He feels positive that from now on Fruitvale will be a surprise and will grow very rapidly. He stated that the Fruitvale Development Co. has contributed for this purpose $1,000; also that the townships of Blue Lake and Montague had contributed another $1,000 and $600 more was promised for next spring. He also stated to the land owners that next year they would find the Montague -Whitehall road completed and that this would greatly benefit the development of the entire country along said "route." Then he spoke of the new boats and freighters now being operated up and down White River and that freight was being delivered from Whitehall to Fruitvale at 50¢ per ton. Nine families are now making their permanent homes in the town of Fruitvale and over 30 houses had been built on various tracts and that next summer a general store would be conducted. The poultry branch at Fruitvale is a great success. The farm has over 6000 "white leghorn hens" and was unable to supply the demands for eggs and chickens for Chicago hotels. M. Parker advised that more people join him in this enterprise and assured them of big profits through co-operation with the company.

Chicken Farm Fruitvale Mich.

Feeding the Chicks at Fruitvale, Mich

The Fruitvale Hotel was doing a big business this summer and it was necessary to make additions to the hotel and camp to accommodate the crowd. The company had this summer erected a greenhouse 30' x 100' and next spring would supply all tract owners with early plants, fruit trees and berry plants. The tract owners now have 80 acres planted to orchard and much more work will be done this fall and early next spring. The report was well received. Reports were also made by other members who were at Fruitvale this summer and all were well pleased with the progress now being made, and from all appearances it seems that ere long Fruitvale and it surrounding tracts will be the home of anew, happy and enterprising community, consisting of live wires who will spare neither money nor muscle to make a success of Fruitvale. After the meeting lunch was served and all present were entertained by good music and other talent."

October 21, 1915

With World War I looming as a dark cloud over the country, little activity was reported out of Fruitvale from its Chicago residents. The thoughts of most did not lie with a second home in Michigan nor the starting of a farm in Fruitvale. Because of this, all news reported was from the local residents of the Whitehall Montague area and their support of the "City."

As with most salesman, such as Harrison M. Parker, the harder the times, the harder they try. So during this time he started the Fruitvale National Farm Loan Association, in an effort to attract more people to the 5 acre Fruit and Poultry Gardens of Fruitvale. As a go between, the Association would take groups of interested farmer's and work to try to secure government loans to start their farms. Also published at this time was a lengthy booklet call "Chickens and Cherries at Fruitvale Michigan." This described how anyone with a little money, $5 down and $5 per month, could be self sufficient in only a few years at Fruitvale. No matter what the method used, few people took up the proposal, and the few that did, only lasted a short time. Today, if you look closely, the remnants of patches of fruit trees can still be seen in the area, but they are few and far between. The soil and the climate of the area, just is not as good as that of the northern sections of Oceana County where the "Fruit Belt" exist today.

Third Annual Picnic Of Booster Club Held At Riverside Inn

"The business men and Booster Club held their third annual picnic at Riverside Inn, Fruitvale last Thursday and from every point of view it was a grand success. Promptly at 11 o'clock nearly every businessman in town closed his doors and said good-bye to all business cares for the rest of the day. Those who had cars loaned them freely and a large number of men were thus accommodated, in all about 130 taking advantage of the outing. The roads were not so bad so the trip was soon made. Shortly after their arrival they formed in line for their march to the spacious dining room where the tables were found to contain the best of good things. Rev. J. W. Steffe invoked the divine blessing and then the men were served the most delicious chicken dinner ever set before a hungry crowd. How they did feast!"

September 6, 1917

Road to Fruitvale Needed

Harrison M. Parker and son Harrison Jr., at Fruitvale

Good Roads are Necessary to Insure Proper Development

Editor Whitehall Forum, Whitehall, Michigan

"Dear Sir: We had occasion to visit Fruitvale and the Big Blue Lake country a few days ago and must say that some improvements are going on all the time in this beautiful place. Mr. Parker's company is again reconstructing the dam at Brown's Pond and has also added a number of new building and out-houses on their 5 and 10 acre vegetable, fruit and poultry farms. What is most needed at the present time is at least one good road from Whitehall to Fruitvale and another to the same place from Montague. Good roads are what interest the farmers now days. Better still would be to again harness the White River at some convenient place and provide electricity for an interurban car line from Whitehall, through the beautiful Big Blue Lake country and then on to Fruitvale and Fremont. This would be the real starter for farm developments and would bring in a lot of new people who by their settlement and improvements would bring business to these towns and add more life and new energy to this part of Muskegon and Oceana Counties. It seems it is time for some body of men, such as the Chamber of Commerce, to take this matter up and act at once. If need be, bond Whitehall and Blue Lake Townships for at least two good roads. The money will be well invested. As it is now no person cares to invest in a country where roads are bad

Beulah Parker at the Parker Fruitvale residence

Mary Parker as a Red Cross Nurse during a WW I fundraiser given by her mother, Edith Parker at their Fruitvale home.

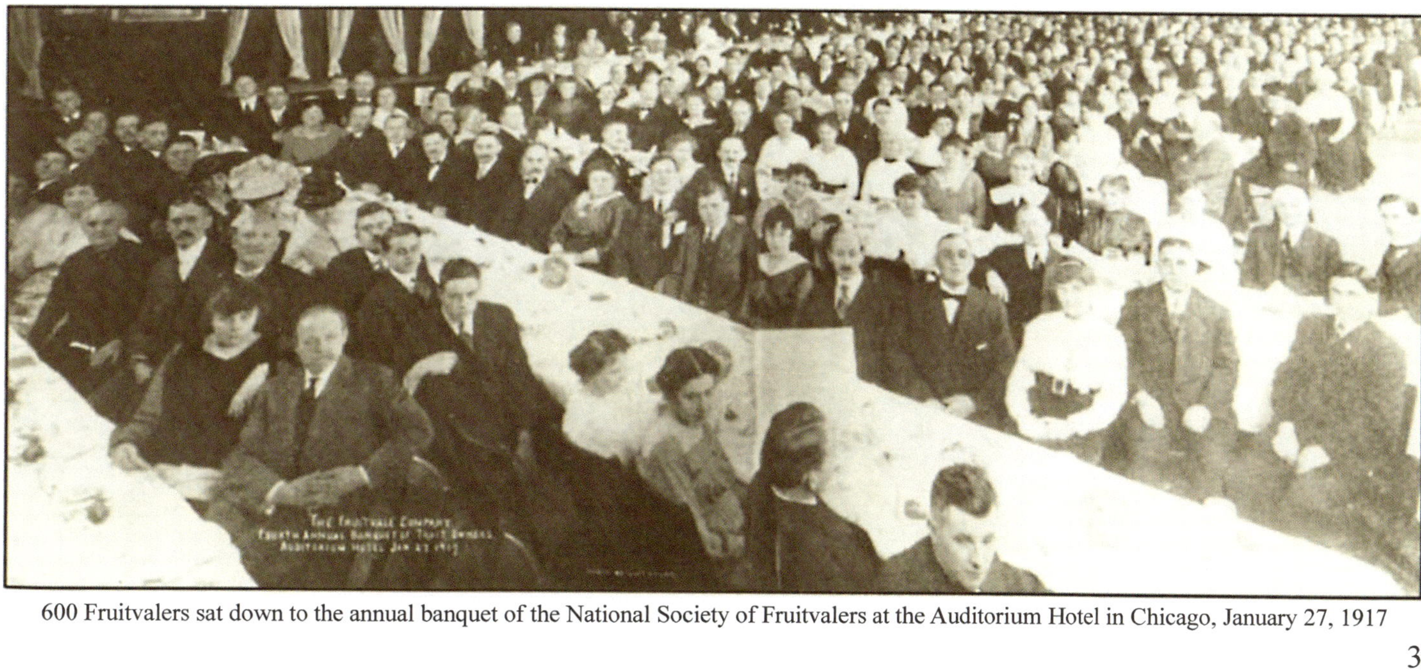

600 Fruitvalers sat down to the annual banquet of the National Society of Fruitvalers at the Auditorium Hotel in Chicago, January 27, 1917

and often impassible. Good roads also would bring more summer resorters and these in tum would spend their funds in Whitehall and Montague Mr. Mossbackwake up! Subscriber."

To hold on to what they have accomplished so far, the Fruitvale Company will mortgage it's holdings to receive needed working capital. From the documents filed at the county courthouse, we can now get a good idea as to the investment and effort put forth by Harrison M. Parker and his partner's, to establish the "City of Fruitvale." The complete list gives a very good example of the life style of the times, and is thus reprinted in its entirety at the back of the book. This list contains just the buildings construct by Harrison Parker and the Fruitvale Co. With many early articles reporting fraud on the part of Parker, these buildings show some of the monies reinvested into the area.

1 - Greenhouse
1 - Barn
2 - Wagon Sheds
1 - Boat House
5 - Boats
1 - Bargc
1 - Office
1 - Store Room
1 - Ice House 18 x 32 feet
1 - Blacksmith Shop
1 - Colony House 12 x 14 feet
1 - Six -room House
1 - 2-room House (office)
1 - Brooder House
1 - 3,000-egg Hall Mammoth Incubator
1 - Duck House
1 - Laying House 14 x 20 feet
1 - Shed 14, x 20 feet
3 - Laying Houses
1 - Breeding House
1 - Brooding House
1 - Store Room 16 x 36 feet
42 – Colony houses 6 x 8 feet
8 - Buses
1 - Hotel
41 - Tent Bungalows
1 - Club House
5 - Cottages
1 - Oil House
1 - General' Manager's Quarter
1 – Superintendent's House
1 - Dodge car

It will not be until the spring of 1920, that any more news or activity will come from Fruitvale. Now as the worlds troubles fade from memory, the residents of Chicago return to their lots, gardens, and the Rochdale Inn.

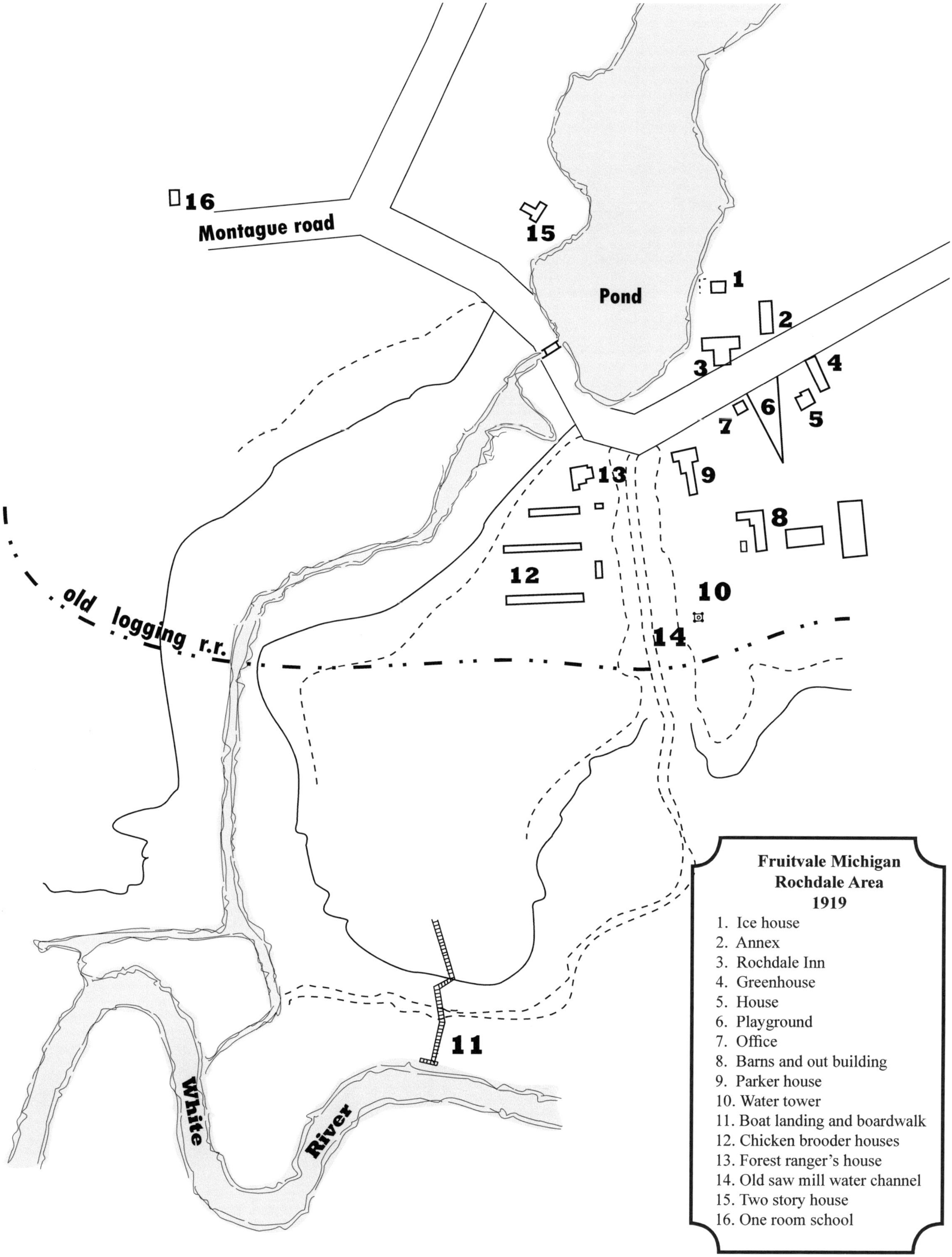
16
Montague road
15
Pond
1
2
3
4
5
6
7
13
9
8
12
10
14
old logging r.r.
11
White River
Fruitvale Michigan
Rochdale Area
1919
1. Ice house
2. Annex
3. Rochdale Inn
4. Greenhouse
5. House
6. Playground
7. Office
8. Barns and out building
9. Parker house
10. Water tower
11. Boat landing and boardwalk
12. Chicken brooder houses
13. Forest ranger's house
14. Old saw mill water channel
15. Two story house
16. One room school

Dear Maggie. This is the hotel where we are staying its lovely here, plenty of boating, swimming, and car rides, I only wish you were here it would do you good I hate to leave it Sat. morning. Mrs W. July, 1918

Dear Sister & Family; We are having one grand time. Taking all kinds of hikes. Leaving for Chi. Sat. morn. have been rowing on the lake back of the Inn. If I get down will tell you all about it, lots of love. Emma Aug. 21, 1924.

The 1920's

Early postcard view of the dam and "Falls" with the stairs.

1920

July 29, 1920

Fruitvale Improvements

Fruitvale this coming right to the front this summer with Mr. Chas. Schierstadt as manager of the hotel. He has about 100 guest at Rochdale Inn at the present time many more are expected before the season ends. Rebuilding of the dam and the comeback of beautiful Brown's Pond are big factors in making this resort popular. Among the latest improvements made for the pleasure and interest of the guest is a large dance pavilion extending out from the hotel over Brown's Pond. A bowling alley and a pool room will be added also to the hotel's amusement features.

July 1, 1920

New Pavilion at Fruitvale

A large dance pavilion has been built in connection with the Fruitvale hotel. It has 2,000 feet of floor space in this all enclosed with screens. Mr. and Mrs. Schierstadt are again in charge of the hotel. The Fruitvale dam has been rebuilt and is about ready to fill, Mr. Schierstadt expects to entertain a big crowd of Chicago people at the hotel on the fourth.

The rebuilding of the dam this year is of major importance not only to the Rochdale Inn, which overlooks the pond, but as a major attraction to the Fruitvale area as a whole. After the dam went out on Tuesday night, August 4, 1914, it was not rebuilt until 1920. For the past six years, only a meandering creek, with scattered mud puddles and numerous pine stumps, greeted visitors and landowners to the area. Constructed by William F. Thieman of Montague, one of the areas most respected contractors, the new concrete structure although showing its age, still holds back the waters of Sand Creek today. During the summer, the steps descending on either side of the dam are constructed, and then in the fall, the pleasure park is added. The park will consist of a large wading pool at the base of the falls, along with trails and footbridges over the creek.

The Fruitvale Gazette

"Mr. and Mrs. A. Loe of Jefferson Park, Chicago, were spending their honeymoon at the Rochdale Inn, were given a great ovation by a host of Fruitvale and most prominent citizens.

The reception committee consisted of the following;

Mrs. G. Galloux, Tin Can Performer
Miss Flo Anderson, Shimmay Star
E. T. Anderson, Star Gazer Aviator
R. W. Christie, Soda Squirter and Daylight Seeker, odervise moonshiner EE. EE Felin – Alias Mary Jane

The above cast was assisted by a most beautiful chorus consisting of;

Tim Wilson, The Holy Ghost
Elleen Houliban, Snake Charmer
Mary Houliban, Baby Bliss
Virginia Sullivan, The Child Vamp
Frances Etty Ratty, Heavenly Twins
Della Shaney, With the Ancient Voice
The 5 Musketeers from Chicago, All for 1 (girl) and one for all.

A mob with horns, tin cans, kazoos and husky voices kidnapped the bridal couple from their bridal suite at bungalow 22, in Lover's Lane under the pine groves. Then the angry mob and blood-thirsty crew marched them to the parlor of the Inn. Jack Hartney took his chances to kidnap the bride, which was done via his tin-lizzie. After the strenuous escapade, the crowd marched to the soda emporium, presided over by Ralph Christie who with magnanimous liberality and great self-sacrifice treated the bridal couple to horse necks and chocolate sundaes, while the mob looked on with parched lips and dry throats, until the greatest benefactors Tom Sullivan and Emil Fellin-the Chicago philanthropist, unable to see the sufferings of the herd came to the rescue and "set' em up."

"The wind-up came with an aeroplane ascension given to the bridal pair, with E. T. Anderson as pilot and a march back to their abode, leaving them to reflect on their folly."

"Ms. Virginia Sullivan is taking her vacation in bed."

"Flo Anderson, the busy body and life of this community, has learned a new shimmy movement called the snake of the wicked hip."

"Miss. Gaselle Schwartz dreamed of worms all night. She has also learned a new stroke and is ready to give swimming lessons to all comers."

"Don't forget the big dance Tuesday night with the celebrated, exasperated Wodoe's Orchestra."

"Ralph Christie has vindicated himself of the acquisition of being crabby and has promised not to knock down any tax receipts."

Edw. E. Fellin, the noted chicken fancier has alienated a squab from Christy and indications are that the Fruitvalers will wetness a mighty battle between the two gladiators.

August 5, 1920

This year also marks the first year in which the taxes for some of the lots in the Original Town of Fruitvale, are being paid by the lot owners direct. Before this, all of the taxes were collected by Fruitvale, and then they paid the county.

Thursday, September 9, 1920

Good Time at Picnic

Annual Festival Takes Large Crowd to Fruitvale

A beautiful day and a large turnout were the welcomed guest at Rochdale Inn, Fruitvale, last Friday, the day of Whitehall's Annual Citizens picnic. Over 40 automobiles and 200 people journeyed to that beautiful spot known as Brown's pond, which by the way is Fruitvale's chief asset has a summer resort possibility.

The happy crowd left Whitehall and about 9:00 bent on a day of pleasure and sport. Shortly after arrival at Fruitvale, baseball games were in vogue. Ladies as well as men played the national pastime and if reports are true, the ladies played a better game.

After two hours of baseball 152 hungry people sojourned themselves to the dining room of Rochdale Inn and partook of dinner. Needless to say they devoured everything set before them, licked their plates clean and even desired more. Such was their hunger.

Then came the sporting events, gun club shoot, more ball games and dancing in the new pavilion. The White family, with three entries in sporting events, took high honors with three first and a like number of prizes. Dorothy and Jean are real athletes, they surely can run and jump.

The sack race furnished the spectators with the most amusement. Just try it once and see how easy it is. Honors and a 25 pound sack of flour, donated by Reed Bros., went to Alex Forsbery who won in a close finish with L. B. Gee second. The finale of the races was stage by Mrs. Gustaf Moovie, contestant in the fat ladies race, who easily won because it was not run.

Next came the challenge of the single men to the married men for a tug-of-war. The married men quickly and gladly accepted. Why not? They were the most husky and heavy. All set. Pull! Then snap! went the rope with such force as to send the warriors into heaping, scrambling and seething confusion. Another rope was secured in the pull again started. Out-weighted and out pulled with the assistance of Jack DeWitt the married men were victors and the single men succumbed to defeat. Single men however were not quitters. They put up a

great fight and are only too willing to have another try. "Next year," said they, "we'll show you."

It was a day well spent and thoroughly enjoyed. As dusk fell the crowd slowly and hesitantly retraced their steps back home, only wishing for another such gala day in the near future. Once a year is to seldom. Why not get-to-gather and have a good time every once-in-a-while, instead of once a year.

BLUE LAKE DISTRICT A GROWING RESORT CENTER

"The Blue Lakes are rapidly developing into a real live resort center of Muskegon County," according to Wm. C. McGinnis in a recent interview with The Forum. Mr. McGinnin, a summer inhabitant of Blue Lake for over nine years, is now permanently located in that beautiful region that is calling many Chicago people to its shores. He says that prospects are bright for the future prosperity of this "land of the beautiful lakes. "

In the past five years, according to Mr. McGinnis, much building has taken place in the Blue Lake region, and he places a conservative estimate of $30,000 as having been spent in construction work there within the past two or three years, not including the 248 Club. Cottages and summer homes have been built by the following Chicago people in this period; Measrs, Cleaver, Kolling, Parmenter, Dystrup, Hogstrom, Peterson, Hyrish, McGinnis, Bowling and Church.

Point Comfort hotel and cottages were also erected last year. The hotel proper is a building 40 x 80 feet, which last summer accommodated an average of 45 guest per day. Ten cottages, 12 x 20 feet, were also constructed to operate in connection with that hotel. A great demand for cottages has developed and all were occupied last season.

The Little Landers also dedicated their new club house this past year and some members spent a very pleasant time in those surroundings.

Mr. McGinnis further says, "I have every reason to believe there will be much construction work next summer." He adds, "Not only does this money spent contribute to the tax-roll but it also adds to the receipts of Whitehall and Montague business firms. Those who are here and those who make a habit of coming here are bending every effort to get good roads in this section, so that Whitehall and Montague will be more easily accessible. When that times comes, which will be soon, Blue Lake will surely be on the map."

April 14, 1921

Mr. Parker in Dock Project

"The people of Montague are very grateful to Mr. Harrison Parker and the Cooperative Society of America for making it possible for us to get the Goodrich boat services to White Lake this season. They are constructing a new dock 200 by 20 feet and warehouse 30 x 50 ft. at a cost of about $5,000, which dock they will rent to the Goodrich Transit Co. They also purchased the Sadony property on Prospect Street in this village in order to be able to have plenty of gravel for the roads necessary to make the dock a success. Mr. Parker has always been a 'bear' for our section of the country and has brought many a dollar to our community. His grand success with the Cooperative Society of America only goes to show what hard work and persistence will accomplish. "

August, 1921

"Mrs. Lexington has completed her house on the County Line road. H. Hauss of Sec. 32 has also completed a home. We wish a few more like these would settle in Fruitvale, then our sections would increase in value and more chances for good roads."

"W. Hammond and family are tenting on their lot at 12th St. and Woodlawn Ave. in the original town of Fruitvale."

"Mrs. Shaw has completed her home this year and has it decorated in a pleasing manner. She also has put up a wire fence around her lots which looks nice."

"The Ladies Aid Society of Fruitvale will attend the bazaar given by the Ladies Aid Society of Montague August 3."

"Miss Alaine Brown and her family of Persian kittens have been at the Wawanaisson cabin for the last seven weeks and expect to stay until snow flies."

"Mr. Sleber had the good luck of landing a three pound bass at the county line bridge Sunday.'

"The Rochdale Inn looks better this year than last with the diving platform and boat pier. The pleasure park below the dam is a very pleasing spot to spend a hot day. It is gratifying to see so many improvements."

"Nick Anderson has a swollen lip as a result of the Montague - Whitehall football game last Friday afternoon."

"Thursday evening October 6th a merry party, composed of residents of Fruitvale and Trading Post enjoyed a bus ride to Muskegon. A fine time was had by all notwithstanding the damp weather."

"The boys of the neighborhood held a meeting Friday evening at the Trading Post school house for the purposes of organizing a basketball team."

October 13, 1921

"The home of Mr. and Mrs. T. A. Smith was the scene of a lively Halloween party last week. The house was profusely decorated with autumn leaves, pumpkins, black cats, witches and goblins. Over fifty guest were present, all masked as fancy dictated. The ghosts, goblins, witches etc, had a very puzzling guessing contest until all were unmasked. Halloween stunts and games were the features of the evening. Refreshments consisted of red-hots, coffee and good old fashioned doughnuts. The part dispersed at a late hour, all wishing that Halloween would come soon again."

November 17, 1921

Challenge From Fruitvale

"The White River Athletic Club is now busy getting its basketball team in shape. Considering that practice is held only once a week owing to the lack of a gym, things are progressing fairly well. All the men are new at the game except Art Henrichs and Frank Stiles. The former played while at Lane Tech., while the latter played with the Wendell Phillips High of Chicago. Ira Ruffer and Tom King the forwards, are new men but both are learning the game rapidly. Ruffer is fast and is a hard man to guard. Stiles plays center where in this position he can captain the team. The guards, Art Henrich and Harry Weisses are both valuable men and should make their opponents hustle to get away from them. As reserves Bob Stanton, Don Walker and Elvin King are ready to step in if any thing goes wrong. The team is looking forward to their first game, and are looking to take on any team averaging from 135 to 140 Ibs. In regards to games write to the manager, Mr. Puffer, Montague, Box 4."

1922

Almost from the beginning of Fruitvale and its co-operative style of "working together," several groups of land owners have organized for the betterment of the community. These clubs consisted of the; "Fruitvalers," with membership open to all land owners, and meetings once a year during the winter in Chicago, the "S. S. S. Club," which built its club house about 1/2 mile West of Big Blue Lake, overlooking a small creek, the "248 Club" on Blue Lake, and the most locally prominent groups, the "Little Landers," and the Blue Lake Co-operative Association.

As most of these organizations where started in concept, during the long off season in Chicago, and died out slowly after a few years, it is not possible to determine their exact life span. Most seemed to be in existence though from about the mid 1910's until about the late 1920's. Based on a newspaper published by the Blue Lake Cooperative Assoc., this group was formed in 1915, while the Little Landers' was started in 1914.

Little Landers Column

President Steiner Explains Purpose of Organization

"In this article, I will endeavor to convey to our readers the objects of our organization.

Since the discovery of Fruitvale, some years ago, a number of organizations composed of Fruitvale lot and tract owners were formed with the best intentions of doing something for their members. And the years passed by and so did these organizations. There was much discussing done but absolutely no action taken. They all seemed to be as far from their ultimate aim when they ended as when they started. One of the main reasons for this failure to accomplish anything, was the entire lack of funds for any kind of purpose.

As a consequence this very important question of settling on their land is for most tract owners as big a puzzle today as it was yesterday, and will be so tomorrow, until they realize that the solution of all questions effecting the future development of Fruitvale, depends a great deal on the property owners themselves. They must begin to realize that it requires the whole-hearted support of every one and that all must share in the cost to carry on the work.

The purpose of our association is to unite and secure the cooperation of tract owners for the purpose of developing their land and for the welfare of Fruitvale in general. This paragraph convey very near the purpose of our organization.

We are incorporated not for profit, and this fact should be appreciated by all Fruitvalers. We have no selfish motives in our endeavor to help in the general improvement of Fruitvale. In order to make our monthly meetings more attractive and interesting we usually add a social feature of some kind. We have for this purpose a standing committee for entertainment.

These social features of our meetings become an event to be looked forward to with a certain amount of pleasant anticipation.

Our annual dance is a big event, as is our annual banquet. I may state here, that our membership is proving its loyalty in helping to make all of our affairs a success.

However, it is not merely the problem of Fruitvale that occupy our minds. We have started in the right direction to make our club a permanent institution, and have our members enjoy all benefits and privileges there from. For this reason we have built a shelter on Big Blue Lake, a small house, which in time will become larger and greater. This little house was built mainly with the money of members that have bought Life Membership Certificates and it belongs to the members, to use it as their home whenever they visit Blue Lake.

The little house, modest as to dimensions stands as a symbol of the spirit that made it possible to erect it. More about our organization in succeeding articles."

Gustav Steiner, Pres.

Thursday, April 6, 1922
Little Landers of Fruitvale

"This week we are introducing to our readers a new column, which is to be a regular feature of our publication. This column is to be devoted entirely to Fruitvale and Blue Lake resort interest and has the support of a large number of new subscribers whose interest lie in the development of that territory.

The Little Landers of Fruitvale are sponsoring this publicity campaign. G. Steiner is president and J. G. Heim, is secretary of the organization. The secretary's office is located at 4300 Calumet Ave., Chicago. Where subscriptions to The Forum will be taken and news items for this column received."

The President's Message

"By courtesy of the publishers of this paper, "The Little Landers of Fruitvale" are enabled to send a message to many that are interested in Fruitvale and that otherwise would not be aware of the existence of this organization and its purpose.

In this column we will register all the news pertaining to Fruitvale as we receive it from our members and friends. We will tell of the activities of our organizations, give an account of our entertainments and report all matters that come up in the course of our meetings and that we deem important enough to be of interest to our readers and to make this column composed of desirable reading.

This association is organized not for profit and our meetings are conducted open to all. Meetings are held every 2nd Wednesday of each month at 912 Masonic Temple, Chicago. More about the purposes of our organization, its underlying reasons and its principles, will appear in succeeding articles."

Gustav Steiner, Pres.

"Secretary J. G. Helm says as follows: "The Little Landers of Fruitvale" are now entering their eight year of activity. They own their clubhouse and grounds on Blue Lake and more improvements are on the way. We are expecting this years events to be the banner year of all. While we are willing to work and do work, we also know how to have a good time. Watch us! We have 'The People' in the Little Landers, we have 'The Time' in the good old summertime and we have 'The Place' on Big Blue Lake."

A box social will be the principle leisure of our next meeting on Wednesday, March 8th. It is understood that the ladies will bring a box lunch for two and that the gentlemen will buy them at auction. All who have attended these affairs, know something of the good times usually had. The doors swing open to anyone interested in Fruitvale and the Fruitvale country, together with its several organizations.

If you hold pleasant memories of Fruitvale and Big Blue Lake, with its entrancing streams and woodlands, you are invited to join us."

March 2, 1922, Thursday
Little Landers of Fruitvale

"In my last article, I explained the object of our organization. Today, I shall give a summary of our accomplishments. When our society was founded, nothing definite could be promised and the members really expected more than the organization was able to give. Advice and morale support, alone, will not build up anything. The spirit of our membership manifested itself right there when the suggestion was made to build a home on Big Blue Lake.

The necessary sum to buy a lot on the lake was subscribed, and then building bonds of ten dollars each were sold. After a time it was deemed advisable to call in the bonds and exchange them for fifty dollar Life Membership Certificates. A number of the members paid up these certificates and by doing so helped to put over the building program. By purchasing one of these certificates the holder is exempt from paying any further dues for the rest of his natural life, is prorated share owner of all the clubs property, and is entitled to all privileges that the club can extend to its members.

Now we own, clear of debt, a valuable lot on Big Blue Lake, which is improved by a house to afford shelter at all times to every member that so desires. These assets enable us at once to occupy the advantageous position of being on the ground to spread · out propaganda for the development of Fruitvale in general, and to live up to our objects, our purposes and our principles."

Gustav Steiner, Pres.

"The Little Landers are busily engaged in a number of activities these days. Principal of which, just now, is our annual dance, to be held Thursday evening, May 25th at Colonial Hall, Chicago. A number of other clubs that are directly interested in Michigan have signified their intention to cooperate with us.

Having observed with great interest, the summer resort activities, as delineated upon through the columns of the Whitehall Forum, which are to be concurred in the coming season we who have interest in Michigan and especially in Muskegon County, are elated to some considerable degree. We are accordingly expected to greater hope and more actual endeavors as regards our interest there, and anticipations of a pleasant and successful vacation this season is already assured.

Many of us have formed a habit of going to Michigan. We have never regretted the expense incurred. Our strenuous activity in the City makes our vacation days an actual necessity. Are we coming? I and we are coming many thousand strong and we expect to leave many thousands of dollars in Michigan. We will do so with no regrets. We expect to pay our way and arrange accordingly.

Space will not permit, nor will words suffice to express how in the near future the summer resort possibilities of Michigan will be so-related with the wonder of Chicago."

J. G. Heim
Secretary of the Little Landers of Fruitvale

Thursday, May 18, 1922

Fruitvale News

"Our recent meeting was well attended and the social feature and supper will long be remembered, and the additional finances derived will fit in very conveniently at this time. Everybody went home evidently well pleased as there was no end to the general chatter and merriment long after the meeting was closed. The summer vacations being over will have a tendency to enhance the activities of our interest during the coming months.

We are looking forward to a lively time on Oct. 11th, as this will be our Annual Election night. The Governing Board have recently met and began laying plans for our future activities as far as they will pertain to the coming years work. All our members should be out at this meeting and learn first hand just what is to be done and be in readiness to co-operate toward the further success of our organization."

OCTOBER 5, 1922

LITTLE LANDERS HOLD MEET

"The Little Landers of Fruitvale meets the second Wednesday of every month in their hall, 912 Masonic Temple Building, Chicago.

The last meeting held October 11, was an important and interesting one. The annual reports of the various officers of the organization were heard and election of officers for the ensuing year resulted as follows:

President - F. A. Ruebner.
Vice President - G. Steiner.
Recording Sec'y - Wm. T. Barnum
Sec'y-Treas. - G. M. Barnum
Trustees - H. Nabel and E. Maggnuson
Members of Governing Board - J. Bartl, R. Schneider, Mrs. H. E. Lonsdale, E. Walter, Wm.C.McGinnis, Miss J. Woelke.

It is the plan of the President to get the Club House, located at Big Blue Lake, in order so that it can be used by members wishing to spend their vacation at that beautiful spot at Big Blue Lake."

NOVEMBER 9, 1922

LITTLE LANDERS COLUMN

"Many of our members returning from Fruitvale are reporting progress there in a general way and of the entire satisfaction accorded them by the 248 Club and the Rochdale Inn. Both Hotels were well patronized during the past vacation season just ended and far exceeded expectations.

The Little Landers meeting to be held Wednesday evening, September 20th, at 8 p.m., will include an old fashion box party. All ladies attending are expected to prepare a box lunch for two and the gentlemen are to buy these boxes at auction. Individual boxes are not to exceed one dollar in price, and receipts are to go into the general fund of the organization. Let's all pull together and see if we cannot outdo some of our former parties of this nature, which have previously proven satisfactory in every way.

As an addition to the entertainment, 1. G. Helm will give a series of select stereoptican views which have been asked for several times. These views will be instructive as well as entertaining. Mr. Heim has had experience in this line for many years and you may expect to hear and see things out of the ordinary.

In the near future a basket picnic will be held in Lincoln Park. Date will be announced later. They say it's to be on The Hill, in the Park, about a block off Center Street. Mrs. A. Thice is chairman of the picnic committee and can give all the details. She is to be assisted by a goodly number of our most handsome ladies. We'll all be there. Who would miss a basket picnic with all the other things that go with it. "

SEPTEMBER 14, 1922

PICNICKERS TO HAVE TIME

"All aboard for Fruitvale. The cars leave Colby Street at 9 o'clock for a day's picnic and fun. All Whitehall is going to enjoy the banquet, sports and pleasure. Entertainment of every variety is being planned and to stay away is to miss one of the best times possible.

Prizes will be offered to make the sporting events an attractive card. Watch the fat man run, the sack race and the ball

games between the married and single men, the tannery and the businessmen and then the play-off. Sure there's going to be lots of events for the women, too."

While the community of Fruitvale sleeps through the cold winter months of 1923, a major change in the ownership and management of the holdings occurs. Although Harrison M. Parker will at this time relinquish most of the control of the company with the sale, he will reappear again in the oil years of the late 1920s. With this new ownership, lots will continue to be sold along with five-acre tracts, but the emphasis will change from the farming of the land, to the recreational uses of the Inn as a resort community.

Parker home, latter called the Lakeview Cottage.

Riverside Inn as it appeared in early 1920.

February 22, 1923

Fruitvale Changes Hands

Fruitvale, Michigan. February 15, 1923
Montague Observer Montague, Michigan

"Gentlemen: as we have received several phone calls regarding the rumor that the Estate of Fruitvale, formally owned by the Co-operative Society of America, has been sold by them, we believe it would probably be of interest to many of your readers to find out about this change of ownership through your paper. The entire Estate of the Co-operative Society of America, with the exception of the Rochdale Hotel, was sold February 1, 1923 by them to Gustave Kopp and William B. Lidke. The Estate consist of approximately 16,000 acres of land in Muskegon, Lake, Oceana and Newaygo Counties, some of this land is improved by farmstead cottages, also the south side of Big Blue Lake, the hotel known as 24S Club and the club building known as S.S.S. Club, and dock at Montague. The Rochdale Hotel has not been purchased for the reason that a clear title could not be obtained by the purchasers on account of a junior mortgage on this property, the hotel, however, is leased to the purchasers for a term of 20 years with the option of purchasing any time during this term, which will be done as the junior mortgage in question will be retired before the term of the lease expires. The purchasers are incorporating at the present under the laws of the state of Michigan, the name of the Corporation will be the Fruitvale Resort Company. The home office will be Montague, Mich., the Chicago office will be in the People's life building. The officers of the Corporation will be Mr. Gustave Kopp President; Mr. George H. Wilkins, Vice President; Mr. William P. Lidke, Secretary and Treasurer. It is the intention of the purchasers to use the entire estate is a hunting and fishing preserve, and as a resort and Country Club. A new clubhouse equipped with pool tables and bowling alleys has been completed, and a second story is being added to the Rochdale Hotel with about 36 more rooms; the dining room is being enlarged so as to accommodate a large number of guest; a large veranda will stretch across the entire front and side of the hotel on both floors; a stable of saddle horses been has been acquired for the use of patrons and guests next summer; soon as the weather permits, and modern large golf course will be laid out and constructed adjacent to the hotel property; it will also be the aim of the new owners to open the hotel earlier in the season and keep same open until October 1st, so as to give the late vacationers a chance to visit the playground of the United States, the State of Michigan.

We sincerely hope to get the support of all the people in this territory to help us and to help make the State a real resort and playground proposition to all concerned!

Yours very truly. Fruitvale resort company by William B Lidke.

April 26, 1923

$100 Reward

$100 reward will be paid for the information being to the arrest and conviction of anyone leaving unguarded campfires or

"A Scotchman's Dream" (L to R) J. A. Caster, Agnes Grabske, Jos. James, Adeline Krause

Vera Myers from St. Louis, Mo.

setting fire carelessly, or with intent, on our property or property under our control.
Fruitvale Resort Co.

MAY 10, 1923

FOREST FIRE AT FRUITVALE

A forest fire near Fruitvale threatened to wipe out that section of the country last Saturday and Sunday when an area of three square miles was burned over and four houses and two garages were destroyed before the flames were subdued. Help to fight the fire was summoned from Montague and Whitehall. Fire Chief, Chas. Obrenberger, with a force of firemen, responded to the call and after fighting the fire for 14 hours got it under control.

Thursday, October 25, 1923

As each year come and goes, so does the leadership change at Fruitvale. In its efforts to survive, the company will add new officers depending on the talent and capital they possess. For 1924, the company is listed as follows:

Fruitvale Resort Company
(A Michigan Corporation)
Martin J. Higgins, President
Joseph H. Gerken, Vice President
John Coe, Treasurer
Gustave Kopp, Secretary and General Manager
Directors:
Joseph H. Gerken
Geo. B. Parmenter
Geo. E. Galloux
L. J. Simmonds
John Coe
Martin J. Higgins
R. P. Sheperd
Gustave Kopp, Chicago Office, Room 805, 130 N. Wells St.

It must be noted that not everyone enjoyed living at Fruitvale. While most of its residents only stayed for a short time during the summer season, a few soles tried to make a living from the land. Some succeeded, while most found the land unforgiving.

July 24, 1924

Woman Takes Own Life

"Mrs. August Beck, of Fruitvale, took her own life Saturday by swallowing carbolic acid. Mrs. Beck had attempted suicide once before and had failed. Despondency was said to have been the reason for her act, Mrs. Beck, with her husband, came to Fruitvale about four years ago from Chicago to operate a chicken ranch. The lonely life, after years of living in the city, was said to have affected the woman. She is survived by her husband and one son, who lives in Chicago. Mrs. Beck was about 45 years old. Funeral services and burial were in Whitehall, Monday."

The next three years for the most part were a quite time around Fruitvale, with little major news being reported.

In 1925, with J. M. Agee, as manager of the Rochdale Inn, an effort was made to attract more local business from the communities of Whitehall and Montague. One group which had several of its meetings at the Inn was the Chamber of Commerce. Also during the summer of 1925, boat races were held at White Lake, with Fruitvale offering bus service from the Grand Stands to the Inn each night for dancing and dinner.

By 1926, the ownership of the Fruitvale Resort Company changes management again to; Gustave Kopp, President and General Manager, Joseph H. Gerken, Vice President, John Coe Treasurer, E. M. Otto, Secretary.

Beside the founder of Fruitvale, Harrison M. Parker and wife Edith Stubbs Parker, Gustave (Gus) Kopp, tried the hardest and worked the longest, to make the resort a success. Born in Iowa in 1882, Gus would move to Chicago, where he would first hear about Fruitvale in the early 1920s and would become an officer of the company shortly thereafter. To Gus, Fruitvale would become his life, and he worked there each year, until his death on September 27, 1968 in Chicago. A kind and gentle man, he had a single focus, to make ones experience at Fruitvale a pleasurable and a memorable experience that would entice the guests to return year after year. During the short summer season, Gus would most often be seen around the Rochdale Inn, with camera in hand, taking pictures of guests enjoying themselves with family and the new friends they made. The idea he had was simple, yet well thought out. He would take the pictures of the guest, then during the long cold

Relaxing in the Falls. (L to R) Bud, Mildred, Alice, Harry

winter months, Gus and his small staff at the Chicago office, would mail the photos free of charge to the vacationers. The idea was to rekindle the memories of the great time had by one and all during the summer, and to ask them to register at that time for the upcoming season at Rochdale Inn.

Being a strong believer in the power of the picture, especially of vacationers having a good time, in addition to the photographs taken by Gus at the end of each week, a professional photographer was hired to take group photographs of all the guest before their departure. Photography also play a strong roll in the sales brochures that Gus had reprinted yearly. All the brochures relied heavily on photographs to sell the message of an enjoyable time in a relaxing atmosphere while having fun with friends. The only pictures on the walls of the dance hall across the road from the Inn, and in the lobby of the Inn itself, were group photo's of resorters. In addition to the photographs, numerous picture post cards were available for sale at Fruitvale. There are nearly 60 different ones known to exist, covering the history and happenings at Fruitvale.

Another idea that Gus had was that of having "business girls" stay at the Inn. The idea was simple, yet very effective. He would concentrate his ads in newspapers for the Inn towards having secretaries and young college girls spend their vacations at Rochdale Inn. Of course, by doing this, the men will not be far behind. This large gathering of young ladies, also attracted many local men, married, single, doctors, lawyers, etc. It is believed by a former manager of the Inn, that the wives clamping down on their husbands and boy friends travel to Fruitvale, helped in part, to contribute to the downfall of the Rochdale Inn!

Gus Kopp, in addition to the photographs he took, during the off season, wrote countless letters to guest, friends, and business people. It is fortunate that today, several of these letters survived. During a period starting in the early 1920s and into the 1940s, Gus was in correspondence with the Messmore - Durringer family of Ohio. The Messmore's owned a large tract of land on the west side of Brown's Pond, and adjoining the Fruitvale holdings. It was Gus's intention to acquire this property from them for further expansion of the most important area of Fruitvale, that being the area surrounding the Rochdale Inn. So during the some twenty years that Gus worked on the purchase of this property, he wrote on a regular bases to the Messmores', not only about the land transaction, but about the conditions at Fruitvale. What makes this even more important to the history of Fruitvale, was the fact that Mrs. Messmore keep not only copies of the letters of reply to Gus, but also the letters he wrote to them.

Gus Kopp with his camera.

Looking west across Harrison (Fruitvale Rd.) at the Rochdale Inn.

The new tennis court at the Inn.

Boat dock at the front of the Inn.

Relaxing after lunch. Manager Raymond Baker standing (L) with white cap and pipe.

Just a note

All of the news coming out of Fruitvale in 1927 was good news. A major fire occurred that year with a loss of seven of the original poultry farm buildings.

April 14, 1927

"Forest fires swept over a large area of land around Fruitvale last Saturday and Sunday destroying many chicken houses on the various ranches along Sand Creek. Dan Gau who lives at Brown's pond, says it was the worse fire that has visited that section since his residence there. His home was also threatened but was saved after fighting the approaching fire for several hours."

Beginning in early 1928, another change in the management of the Fruitvale Resort Company occurs. Gustave Kopp remains as President and General Manager, with a new Vice President in the naming of Frederick Seaberg, and Treasurer George E. Galloux, while E. M. Otto continues as Secretary.

This year also marks the beginning of a close cooperation between Gus Kopp and the Chicago Area Boy Scouts of America, which will last for some 40 years. In an effort to shore up slacking revenues, Gus will attempt to sell several hundred acres of White River frontage in Oceana County to the scouts for $22,350.00. This is the first major land purchase from Fruitvale, that the scouts made to expand their Owasippe scout camp. But in a letter written by Gus in September 1931, the 'deal' is still pending.

Even though Gus writes, "the weather has been unusually warm down here (Fruitvale) as well as in Chicago, consequently we have been able to do a capacity business; in fact, we have been turning them away the past several weeks."

Fruitvale and the Rochdale Inn never seemed to make money. With a very short resort season, late June to the first weekend of September, weather played a major role as to the turnout of resorters. Also figuring into the financial stability of the resort, was the large staff that Gus maintained. Normally about 50 employees were hired each summer. The staff consisted of; cooks, kitchen help, waitresses, managers for the Inn, cleaning staff, recreational directors, general staff, and of course the bands that played each night. Most of the staff consisted of young college students that were brought in for the summer from out of the state. With poor transportation

Horseback riding in front of the Fruitvale stables.

The ladies enjoying a game of bridge in 1929. Fruitvale Resort Co. Land Office (L)

Vacationers at the Rochdale Inn.

in the area, this insured that the staff would stay the summer, regardless.

Another area of major expense, was that of the food cost at the Inn. No matter who you talk to, or whatever article you read, the quality of the food was always given high praise. Many local residents still have fond memories of going to the Rochdale Inn for their Sunday chicken dinners.

August 16, 1928

Guest of Rochdale Inn

The Progressive Club, were guest of Gustave Kopp at the Rochdale Inn, Fruitvale, Tuesday evening. After partaking of a fine spread the club was treated to an interesting travelogue talk by George W. Davies, secretary of the McLaughlin for Congress club, of Muskegon. The hotel orchestra furnished some exceptionally fine music during the dinner hour. Some of the boys repaired to the ballroom after the meeting and indulged in the light fantastic. Rochdale Inn is filled to its capacity at this time with resorters. This resort has been greatly improved and beautified under the present management and is becoming more popular every season. The spacious dining room accommodates a large number and the hotel has a capacity of about 250 guests. The surroundings, are delightful, there being plenty of opportunity for recreation in the surrounding woodland, and the sylvan waters of Brown's Pond and Big Blue Lake where fishing, boating and bathing afford great sport to the resorters.

AN ADVANCE "X-RAY" OF THE 1930 SEASON

RAY BAKER

Our Popular Assistant Manager

will be at Rochdale again this summer, to help make your visit a pleasant and comfortable one. He's there, waiting to welcome you Decoration Day, so plan now to spend the vacation at Rochdale.

X: "Hello, Ray! Appears like we'll have a great crowd up Decoration Day, eh what?"

Ray: "Sure does, X. Reservations look as though we'll see a good many of our old friends soon."

X: "Well, I've a lot of surprises planned. It won't be *my* fault if they all don't have the time of their lives!"

Ray: "Mine either. But you don't need to worry—judging from last summer. Mac (the Chef), who is already on the job, is planning to outdo himself with all kinds of wonderful food. And have you noticed all the new improvements around here—beautiful flowers and everything?"

X: "You bet I have! The Inn looks wonderful this year. By the way, did they get that good orchestra for the Decoration Day dance?"

Ray: "Yes sir! Just wait 'till you hear it. That ballroom will be in an uproar!"

X: "It'll seem good to see a lot of familiar faces."

Ray: "You bet—and a lot of new ones, too."

There won't be a dull moment at Rochdale Inn over Decoration Day, and during the rest of the season, too, if these enthusiastic gentlemen have anything to say about it. And Mr. J. E. McKay, Rochdale's famous chef-steward, is anxious to do his share with tempting additions to his always excellent cuisine. Let them prove to you how much real fun a vacation at Rochdale this summer will be.

X Y Z

Our Famous Athletic Director—

will greet you at the Inn Decoration Day. Here he is, smiling a welcome to everyone of you. You'll learn new tricks of fancy diving and a lot of interesting Outdoor things under the competent instructions of "X." "Every girl a swimmer," is his motto.

SPECIAL DECORATION DAY OUTING—LEAVING CHICAGO THURSDAY NIGHT, MAY 29TH; RETURN TRIP, LEAVING SUNDAY NIGHT—ALL EXPENSES PAID—INCLUDING STATEROOM—$26.25.

ROCHDALE INN - - - - MONTAGUE, MICHIGAN

Reservations Made at Chicago Office; 130 North Wells Street, Room 801 - - - Telephone Dearborn 5498

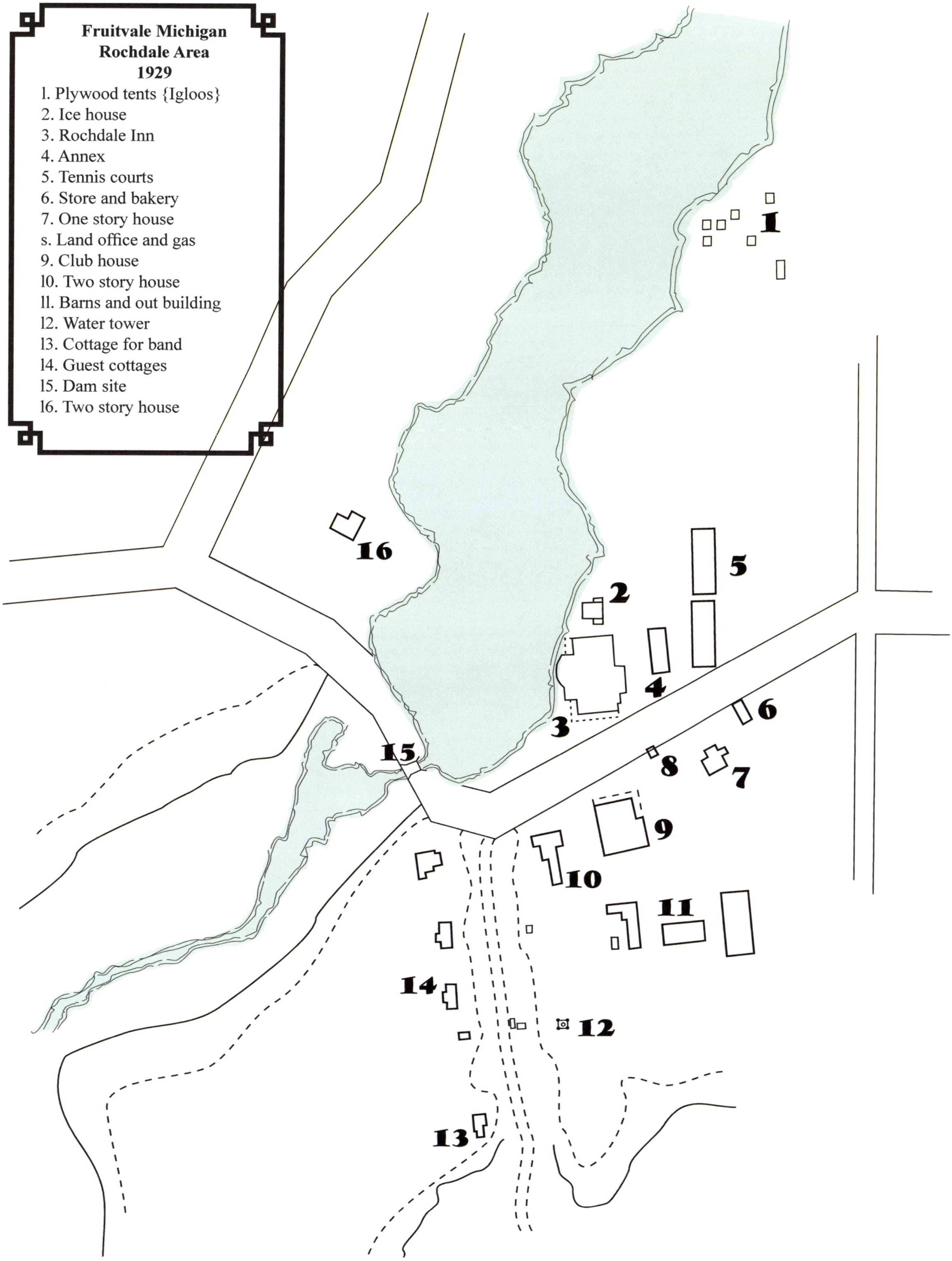
Fruitvale Michigan
Rochdale Area
1929
l. Plywood tents {Igloos}
2. Ice house
3. Rochdale Inn
4. Annex
5. Tennis courts
6. Store and bakery
7. One story house
s. Land office and gas
9. Club house
l0. Two story house
1l. Barns and out building
l2. Water tower
l3. Cottage for band
l4. Guest cottages
l5. Dam site
l6. Two story house
1
2
3
4
5
6
7
8
9
10
11
12
13
14
15
16

Lobby of the Rochdale Inn

South wing of the dining hall, Rochdale Inn

The 1930's

From all the people that I interviewed, and the articles written about Fruitvale, never was it reported that anyone was disappointed with their stay at the Inn. One such visitor in the fall of 1931, was Agnes Nugent Diesel. From the diary of her vacation, we can get an idea as to the activities and good times, had by all.

Interior of the Clubhouse showing the soda bar. Tables were moved to allow for dancing.

Vacation Days

"One June day in 1931 two girls sat in one of the cozy little rooms of an apartment which housed a great many girls who were reading over the replies from many vacation resorts to which they had written. One in particular seemed to meet the approval of both and plans were quickly made for their departure, early in August. To travel by bus seemed to be the better way as one of the girls refused to travel by boat, the train that took its passengers to that part of the country was so slow and might be classed as the "Slow train through Arkansas" Someone bright morning in the early part of August they left the Windy City, by bus, at seven o'clock and after having many detours and long waiting, we reached our destination just in time for dinner.

Rochdale Inn is a very lovely resort, located not far from Montague, Michigan, and just a nice drive from Muskegon, where the boats land. It has an authentic romantic setting and is perched on a little hill overlooking a deep body of water known as Steadman Lake. Many pine and oak trees aspire very tall, with large straight trunks which have been treated to a white "summer coat," and I may say, adds much to its attractiveness. The Inn itself is a very nice bright place with a very pleasant atmosphere, and the proprietor is a most capable gentleman, a German I believe (Gus Kopp), judging from the name, but good American food is served if your appetite is not increased during your stay – well – it just is not their fault. The Inn has found it expedient to engage an orchestra for the season and this year the music of "Hal Chase and his Ramblers" was chosen, which furnished a nice concert during the dinner hour, and later for dancing. Through the french window of room "105" one could look out over the quiet water of the lake that was most beautiful on moon light nights or early mornings and hear the rush of the falls that was always pleasant music to the years in which carry one far off into dreamland, to awaken in the morning feeling very much invigorated and ready for a day of activities which was sure to follow. One thing of utmost importance is to get through the dining room door before the eleventh hour or you would be out of luck with "Al," the headwaiter, which meant, you must partake of light lunches at the clubhouse, which was just across the way. Days were taken up with hiking, which range from three to thirteen miles, swimming, rowing, volleyball, tennis, horseback riding, for which "Queen" was the favorite, while the nights had planned activities as well, which were marshmallow roasts, and as Ripley would say "believe it or not," snipe hunting, which always had a large following, trip to the haunted house, moon light parties, masked ball and their social dance with took place every evening from 8:30 to 11: 30 p. m. for which there was room left for discussion and imagination, not mentioning what one can see with their own eyes. And spending three weeks at the Inn one makes numerous acquaintances and we found some to prove real friendships, which I've always maintained proves that you spend your vacation well, whoever may read this epistle may think this illogical, but I do not. Some day the familiar call would be heard from the bus driver who would pilot the God-fearing people to the various churches in Montague. Sunday afternoons were carefree with the usual four o'clock swim and dip in the falls after the club fans had listen to their favorite ball team over the radio. Crowds would gather at the clubhouse for light lunches, and refreshments were always in readiness – no – you did not have to drink your ginger ale there. Each week would find the crowd making their departure, vowing to spend a longer time the following summer, to those remaining crowd, moved, sang the "So Long Song" and the deluxe bus moved taking them to their various stations. New arrivals would come on the afternoon boat, and also the many who would come at different intervals during the week and for the weekends. The newcomers always received a hearty welcome and Andy was always on the job to help them to their rooms with their baggage. We enjoyed our stay at the Inn very much and hope the next time it can be for a longer stay. Amen."

Afterwards, Agnes purchased several lots nearby, bought a deluxe bungalow for $75.00, and had it moved to her property. The cottage is still owned by the family today.

But as Gus had stated, a resort can only prosper, when the country does, the years of the Great Depression, hit the Fruitvale resort hard. The following is a letter from Gus, to the Messmore's on his land purchase for which he is still paying on. Sometimes Gus sends them money for the payments, while often the Messmore's will take a vacation at Rochdale in lieu of the money that Gus is short of.

As a country went through several years of economic depression, so did Fruitvale. Most landowners were unable to pay their taxes, and fewer still had money for vacations to Fruitvale. Without the Fruitvalers, from 1930 to 1935 there was no news reported from Fruitvale as it tried to survive.

In letters from Gus, we can get a feeling as to his effort he made to keep the resort afloat.

January 31, 1934

Our rate will be the same as last year, unless the NRA Hotel Code should

Bathing beauties at Rochdale Inn

The latest in 1929 swimwear (L to R) Al Grant, Gard Weston, Herman Grant

Summer staff at the Rochdale Inn (L to R) Bob Beard, Rachel Chalfonte, Jan McKay, Frank Termer, John Lahmzes, Gin Batteron, Esther Bozarth, Byron, Libby, Gwendolyn Belding, (seated) Eve Faulkner, Cora Ann Nimm, Maxine Jenkins, Dot Trent, (front) Harold Phillips, Don Werner, Tom Beeli.

Postcard reminder mailed to guest.

force some changes. We don't know as yet how it is going to affect us, but hardly believe that any changes will be severe enough to warrant our raising the rates.

One of the few groups that had the resources to use the Inn when others couldn't was the Episcopalians. Starting in 1929, they would use the Inn for their yearly summer conference. "I am sure that by having this group at Rochdale during this time helped keep it from going under."

"This will be the fifth year we entertain the Episcopal Conference, all young folks, lasting from June 24th to June 30th and I know them so well that I can arrange it in a manner that will make it a never to be forgotten event.

April 21, 1934

"The Episcopalians have no objection to our having guests to whom they have always extended cordial invitations to join in their lectures and programs."

"The business outlook is much better than a year ago, and, while the World's Fair is again going to cut down our attendance, still I do not believe it will be as great as last year."

July 24 Lodging Cost

One of the activities at Fruitvale for guest and landowners was of course fishing. With several lakes, streams and the White River, there were plenty of spots to try one's skills.

> THE ROCHDALE INN
> Situated in the heart of the scenic White River valley on Stedman Lake. Invites the members of the Golf and Yacht Club to spend an evening at this unusual hosterly.
>
> DINE AND DANCE NIGHTLY
> Ball Room serarate from Dining Room
> Phone 158F3 for reservations

June 18, 1934

"If any of the crowd are planning to do any fishing, they had better bring their own worms with them, because, you know our soil will average about a can of worms to 2 acres of ground and that is a lot of spading to do."

As with any resort, the season and the weather during that time, played a major role in the numbers of resorters that showed up.

September 24, 1934

"We haven't had a real killing frost as yet, but no doubt will before long. The woods will begin to get their real autumn colors, a sight well worth seeing. It's too bad we can't prolong the season so folks could enjoy the best part of the year. Someday perhaps, they will learn better and come up and see us when nature puts on a real show."

During most years, Gus would lock up the resort along in September and return to Chicago, where he had an apartment. As winter set in, it was the time for Gus to plan for the coming season by contacting past clients, sending out new brochures, and mailing photographs taken of resorters during the summer. Due to financial strain of the times, Gus would stay at Fruitvale during the winter of 1934–35.

September 13, 1934

"I'm thinking seriously of remaining up here this winter, and it now looks as if I'll have to have a housekeeper to, that is if I want to stay. The regular caretaker we had last winter, Mr. VanDerVort wants to go to Chicago, and since his wife does the cooking, I'll be in a helluva shape, if I don't get somebody. Us single old fellows, do have a rough time of it, don't we?

October 3, 1934

"There are four of us at the Inn at present, all men. We are making the best of it, and if you want to go on a diet, you just join our happy party. I hate to tell you what the cooking is like, and how much of it you get! You almost can see our waistlines melting away!"

Here I is at last Kiddo-am certainly having one real time-altho the other year was considerably more interesting-well-only one more week to go-& then maybe I will come back to work a full fledged chauffeur-Will see you soon Love Thelma, Aug 13, 1934

ROCHDALE INN

MONTAGUE, MICHIGAN

GUSTAVE KOPP, Manager · PHONE 158-R

★ ★ Chicago Office, 160 North LaSalle Street Phone, Dearborn 3613 ★ ★

Dear Friend:

A hearty welcome awaits you and your friends at Rochdale Inn. We are sparing no effort to make this season the greatest and happiest in our history--and we hope that you will take advantage of every opportunity to join our jolly family again this summer.

You will be glad to know that we have engaged, what we believe will be, the best orchestra that Rochdale has ever had. Ivan Combe and His Purple Knights, Northwestern University students, comprise the group, who will furnish the music for our nightly dances.

Then, for the benefit of those who like to dance later than we have ordinarily danced in the ballroom, we are turning the Club House into something of a Night Club. The orchestra will play in the ballroom during the early part of the evening and after 11:00 P. M. will continue their performance in the Club House, where a special dance floor has been installed.

Sun bathing, atop the Inn roof, will be an added thrill for our guests. A portion of the main roof has been carefully screened and you may enjoy the full benefit of the sun's ultra violet rays in strict seclusion. Certain hours will be set aside for the ladies and certain hours for the men.

We will again feature our popular fixed cost outings at no increase in price. You will have your choice of travel by boat, bus or train. A new steamship line will operate between Muskegon and Chicago and we have been promised the finest service in years. Full particulars will be sent to you as soon as the new schedules are available.

Reservations may be made whenever you wish for a small deposit of five dollars--either by mail or at our Chicago office. Upon full payment, you will receive your ticket, covering all expenses of the trip you have chosen. We are enclosing a reservation blank, and would suggest that you send it in as soon as possible, to be assured of your favorite room. The deposit will be refunded should there be any upset in your vacation plans, so do not hesitate to make your reservation now.

Nearly all of last year's staff, including Ray, of course, is back this summer to welcome you.

Very cordially yours,
GUSTAVE KOPP
Manager

MONTAGUE
MICHIGAN
PHONE 158-F

GUSTAVE KOPP, MANAGER

CHICAGO OFFICE
160 NORTH LA SALLE STREET
PHONE, DEARBORN 3613

A. W. Messmore Account with Rochdale Inn
From August 1st to August 27th, 1935

MEALS

Mr. and Mrs. Messmore				
	2	Breakfasts	$ 1.00	
	12	Lunches @ 50¢	$ 6.00	
	42	Dinners @ 75¢	31.50	
8/3/35	3	Extra Dinners	3.00	C. Miller
8/14/35	1	Extra Dinner	1.00	B Gardner
Mrs. Gardner and Family				
	29	Dinners at $1.00	29.00	
	45	Dinners at .50	22.50	
George Messmore				
	2	Lunches @ $ .75	1.50	
	5	Dinners @ 1.00	5.00	
Mr. and Mrs. Cripe				
		Meals	18.00	
Mrs. Cripes Daughter				
		Meals	4.50	
Mr. and Mrs. Chester Messmore and Daughter				
		Meals	22.00	
		TOTAL	$145.00	
		Sales Tax on Meals	4.35	
				$ 149.35

George Messmore	Lodging	2.50	
Mr. and Mrs, Cripe	"	10.00	
Mrs. Cripe's Daughter	"	2.50	
Chester Messmore	"	9.25	24.25
		TOTAL....	$ 173.60

"THE PLACE YOU'LL LOVE FOR YOUR VACATION"

The adventuresome drive to Fruitvale.

Even by staying at Fruitvale for the winter months, Gus was always looking for other means of raising capital to keep the resort from failing.

November 12, 1934

"Seriously speaking however, if you have that much (money) you can spare, I'll gladly play regular loan shark rate of interest payment back out of the first funds received when the Inn opens and secure it with a mortgage on the strip of land we own which takes in the bungalows on the lake, the tennis court and extends back to the river.

January 21, 1935

"Right now we are in the midst of a sub zero cold wave that is anything but pleasant. I am hoping however that it will freeze the old lake at Fruitvale and that we will soon be able to harvest the ice, of which you know we need plenty."

Ice cut each winter season form Brown's pond, is packed in either sawdust or straw for the summer's use. Used for preserving food at the Inn, Gus also made sure that ice was always served in the drinks.

Business conditions seem to be slowly improving and we are looking forward to a very satisfactory season. Most of the old employees will be with us again, including the orchestra."

"The winter months are always the most trying for us, and I certainly will be glad when they are over."

February 15, 1935

"Business seems to be getting better, and I look for a good summer which we surely can stand. The country had plenty of snow which ought to spell bountiful crops. I don't like the steady rise in food prices however. It won't be possible to raised rates, and every advance cuts into your earnings."

"If you come across any stunt or novelty that you think would be in order at Fruitvale, I'll be glad to hear about it. We want to keep up with the times and give our guests the utmost in amusement and entertainment."

February 27, 1935

"Also want to thank you (Mr. Messmore) for the shuffleboard information. Looks as if it might be an interesting game, if I can possibly manage it, will try to install a court and see how our guests take to it."

The court was never installed by Gus, due to financial reasons.

April 20, 1935

"A week from Wednesday the trout season opens, and we have quite a few reservations so it looks like a big day. We usually keep open all night and serve 'hot dogs and coffee ' in the kitchen. If it's a cold night, business will be good."

May 4, 1935

"The fishing season notwithstanding that it was cold and wet, went over big for us. We had one party alone of 35 men for a special dinner and kept open house all night. Too cold however, for many fish to be caught."

Although Gus was always, it seemed, fighting for the survival of Fruitvale, he writes very little about his own personal hardships during that time. One of the few times he does though, is in a letter to the Messmores, about Mr. Messmore becoming a grandfather..

"I quite agree with you that it must be a great honor and privilege to be called a grandpa and what a joy it must be to the youngsters when they see you coming! All my grandparents passed out of the picture long before I was born, and having ceased to have a real home since I was a kid, I suppose is one of the reasons why I am not in your class today."

But please don't hold that against me, I might at least make partial amends by following in your foot steps even at this late date!"

At this time Gus was 58 years old, being born in Iowa in 1882.

November 16, 1935

"This past year was really the first good season we have had in some four years and I believe we are now due for a big "come back" in the resort business."

1936
ROCHDALE INN STAGES BIG CHICAGO PARTY

"Mr. Gustav Kopp, manager of the Rochdale Inn, did things up brown in a social way for the patrons of his famous and hospitable Inn on White River, when he staged a ball in the "Hanger" room on the 19th floor of the LaSalle Hotel in Chicago on the evening of January 11. Over six-hundred people who are former patrons of the Inn, gathered under the Rochdale Moon (which by special arrangement was anchored over the LaSalle for the night), for an evening of retrospect and fun. Three one-week special two-day cruises on the Missouri, and many other prizes were presented to the holders of the lucky tickets. Colored motion pictures of the many activities and guest of the hotel during the past summer were thrown on the screen, while George X whose real name is George Scheuchenpflug acted as master of ceremonies. Herbie Mintz' famous dance band played the event which lasted from 9:30 to 1 o'clock. A style show was another feature event. The event was considered a huge success from every angle and everyone is enthused over prospects of the coming season at the Inn."

In a letter from Gus to Mr. A. W. Messmore, Gus tells us of his impression of the dance.

January 25, 1936

"The dance while we did not make any money in connection with it, from a publicity standpoint was a big success. Almost 700 Rochdalers turned out to live over again the good times they had at The Inn. It was a lively crowd and they all seemed to be having a wonderful time and enjoyed the style show and bathing beauty contest. Had you been there, with

S. S. Alabama, Palatial Flagship of Goodrich Fleet

All-Expense Trip "A" De Luxe

Daylight Run Both Ways on the Finest of the Goodrich Fleet through Lake Michigan, Muskegon Lake and White Lake

EIGHT DAYS OF JOY ON WATER AND LAND — $33 50 — SATURDAY MORNING TO NEXT SATURDAY NIGHT

Our De Luxe Daylight Trip offers complete travel and vacation luxury for eight days at a startlingly low price.

Leave Chicago any Saturday at 1 p. m. on the S. S. Alabama—regal Queen of the Goodrich Fleet. Leave all care behind and enjoy a day of nerve quieting repose on the steamer's spacious decks.

A special dinner will be served Rochdale Inn guests in the main dining salon of the boat. This is included in the cost of the trip. Dancing offers an added delight.

The Alabama arrives at the port of Muskegon about 9 p. m. Then a wonderful moonlight ride in comfortable busses through Muskegon, Whitehall and Montague out over the country to the Inn.

Now for a glorious long week the delights of this Summer Paradise are yours. The management is always on the alert with every courteous effort to make your vacation a memorable one.

The following Saturday morning after breakfast the bus will take you to Montague, where the S. S. Carolina will be waiting to give you another exhilarating day on the water, reaching Chicago at 5:30 p. m.

THE COST OF THE TRIPS FEATURED IN THIS BOOKLET INCLUDES ROUND-TRIP FARES, STATEROOMS ON NIGHT TRIPS, ALL BUS FARES, MEALS AND LODGING AT THE INN DURING LENGTH OF STAY, FREE USE OF ROW BOATS, CONCRETE TENNIS COURT AND FREE ADMISSION TO BALLROOM.

your wife's permission of course, we would have nominated you as one of the judges!"

With the new year ahead, and more successful season just completed in 1935, Gus again seeks new ideas to help the ailing Inn. One of the suggestions, that was really part of the original concept of Fruitvales' founding 25 years earlier, Gus writes ...

Episcopal services on the bank of Brown's Pond.

February 24, 1936

"For some time I've had in mind the idea of a fruit and vegetable garden for the summer. What do you think of it? What I am interested in most, is getting a big ever-bearing strawberry patch under way, the kind that has the berries ripening the latter part of July and in August when they bring a good price. As you know we have plenty of ground, and if the irrigation part were given due consideration, it might be possible to make that a regular business, and figure on not only supplying us but all the hotels and summer cottages on White Lake as well. And if we could add to it raspberries or blackberries, crops that go big with the resort population, and later on perhaps chickens, within a year or two would have a profitable business."

Again with good ideas, and no money to institute them, the berry idea died on the vine. As to the conditions at the Inn during the winter, he states...

"The country around the Inn has been buried under ten to fifteen feet of snow, and for three weeks it was impossible for a car to get in or out. The road is now open again, and I hope this week will see the village gang putting up our ice. They are a real bunch, do the work now, and I pay them during the summer." A lack of monies has never stopped Gus from 'dreaming about making a success of the resort, so even without it, he seeks other means to obtain his goals.

March 17, 1936

"I fully agree with you that berry farming ought to be profitable, but in the past it has been impossible to get anyone to look after it. This year however, I believe I have a good man, the one Mr. Parker had in the old days and who started the first berry patches, hence knows all about the soil, conditions, etc. He's not a youngster by any means, but being anxious to get out of Chicago, I can get him for about his room and board. This man is an expert along fruit and flower lines."

For the first time in several" years, there is news from Fruitvale in the local papers. This time it is not about the resorters nor the land owners, but of local interest. Due to the vastness of the area that still lies undeveloped, and the numerous waterways, Fruitvale was a favorite spot for local sportsmen.

SEPTEMBER 17, 1936

SPORTSMAN WILL NET NOXIOUS FISH IN FRUITVALE POND

"Acting in the capacity of chairman, in the absence of President Clinton Gasahl, Ben Dreskey, director of the organization of Whitehall, conducted the September meeting of the White Lake Sportsman's Club, held Tuesday evening at the High School auditorium. Due to election night and inclement weather conditions only a small attendance was present, but two projects--cleaning of Brown's pond and wintering of a flock of pheasants was undertaken. Brown's pond, at Fruitvale, which is habited by trout, and by various noxious fish, and which is fonned by the damming of Sand Creek, will be drained by conservation officers and during the weekend of October 3 and 4 sportsman of this area will assist in netting and removing noxious fish and suckers and the placing of them in the water below the dam. The bed of the pond will also be cleaned and the water again raised. Everyone interested in this work is asked to offer aid."

OCTOBER 1, 1936

SPORTSMAN URGES To HELP IMPROVE FRUITVALE POND

"Sportsman of this area, whether members of the local Sportsman' Club or not, are urged to take part in the work of cleaning Brown's Pond, at Fruitvale, and brushing Sand Creek above the pond, this week Saturday and Sunday. It is hoped that a large attendance will be on hand to do the job properly. Originally it was intended to attempt only the cleaning of the pond and the netting of noxious fish, but the promise of a large crowd has influenced the decision to attempt work on the creek also, and workers are requested to bring rakes, saws, axes and boots. The crews will be organized into two separate units under supervision.

Although there is no particular time set to begin the work. It is hoped that as many as possible will spend all the available time at their disposal at the pond during the two days."

The dam as last rebuilt, was finely constructed of poured concrete, well designed and landscaped to offer a relaxing site for the resorters. One of the features of the dam, was that it contained a spillway and a control value, that when opened, would allow for the lowering of the water level in the pond.

1937 brings the only news from the resort; that of the eleventh annual church conference held at Rochdale. As the

group with the longest record of support, again in 1938 for the 12th annual summer conference, the Episcopal churches meet at the Inn. During the hard times and the good times, the conference helped Gus keep the Inn open, even if on shakey ground.

RECORD NUMBER AT CONFERENCE NEARLY 170 ENROLL FOR EPISCOPAL MEETING THIS WEEK

"Church officials, layman and juveniles numbering 168 registered yesterday at Rochdale Inn to make the 12th annual summer conference of the Diocese of Western Michigan Episcopal churches the largest in its history. The Rt. Rev. Lewis Bliss Whittemore, bishop of Western Michigan is in charge.

Sunday's program consisted of registration, room assignment and enrollment in the various religious courses to be offered during the week. A conference assembly held in the evening introduced instructors to the group and gave members a chance to determine the nature of the subjects.

These courses are to be discussed by prominent officials in the Episcopal Church including Prof. R. 1. Colbert, head of the sociology and extension bureau at the University of Wisconsin; Rev. Charles C. Jatho, Royal Oak; Rev. H. P. Krusen, Manistee; Rev. W. Hamilton Aulenbach, Bloomfield Hills; Rev. John S. Higgins, Chicago, Ill; and Mrs. Derrill Darby Taber, national field secretary, Women's Auxiliary.

More than 25 members of St. Paul's Episcopal Church of Muskegon, visited the conference yesterday and similar groups expect to attend various programs during the week. Nine official delegates from St. Paul's were registered."

EPISCOPAL MEET ENDS AT ROCHDALE CERTIFICATES GIVEN TO 160 FOR COURSES AT CONFERENCE

"Many sun tanned high school students and more youthful clergy left Rochdale Inn this noon after the week's summer conference of Episcopal churches of the Western Michigan diocese. About

(L to R) George "XYZ" Scheuchempflug, athletic director, Gustave Kopp, owner, Ray Baker, manger

Costume party held in the lower level of the Rochdale Inn.

160 took the various courses offered during the week and received merit certificates at noon luncheon today.

An amateur circus last night entertained the conference and featured acrobatics, swimming fetes and other stunts by members in addition to tricks by a string of trained horses, kept at Rochdale.

Last Wednesday, Women's Auxiliary day, brought more than 60 women to the conference grounds who were entertained at tea by Mrs. E. D. Taber, national field secretary of Episcopal auxiliaries. Bishop Lewis Bliss Whittemore, of the West Michigan diocese, addressed the woman on the subject, "Woman's Work in the Church."

THE MUSKEGON CHRONICLE JUNE 1938

NEW ROCHDALE CLUBHOUSE POPULAR

"In keeping with the increasing popularity of the nightly dances at Rochdale Inn, the management has improved and enlarged the Clubhouse. The 1250 square feet of dance space means that the floor is over twice as large as last year.

Joe Gerken and his orchestra have opened their third season at Rochdale Inn. They bring a type of music with them in the augmented orchestra, that has been known as "something new and different" in the hotels where they have completed engagements, among them The Nelson and the Faust Hotels at Rockford, Illinois, Normandie Park at Wausau, Wisconsin and the Brevoort Hotel in Chicago. For those of you from Chicago, the band is scheduled to open at The Bismarck Hotel next Labor Day."

It seemed that no matter what Gus tried to do in behalf of Fruitvale and the Rochdale Inn, it just was not financially strong. The resort that had become his life and family, by 1939 still had not improved. So in as a last ditch effort to save what he loved, Gus sold the Rochdale Inn and cottages to Mr. and Mrs. Norman J. Larson. Gus Kopp though, would remain as manager of the Inn and owner of the remaining Fruitvale properties.

MAY - JUNE 1939 ISSUE - WHITE LAKE YACHT CLUB NEWS NEW PROPRIETOR AT

Rochdale Inn Gustave Kopp To Manage Resort

Mr. N. J. Larson, of Chicago, who recently took over the Rochdale Inn properties at Fruitvale, will be the new proprietor of the Inn this summer. The services of Mr. Gustave Kopp, who for years managed the properties for the owners, will be retained at the Inn as manager. Through a medium of an all-expense vacation originated by Mr. Kopp, the Inn has become famous in Chicago and vicinity and each season is crowded to capacity during the resort season. A big get-together dance is held each winter in Chicago at the Hotel LaSalle for the guests of the Inn. The Rochdale Inn clubhouse across the street from the hotel has become famous in Western Michigan as a high grade night club and a favorite rendezvous during the summer months when dances are held nightly. Mr. and Mrs. Larson arrived early this spring and have made many improvements to the hotel cottages. An electric light plant has been installed in the clubhouse which will operate a 32 volt phonograph during the hours the orchestra is not on duty. A new tennis court has just been completed and many other improvements made to the hotel and clubhouse. Buddy Friend and his Orchestra from the University of Michigan will play the dinner music and dances this season.

As to the "new" tennis court that is mentioned in the above article, this refers to a second court that was added just to the north of the first one.

CAN FRUITVALE BE SAVED? JULY 1939 ISSUE ROCHDALE A POPULAR SPOT

"According to all indication, Rochdale Inn and clubhouse with Buddie Friend and his University of Michigan orchestra will be a popular spot with the younger set around the lake this summer.

A new electric lighting plant has been installed which lights the clubhouse and lobby of the hotel. The management is considering installing a turbine at the water falls that will be powerful enough to light and power all the properties in the entire group. The clubhouse has been completely redecorated and has all the earmarks of a high grade night club. The orchestra plays nightly at the dinner in the large dining room overlooking Steadman Lake, later playing the dance at the clubhouse."

Can Norman Larson save the Inn, or is it too late to help, even under new management? Another dark cloud hangs over the horizon, in that of a war overseas.

For 1940, all is quite, as Mr. Larson and Gus try to continue with the business of providing the best service that the resorters have come to expect. But all is not well, bills are not being paid, and there is some unrest among the staff and band members

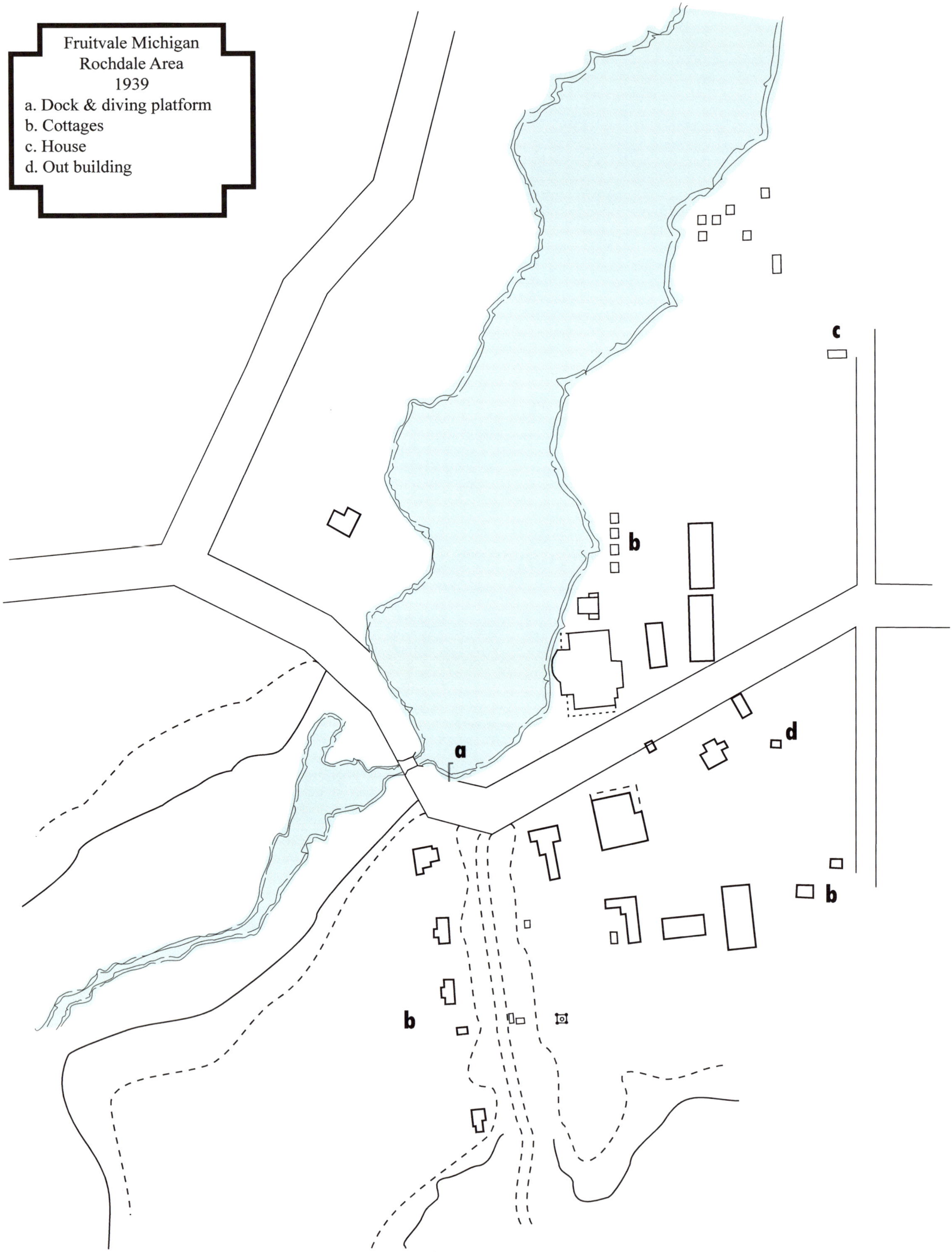
Fruitvale Michigan
Rochdale Area
1939
a. Dock & diving platform
b. Cottages
c. House
d. Out building
c
b
d
a
b
b

The 1940's

Frank Ehdett and his Orchestra at Rochdale.

JUNE 6, 1940 JUNIOR C OF C MET AT ROCHDALE

"Twenty members and two guests were presented Monday night at Rochdale Inn, at the regular monthly dinner meeting of the Montague Junior Chamber of Commerce. Following the dinner, served in the main dining room, a short business meeting was held."

1941 - A YEAR OF HOPE, A YEAR OF DESPAIR.

The problems of the Inn not being able to pay its own way, due to high overhead, such as labor and food cost were not solved by Mr. Larson. The ship that was taking on water for so many years, was now sinking.

In a letter to Mrs. Oveta W. Duerringer before the season starts, Gus puts in this way.

April 17, 1941

"We arc getting ready for what I hope will be a very good season and we surely need it! I certainly put in a tough winter and if things don't break better next fall, Mr. Duerringer will have to find me a job around the station house (he was a fireman)!"

JULY 31, 1941 STANDARD OIL MEN HELD ANNUAL OUTING, TUESDAY AT ROCHDALE RESORT

"Approximately 80 Standard Oil representatives of the Standard Oil company attended the annual outing, held at Rochdale Inn, Tuesday. The meeting was an all: ... day one and swimming, baseball, games and contests were enjoyed by all of the "pumpers" who laid aside their dignity for the day and entered into the fun.

A delicious steak dinner was served in the dining room at 7:00 0' clock.

During the evening the guests enjoyed the music of Hal Wasson's Orchestra and the special entertainment made possible through the cooperation of Casey Dillon of Muskegon. Major Bowes' amateur program winner, who gave impersonations of the worlds' most famous people. Mr. Dillon a guest for the evening, offered his services to the management in an effort to help entertain the oil men."

On September 15, 1941, in what was to be the final chapter of the Rochdale Inn, in its 29 year history, two "WRIT OF ATTACHMENTS" were filed at the Circuit Court for the County of Muskegon. The first one was filed by "Joel O. Berglund," doing business as Berglund Food Stores and Port City Jobbers, against Norman J. Larson and the property south of Montague Road (Fruitvale Road) which included the Clubhouse. The amount of the debt owed by Mr. Larson was $2,402.35.

The second Writ filed on the same day covered the Inn property, and was against the Fruitvale Resort Company, a Michigan corporation, and Gustave Kopp for $159.50. Both of these writs were for unpaid grocery bills for the past two years. Filed to prevent Mr. Larson or Mr. Kopp from selling either place, they were also Mr. Berlund's way of saying, it's now time to pay-up.

The writs, by court order, will allow the contents of the Inn and clubhouse to be sold to cover payment of the past due bills.

As if the death of the Inn was not enough at this time for Gus, news comes of the passing of one of the few long time residents of Fruitvale ...

GEORGE GALLOUX, FRUITVALE, DIES IN MUSKEGON TODAY

Montague, Oct. 11 - (Special) -"George Ernest Galloux, 60 years old, a resident of Fruitvale the past 22 years died today at Hackley Hospital, Muskegon. He was born in Montrechard, France, October 3, 1881, and was married to Gerta Erickson, in Chicago, January 3, 1906. He is survived by the widow; a daughter, Mrs. Helen Wooten, Muskegon; two sisters, Mrs. Ruth Willen, Chicago, and Mrs. McSweney, in Paris, and two brothers, Albert and Edmund, in Paris."

Gus, always seeing a silver lining in each cloud, almost at once started to rebuild the resort with new vigor, and a desire to save what was left of Fruitvale. In a letter dated November 8, 1941, Gus explains ...

"In the matter of a cottage, I'm certainly sorry that you didn't let me know about this (the desire to purchase a cottage) sooner. In order to get some money I practically had to give away the bungalows and sell the big shed."

"The Club idea mentioned in my former letter has taken a good hold and I believe will go over. Several meetings have already been held and another is scheduled for Friday night of this week when it is expected to organize and get ready to be incorporate. The owners of the property have approved of the idea and are willing to go along with them so it looks very much as if I may get the job of manager and help with the promotion work."

"The memberships are to be $10.00 each, non-assessable, with dues of $2.00 yearly and a probable limit of 500 members which should give the Club enough money with which to Operate. The first 100 memberships will be sold· at $10 each and it is quite possible that the next 100 membership will be sold at $12.50 or $15.00, stepping up each 100 memberships a few dollars. The Club is to be incorporated as a non-profit organization and the profits from its operations will enable it to give the members greatly reduced rates and otherwise favor them over outsiders who will still be permitted to come because the Inn naturally must be filled well to capacity to make money and for the first few years, the membership alone will hardly be able to do this."

"Many of the Club members will bring in their friends and this means a much better clientele than we have had heretofore."

"The prospects are very good that the one hundred memberships will be taken care of the first meeting. Only Chicago guests have been invited so far and it is planned to take in the country and out of state guests later on."

In less than a month, the United States will enter World War II, with the bombing of Pearl Harbor by the Japanese, and the Rochdale Inn will never again open its doors to the resorters of the Midwest.

Even with the country at war in 1942, Gus does not give up on the Inn. In his letters to the Duerringer's, he continues to search for new ideas and capital that will allow the reopening of the resort.

March 30, 1942

"As you probably know The Rochdale Inn Estate is on the market at the present time for sale or lease to any responsible party with ample financial means to operate it."

"All the equipment has been removed which means that the party or parties taking it over will have to consider the matter of furnishing it which also includes the cottages, kitchen and dining room, all of which will amount to a considerable item."

April 3, 1942

"The present owners of the property will not spend one cent in fixing it (Rochdale Inn) up. They fared so badly

Chicago, Illinois, October 29, 1941

Mrs. Oveta W. Duerringer
1525 Macomer Street
Toledo, Ohio

Dear Mrs. Duerringer:

Events have been moving rather swiftly at Fruitvale since the close of the season, and not knowing whether or not you have any contacts which might give you the news, I am going to take the liberty of giving you a few items which may be of interest to you.

First of all, the season as a whole was a big disappointment and it was only by sheer good luck that we were able to pull through the closing days which of course included Labor Day. The help not being paid went on a strike Sunday morning before Labor Day (Monday). The county prosecutor with whom a committee of the help had held previous conferences, arrived on the scene early at our urgent request and finally induced the crew to go back to work and we began serving breakfast about ten which was'nt so bad at that! The prosecutor put a man behind the desk who collected all the money which was to apply on the pay roll when settlement was made late Monday afternoon but unfortunately the amount collected amounted to only 20% of what was due so you can appreciate the mood the help was in. Mr. Larson was in Chicago a t the time trying to raise money and it probably was fortunate for him that he was'nt on hand because it was a most trying situation.

Beside the pay-roll there were some unpaid accounts to contend with too and much of this grief finally found its way to the owners of the property who realizing the impossibility of collecting any rent apparently have decided to either sell or consider a new lease with responsible parties.

A wholesale grocer from Muskegon attached the equipment. He also after Labor day bought the first mortgage covering the contents and then proceeded to fore-close and at the sale held sometime ago, bought it in. This party now owns the contents and rather than sell piece meal to get his money will consider any reasonable offer by a new tenant and sell it to him on time.

This brings up the thought that you folks with your large holdings nearby, might know of someone whom you could interest in The Inn property, or perhaps your husband might want to retire and go in the hotel business! The place as you know has possibilities and its well worth your giving it some thought. I will be very happy to supply more detailed information in the event you are interested or know of some one who could be induced to tackle it.

Some Chicago guests have a plan afoot to organize a Club and try and take it over. Whether or not they will succeed remains to be seen and in the meantime I of course am doing all I can to try and get something under way.

Another item and a most sorrowful one is thatof the passing on of George Galloux whom you no doubt remember quite well. He was operated on at one of Muskegon's hospitals and died several days later. His appendix and a further complicated condition I believe was the cause.

My plans for the future are still very uncertain but I am hoping that things will clear up soon so that I will know where I am at. This business of being terribly up against it is quite trying and I certainly don't want to go through another summer like the one just closed.

The Inn property I am sure could be leased on very reasonable terms or for that matter bought at a big sacrifice of what it is actually worth. Mr. Duerringer often talked about the place and had some very constructive ideas about it and if he's still interested along those lines, he'll never have a better chance than now to put them into execution!

Trusting that this letter will find you all enjoying the best of health and that I may have the pleasure of hearing from you soon, I am,

Very sincerely,

Gustav Kopp

Please address: C/O Hotel Newberry
817 N. Dearborn St
Chicago, Illinois

MEMBERSHIP APPLICATION

THE ROCHDALE CLUB

To be
Incorporated Not For Profit

HEADQUARTERS: Room 808, 160 North La Salle Street
CHICAGO, ILL. Tel: Dearborn 3613

OBJECT OF THE CLUB

The object of The Club shall be to bring together in common understanding and purpose, former guests of ROCHDALE INN and their friends and other persons; to further their acquaintance and fellowship; to develop social and recreational activities and to promote and maintain a high standard of Club membership and management.

I hereby endorse the principles for which The Club stands and wish to apply for membership in the same. If elected, I agree to abide by its Constitution and by-laws.

Date	Signature of Applicant
Employer	Address
Business Address	City and State
Telephone	Telephone (Home)

AMOUNT OF FEE WITH APPLICATION $ ________

the past three years that they want to get rid of it. No one has yet has offered to lease or buy it in with all the equipment: you can appreciate that it isn't going to be an easy matter to find a prospect who will tackle it. The property, Lake frontage (approx. 1/4 mile), cottages, in fact everything on the 40 they own the clubhouse is the only parcel missing in this 40 can be had for $7500. Which you must admit is giving it away. In fact you couldn't build the Annex for that amount. In $2000 down payment will swing the deal and the balance can be had on any kind of reasonable terms.

The equipment situation can be handled with a few thousand dollars because there are companies who furnished houses were resorts on a three-year contract with a few thousand dollars. $8,000 at today's prices would be ample to equip everything and the fact that all the old junk is gone would help a lot. You know from your own experience that the beds and equipment we had in most of the rooms were of such poor quality that they should have been thrown out long ago. It would be a great ad for Rochdale to announce "NEWLY EQUIPPED AND FURNISHED". It would pack them in this summer for sure.

The hotel room furnishings that Gus referred to in this letter amount to in each small room; a narrow metal bed with mattress, a little table and a chair. There was no heat or air conditioning in any of the rooms, and lighting was provided by a gas lantern that was lit each night by a staff member. Few guests spent much time in their rooms, due to a full day of activities by the recreational staff that would keep the guest occupied until was time to go to sleep. Gus writes...

The things that worry me is that one of these days someone will come along and buy it at a bargain and probably turn the place into a "Honky-Tonky" joint running it wide open. Surely Rochdale deserves a better fate than that.

The Club idea is workable, but I was hampered by lack of funds and I couldn't call the meetings like I wanted to "pep" them up and keep the interest in the Inn worked up the way it should have been. However I found out that if someone will make the start by buying the place, and from then on it will be much easier to get the money. In fact the drive were made for deposits on reservations for the purpose of getting money to buy new equipment, I'll venture to state that inside of two weeks we will collect several thousand dollars. No cut rate would be offered and from the way many of the guest whom I've contacted have expressed themselves, they wouldn't be expecting it this year."

May 30, 1942

"The proposed deal for the Inn is still pending and with the war situation cutting down on travel and rubber it's getting to be quite a complicated problem. However I still hope that a satisfactory deal will be made, and that the summer months will see activity of some kind at Rochdale."

June 10, 1942

"At this writing it looks very doubtful as to whether the Inn will be open or in a position to take care of guest no matter how few in number."

As the ship sinks further into the water, the few remaining staff of the Inn are forced to find work elsewhere..

"Our mutual friend, Bert Kerkhof, our famous house carpenter and all-around handyman joined forces with another party and bought the Bellevue Shores Resort on the Whitehall side of White Lake. Its a few miles this side of the White Lake Yacht Club and you remember the spot. He's fixing it up and I surely hope he will make a go of it. Mrs. Larson, too, expects to open Glen Villa, although Mr. L. Who is employed in the city (Muskegon) expects to remain here on the job which I believe is a good idea.

No matter what methods that Gus tried, and all the contacts he made, there were no takers for the Inn. Boarded up, and let to sit has a skeleton of its former heydays, the only one left at the end was the Strmic family. As the caretakers, they lived their in behalf of the owners. It wasn't again until December 23, 1944 that the Inn was in the news..

Fire Destroys Rochdale Inn

By Staff Correspondent

Montague, December 23 – Rochdale Inn, popular resort for several decades, not far from the White River, was completely destroyed at 1:30 a. m. today with an estimated loss of between $30,000 and $40,000. The clubhouse and cabins were not destroyed.

Thousands of Middle West resorters, and especially business girls from Chicago, had spent summer vacations at the Inn. Operated by Gustave H. Kopp of Chicago, for many years, the Inn offered vacations of swimming, dancing, and other activities until it closed in 1941 following financial difficulties.

Rochdale Inn also was the most popular place with Muskegon residents. Many parties were held at the Inn while others spend weekends there. Although not far from Muskegon, it offers seclusion and a place to relax. The fire was discovered by John Strmic, Junior., son of the present owner, John Strmic, Sr., of Chicago, who makes his home there with his wife and baby. The family was having a party and all guests, got out safely before the two-story building raged in flames. It was an old frame structure and burned rapidly. An overheated chimney is believed by Montague firefighters to have been the cause. The Montague fire department was called but was unable to save the large Inn, which overlooks Brown's pond. Insurance held by a Muskegon agency on the Inn was canceled several years ago it was not known today whether any of the loss was covered. The Rochdale Inn was constructed and started operation about 30 years ago by Harrison M. Parker, of Chicago. He sold several years later to Mr. Kopp, also of Chicago. Before the war the Pere Marquette trains from Chicago weekly would transport young people under a plan whereby transportation was included in the vacation fee. Seven charges of failure to pay wages were brought in 1941 by employees against Norman J. Larson then the lessee and operator. The furnishings of the Inn were sold also in 1941 to cover grocery bills of the 1939 and 1940 seasons. The nonpayment charges later were dropped in Muskegon Municipal Court when Mr. Larson gave notes in six cases. Mr. Parker, the originator, had a unique plan for the growing and supplying of produce from the area to a chain of grocery Chicago stores. He plotted the area and gave way five and 10 acres to persons who would pay for the deed and abstract, and agreed to sell him the produce. Mr. Parker also operated several barges on the White River to take resorters up to the Inn. When the truck gardening scheme failed, he sold out and was frequently in the limelight as a result of litigation.

At the time of the fire, the Strmic' were having a get-together in the staff dining room, just across the hallway from the kitchen. John Strmic, Sr., who placed a large pine knot in the kitchen stove, which overheated and caused the fire, either from being overheated or from creosote build. The exact cause was never determined.

From that dark September in 1941, when the Inn was closed for the last time the Rochdale resort area will be plagued by tragedy and misfortune until it's completely gone...

THURSDAY, JUNE 13, 1946

ROCHDALE DANCE HALL WILL SOON BE READY To OPEN

"Victor Hugo Ruzicka and Arnold Lipps, both of Lakewood, purchased the Rochdale Inn property on the Fruitvale Road some time ago. It consists of the former dance hall and several cottages.

It is their plan to operate the property again as a resort and dance hall. Sale of drinks is also in the plans. Work of remodeling and decorating the old dance hall is about complete and the place probably will be ready to open soon.

There is a large dance floor in the hall, also a huge 37 foot bar. They have added a kitchen with modern cooking equipment, installed a new electric power plant, and built in two toilets. Both the exterior and interior have been repainted and decorated.

It was reported that the cottage on top of the knoll was sold, but work of restoring the cottage nearest the dance hall is now in progress. This will be used for living quarters. Mr. Lipps stated shortly after the purchase that they intended to restore the entire site. He did not indicate, however, that the old Rochdale Inn building would be rebuilt. There are some reports that liquor by the glass would be served there in addition to beer and wine, but this report was not confirmed. Mr. Ruzicka formerly operated the Victor Hugo drink establishment at Lakewood for several years, and Mr. Lipps was employed for some time at the White Lake Sportsmen's Club at Lakewood."

THURSDAY, NOVEMBER 6, 1947

ROCHDALE TAVERN BURNED DOWN. HAD No FIRE 'PROTECTION

"About 6 p.m. Friday fire destroyed the Rochdale Tavern located across the road where once stood the famous Rochdale Inn. The dance hall, then a part of the resort center on Rochdale or Fruitvale Road, long idle, was put back into service in July, 1946, by a group headed by Victor Hugo Ruzicka, formerly operator of Victor Hugo's at Lakewood.

The dance hall was remodeled, and a bar installed, also a kitchen for preparing lunches. Mr. Ruzicka stated the fire started in a small room at the rear of the hall which housed the lighting plant. This was powered by a gasoline engine, and he thinks a spark may have ignited the gasoline in the tank. Noticing smoke, he opened the door to the power plant, and flames belched forth. He was alone at the time and attempted to put out the fire with several fire extinguishers. Motorists and neighbors rushed to aid, but the fire fanned by a brisk wind soon enveloped the entire structure.

For a time it appeared as though they might save the 8 room house nearby, and a bucket brigade was formed. However, when the wall of the dance hall nearest

the house fell, the house was soon on fire. Much of the furniture was removed, but the contents of the dance hall and bar were destroyed. The loss was estimated at $21,000, on which there was $6,500 insurance.

The tavern was located in Blue Lake Township of Muskegon County. Calls for help were made to the Montague Fire Department, but as the department was not authorized to make the run by township officials, the buildings were permitted to burn.

When the Rochdale Inn burned on Christmas Eve, 1944 the Montague fire department was called and made the run. They succeeded in saving the Annex, but not the hotel building proper, as that fire had too great a start. Friday evening they might have saved the house, but very probably not the tavern.

After the Rochdale Inn fire, the City of Montague sent Blue Lake Township a bill for $75 for services of the fire truck and the firemen. Blue Lake Township officials refused to pay the bill, stating they had not authorized the call for aid.

Montague Fire Chief John Thieman stated that in view of the attitude of the township officials, the department could not afford to jeopardize the truck and safety of the men to make the run. Both White River and Montague townships pay for runs in their areas. In fact one of the trucks in Montague is the property of Montague Township, and White River township pays the City of Montague $100 per year for upkeep of equipment, plus the charge for each run into the Township."

AUGUST 26, 1948

RUZICKA REBUILDING ROCHDALE INN

"Hugo Ruzicka has started to erect a new building on the former site of the old Rochdale Inn on Rochdale road in Blue Lake Township. Late last week walls of cement blocks started to raise upon a cement foundation where the old hotel formally stood. The old Rochdale Inn burned down Christmas night in 1944.

The new buildings will be sort of a Rathskeller on the first floor, a lounge and three rooms and office on the second floor, also six rooms on the third floor. The first floor walls will be of cement blocks and the upper floors of lumber. Ruzicka stated he hoped to have the first floor completed by early October. He plans to operate a bar on the first floor, and a small hotel on the second and third. Installation of a large lighting plant is now in progress. This will be housed in the old ice house connected with the old hotel.

Ruzicka purchased the Rochdale Inn property some time in 1946, and remodeled the old dance hall across the road from the hotel. He operated the dance hall and bar until it burned down Friday, October 31, 1947. The dance hall was partially covered by insurance. Ruzicka then had a resort liquor by the glass license. He has kept the license in force ever since the fire, with the intention of rebuilding. The new structure, which will stand beside the waters of the pond or small lake formed by the Rochdale creek at this point will have an attractive setting."

OCTOBER 18, 1955

V. H. RUZICKA, BLUE LAKE LEADER, DIES

"Montague, October 18 - Victor Hugo Ruzicka, 59, Blue Lake Township building inspector and former Lakewood school board member and postmaster, was found dead Monday evening in the Rochdale Inn, Fruitvale, which he was remodeling.

Coroner John DeHorn said Mr. Ruzicka had died from a heart attack and said death occurred sometime Saturday. His body was found by neighbors. Mr. Ruzicka had purchased the Inn recently and had been living in it while fixing it up for opening next summer. The Inn had been closed for a number of years. Mr. Ruzicka was a carpenter and builder by trade. He also had operated a tavern in the Lakewood district.

Mr. Ruzicka was born in Chicago and married Esther Sweers in Lakewood in 1920. He and his wife had been separated.

Besides his wife, he leaves a daughter, Jeanne of Muskegon, a son, John of Chicago; and two brothers, Milo of Mesa, Arizona, Charles of Muskegon.

Funeral services will take place at 2 p.m. Wednesday from Gee Chapel with burial in Oakhurst Cemetery."

"Sportsman's Club as built by Victor Ruzicka on the foundation of the former Rochdale Inn, after it burnt. Muskegon Chronicle photo

The Annex as it looked in 1968 just prior to being torn down along with the Sportsman's Club. Muskegon Chronicle photo

The 1930's

The Parker Cottage nearly destroyed after the enlarged "wooden" dam washed out.

PEOPLE V. PARKER

Harrison Magowan Parker born July 9, 1877, was the son of Thomas Harrison and Mary Owings Parker of Ross, California. Thomas was the son of an architect, and at the age of 13 was a messenger boy for the Confederate Army during the Civil War. While serving in that capacity, Thomas was shot in the lung and developed tuberculosis. Because of his illness, Thomas gradually headed west in search of warmer dryer climates, when he settled in the community of Ross to raise his family. According to his granddaughter, Beulah Parker Will, "Thomas was said to be a man of considerable vision in regard to real estate prospects, and intermittently did very well in real estate trades, but he also lost a lot of money about as frequently as he did well, and what with intermittent recurrences of his TB, was not a very reliable provider for his family." With this uncertainty of financial responsibility, Harrison became the main provider for the famil y from an earl y age, and continued to look after his father until he died at age 85 in Fairfax, California about 1928.

Harrison was the second child to Thomas and Mary, with Gertrude being the first and Lewis the third and last child. Gertrude married Will Landrum, a jewelry salesman from California. Although I can find no mention that Gertrude ever visited Fruitvale, there are a few deeds recorded in which Edith, Harrison's wife, transferred ownership in the Rochdale Inn to Gertrude in 1929, then a year later, Gertrude deeded the property back to the Fruitvale Resort Company. Lewis, Harrison's brother, died at a young age in California.

Harrison, in addition to helping to provide for the family was a bright and above average student while in school, and was accepted into the Delta Kappa Epsilon Fraternity while still in high school and would thus spend his senior year at the University of California in San Francisco. At the age of 23, Harrison would marry Edith Stubbs in San Francisco, October 23, 1901. The Parkers would move several times around the country before settling in Chicago. Harrison and Edith had three children; Mary, born 1903 in Louisville, Kentucky, Harrison M. J r., 1907 and Beulah in 1912, both born in Chicago. As of the writing of this book, Bealuh is the only surviving member of the family.

In 1911, the first year of Fruitvale, Harrison is already listed in 'The Book of Chicagoians,' a yearly directory of who's who in business from Chicago.

"Parker, Harrison Magman, Advertising agent: born San Bernardino, California July 9, 1877 son of Thomas G. and Mary (Owings) Parker: education high school, San Francisco, and University of California Married Edith Stubbs of San Francisco October 23, 1901. Two children, Harrison M. Jr. and Mary Stubbs. Began in business department of The Wave, San Francisco 1895, later was in business office of Chicago Times Herald, Chicago Daily News, Collier's Weekly, was business manager Philadelphia North American, Chicago Tribune; vice president Stack - Parker Company since 1909. Republican, Methodist, member United Woodman. Clubs Union League, Mid-Day. Recreation fishing and hunting. Residence 455 Deming Place Offices: 1500 Heyworth Building and Commercial National Bank Building."

Even though shrouded in controversy and threats of legal action for being a fraud, Harrison didn't treat his city of Fruitvale as a get rich quick scheme. One of the first buildings constructed was his families summer home, just across the street from the Inn and next to the old creek bed that was dug during the days of the saw mill. The Parker family would come up to Fruitvale each summer for the season from 1912 until about 1918.

In a ,letter from Bealuh Parker Will, dated November 12, 1988, she recalls as a young girl her fond memories of Fruitvale;

"As I remember it, we were there all summer. My father was supposed to come up every weekend, but only managed to make it a couple of times in any year that I can remember. In addition to my mother and the three children, there were usually several guests. Our cottage had a living room, kitchen and a large upstairs bedroom in the main part of the house, and six or eight small bedrooms facing onto a long screened porch. My nurse and I had the big bedroom, everyone else was downstairs. I don't think there was running water, as I can remember having sets of pitcher, washbowl and slop bucket in every room, along with chamber pots under the beds, and a pump outside the kitchen where we got well water. I could almost draw you a picture of everything in the cottage. We all loved it, although I imagine my poor mother was pretty lonesome most of the time, and occupied herself by nursing wounded birds back to health inside the screened porch, and collecting butterflies and wild flowers which we learned to press and set into wicker-edged glass-covered trays. We children collected choke cherries to feed the birds! The rest of the time we ran quite wild around the farm and chicken yard - helping to find eggs that the chickens laid outside the chicken houses. I believe there were several thousand chickens, and can remember loving to go into the incubators to see the chicks hatch."

"After the United States went into World War I, mother put on a number of fund-raising events in which the grounds were strung with hundreds of Japanese paper lanterns, and a man by the name of Jack Hart, I think, entertained with jokes and magic tricks. Many people came, and I can remember watching all the lights and gaiety from my upstairs room after dark came and I was supposed to be in bed. My sister (Mary) dressed up as a Red Cross nurse, and helped with the refreshments."

"When I was two years old, which would have been the late summer of 1914, the old dam broke, and the water from Brown's Pond flooded the stream that ran in front of our cottage. It must have made a vivid impression on me, because I can actually remember being carried out of the cottage in the middle of the night when it looked as though the cottage would fall over the bank. For a couple of years, until a new dam was built, the pond was nothing but a mass of mud with old dead tree trunks sticking out of it, but the flood created a number of little sandy islands all around, where we children used to play and built overnight camps. Anyway, our cottage was cut in half and pulled back into the onion patch; for a long time afterward onions used to grow up between the boards in the kitchen floor."

"About half way from our cottage to the Inn, on the same side of the main road (Fruitvale Road) which was then nothing but sand, stood a little cottage where my grandfather Parker lived for at least one summer. In back of that was a very large vegetable garden, and further down the barns which housed the work horses and my brother's pony, Beauty, who was little bigger than a large dog. Somewhere around there was the potato house, underground with only the peaked rook above which we children used as a slide. Along the side of the creek opposite our cottage was the little house of the chicken farmer and his son Homer, who was my constant playmate."

As a businessman, Harrison had envisioned the idea, raised the capital, purchased the property, laid out the 'City,' promoted the dream, and assembled qualified business leaders to run the day to day operations of Fruitvale, while he continued to work in Chicago.

During the years that Bealuh remembers the family vacationing at Fruitvale, her father's occupations were listed as; Vice President Stack -Parker Advertising Agency - 1912, President Evening American Publishing Company - 1913 and 1914, President The Chicago American News Paper, 1915 and 1916, and in 1917 the last year he was listed in the Chicago City Directories, President of the Fruitvale Grocery and Market Company. Also in 1917, Edith was listed as the Secretary of the Woman's

Exchange of Chicago. This last listing for Harrison, of the Fruitvale Grocery and Market Company, is the only mention other than in Western Michigan newspapers, of Harrison's involvement or any connection of him to the Fruitvale land development. In all the articles written about him or even bio's written by him, until his death, Fruitvale is never listed.

Sometime in the early 1920's, Harrison went to work as business manager for Medill McCormick at the Chicago Tribune, and enjoyed a very good working relationship with Medill. After Medill's death, his brother Robert took over, Harrison had a falling out with Robert over his business practices. A short time later he left the Tribune, and would never forgive Robert McCormick and the way he operated.

Although during this time, Harrison's name rarely showed up in the local papers about Fruitvale, and it appeared that it was being run solely by changing leadership, Harrison was still very active in the land sales side of Fruitvale. A check of Fruitvale deeds that were recorded both in Oceana County and in Muskegon, have both Harrison's and Edith's signatures on many of them as both the seller and in some cases, as purchasers. It was not uncommon, that if a 'Fruitvaler' was unhappy with their purchase, their land would be repurchased and then sold to someone else.

The last time that Harrison will appear in the local Michigan papers, was in the late 1920' s, during the time of the oil boom days when the following was written.

TRADESMAN KNOWS HARRISON PARKER

"The notorious Harrison Parker has evidently returned to Chicago from New York, where he made a miserable fiasco after organizing an alleged bank and trust company. His record and methods were exposed by the New York Times and New York World, which he sued for $1,000,000 apiece, but the courts threw both cases out of court. Parker and associates from Fruitvale, recently promoted an oil stock deal which they proposed to foist on Muskegon by using the name Better Business Bureau. The Detroit organization doing business under the same name, secured an injunction prohibiting the use of that name by the Parker gang.

Harrison Parker sued the Michigan Tradesman for $50,000 damages in the United States Court about fifteen years ago, because it exposed the swindling tactics pursued by him in connection with the inauguration of Fruitvale, an alleged summer resort town in Muskegon County. The Tradesman went to considerable expense to defend the suit, but Max Palm, the criminal lawyer of Chicago, slipped over to Grand Rapids the day before the case was set for trial paid the Tradesman the money it had expended in preparing for the trial of the action, paid the Tradesman's lawyer his fees, paid the court costs and dismissed the case. Parker is yellow all the way through and has swindled the American people out of millions of dollars. Anything his name is connected with is an object of suspicion which should be carefully avoided."

-The Michigan Tradesman.

(Editor's Note-Several citizens of this vicinity were victims of Parker's proposed oil stock scheme, evidently urged into his association by much smooth talk, for which he is adept. They, when learning the real status of conditions, absolved themselves of his company, by going to court and acquiring a dissolution of the Better Business Bureau.)
The White Lake Forum
May 30,1929

Without mentioning this article to Harrison's daughter, Beulah, in her letter to me on November 12, 1988, she states, "my mother moved with me to New York and later Connecticut near where my married sister (Mary) lived. Both she and my father felt that their separation was temporary, but it persisted for twenty-five years." Still bitter about Robert McCormick, Harrison would spend these twenty-five years of his life in a battle that would change him for life. He would spend every available minute researching the past history of the McCormick family, Chicago politics and the effects they had on the tax prayers of Illinois. With this knowledge, Harrison filed a 100 million dollar law suit against the Chicago Tribune and when not in court, he would talk to whatever group would listen to his cause. In a booklet that was sold to help spread the word and support the cause, Harrison states the following.

"If That Be Treason, Make the Most of It"

by Harrison Parker

Speech Before Citizens and Taxpayers of Alton, Illinois, Thursday evening, August 27, 1936, on the spot where Lincoln debated with Douglas.

PUBLIC ENEMY NUMBER ONE

"The chief enemy in Chicago of William Hale Thompson is Col. Robert R. McCormick, the publisher of the Chicago Tribune, who is now known in Chicago as Public Enemy No 1. His business aid, Al Capone, used to be known as Public Enemy No.1. He is now on A1catraz island for cheating and defrauding his government of less than $100,000 in taxes. In a bill that is now pending in the Circuit Court of Cook County, it is charged that the Chicago Tribune, under the administration of Joseph Medill, the grandfather of McCormick, cheated and defrauded the State of Illinois of capital stock taxes of the approximate sum of thirty million dollars in money that was paid as cash dividends to the seven stockholders of that newspaper. Under the administration of McCormick it is charged that the Chicago Tribune has cheated and defrauded the State of Illinois of capital stock taxes an approximate sum of fifty seven million dollars that was paid as cash dividends to the same seven exceedingly rich stockholders. Now thirty million dollars plus fifty-seven million dollars is eighty seven million dollars. So you can see why McCormick is now called Public Enemy No.1, instead of Al Capone."

Col. Robert R. McCormick

"I want to tell you some more about McCormick, in order that you may decide whether you want his kind in control of our government, with McCormick as dictator and Curly Brooks as his front."

"This McCormick is probably the richest man in Illinois today. Last month, while our babies were starving for lack of milk, he paid $500,000 in cash for his home lot on Michigan Avenue in Chicago."

"In all Chicago there is not a monument that he has erected. There is not a hospital bed that is maintained or endowed by him. There is not a tree in a park that was planted by him, nor is there a flower in a public garden, nor a book in a public library that was contributed by this enormously opulent man whose fortune approaching a hundred million dollars, is largely from dividends received from the Chicago Tribune."

In a latter section of the same publication, Harrison states that although McCormick was rich, after leaving Yale University, he moved in with a "poor kinsman named Ed Adams," according to court records. After living with Adams for several years, "as a non-paying guest," "McCormick left with Adam's wife." The booklet then states, "When I was the President of a Chicago newspaper, Medill McCormick, brother of (Robert) McCormick, came to me and said, "My brother is in an awful jam with an irate husband. A federal judge has agreed to help Robert out of his jam by ruining the outraged husband with a crooked court order. But the judge refuses to do the dirty job unless all the Chicago newspapers will agree

HOW THE

CHICAGO TRIBUNE

Cheated and Defrauded the State of Illinois of 87 Million Dollars in Capital Stock Taxes

The small home owners and the farmers of Illinois had to pay the taxes that the Chicago Tribune avoided by fraud.

PRICE, 10 CENTS

to suppress all the news of what shall be done in that courtroom."

"I said to Medill, "I am a hired man; I can't suppress such news, unless I first communicate with the owner of this paper." Medill McCormick left me vowing vengeance by him and his brother Robert. Later he returned and said, "Your position is right."

"Whereupon I telephoned the story to the owner of the newspaper, who ordered the suppression of the news of that dreadful proceeding in a crooked Federal Court that destroyed a human being to aid this McCormick to extricate himself from a jam into which he had gotten by his own unmanly conduct."

This last statement by Harrison, would indicate why he developed a friendship with Medill and the resentment of Robert McCormick.

The biography of Harrison and the reason for the booklet was written as follows;

"Harrison Parker was the business manager of the Chicago Tribune and left its employ and a tremendous salary, rather than take a part in the destruction of the Republic. His direct ancestor, Deacon Thomas Parker, fled his England to escape the tyranny of the Sturat Kings and arrived in the Colonies in 1636 on the "Susan & Ellan" to do his part establishing Constitutional Government on the American soil. Except in the last war, when Harrison Parker was too old and his son was too young, the children and grandchildren of Deacon Parker enlisted as privates in every war, since the French and Indian War, that had for its object the maintenance of the Constitutional Government that this race of men fought with gun to establish. Captain John Parker, a grandson, of Lexington, Massachusetts, fired the first shot in the American Revolutionary War; his grandson, the Rev. Theadore Parker, fired the first blast of the Civil War in the United States, and Harrison Parker, the last man of that illustrious race of men, except his son, has taken the torch of Liberty in his hand, and if necessary to assure his fellow men to the crisis that our country is in, he will walk barefooted with bleeding feet from town to town to awake his fellow Americans from their lethargy, before it is too late to save our lovely country."

"This pamphlet containing one of the most important messages ever delivered in the United States, was sent to you by reason of the fact that a decent American paid for its delivery to you. If you, too, are interested in saving what is left of this Republic, mail $1.00 to Harrison Parker, 732 Sherman St., Chicago, and acopy of this address will then be mailed to 10 decent Americans.

As Paul Revere of old rode from house to house to arouse the then Americans, this speech should be passed from house to house to arouse the decent Americans to conditions that they must know and correct, if this Republican form of Government shall endure as it was founded by our ancestors."

In Harrison's zealousness to state his case, he had sent a lengthy letter to a grand. jury that was hearing the matter but had not requested the information from Harrison to be sent. Because the letter was not equested, court action was taken against him for contempt of court charges. Harrison did appeal the case, but it would take nearly ten years before the final ruling would be made by the United States Supreme Court.

PEOPLE V • PARKER SUPREME COURT OF ILLINOIS OCTOBER 11, 1940

Contempt

"The sending to a grand jury by a citizen, letters charging that newspaper and certain individuals had entered into a criminal conspiracy to defraud the state of revenue by illegal omission of personalty from tax rolls,"

Jones, Chief Justice.

"Harrison Parker was adjudge guilty of criminal contempt in the criminal court of Cook County, and sentenced to imprisonment in jail for a period of ten days."

"The letters are quite lengthy and are couched in exceedingly vicious and inflammatory language."

"The letters also charged the above parties, (Robert McCormick, Thomas J. Courtney, State's attorney of Cook County and others) or some of them, with perjury, subornation of perjury, bribery, malfeasance in office, and specifically charged The Chicago Tribune with "influencing, intimidating or bribing the courts to prevent a trial on the law and the facts." One of the letters states that McCormick, "under whose directions this enormous steal has been effected, is a coward, a liar, a cheat, a thief, a court -fifer and an all-around scoundrel who, after he has cunningly robbed the State that shelters and protects him, will pollute the Channels of Justice to hide his thefts." Parker stated three attempts had been made to murder him, but neither the allurements of fortune nor the terrors of death could deter him from doing his duty."

The court responded in their decision as follows;

"They (the letters) are replete with malignant accusations against private citizens and public officials and are, in all probability, the result of personal enmity. Couched in the language they are, they could serve no useful purpose. Rather they expose the grand jury to the danger of being misled and abused by one motivated by personal animosity." The lower court ruling is affirmed.

PEOPLE V. PARKER APPELLATE COURT OF ILLINOIS. FEBRUARY 14, 1946

"Harrison Parker was found guilty in two separate judgment orders of a direct contempt of the trial court, and he brings error."

"First judgment order affirmed, the other reversed."

"In each Harrison Parker, plaintiff in error, was found guilty of a direct contempt of the trial court, and the punishment imposed was ninety days in the county jail." Harrison writes, "that for fixing crooked judges to write crooked opinions," McCormick "should be either incarcerated in a insane asylum or taken out by a posse of indignant and robbed fellow citizens, and either shot or hanged to an oak tree," while the court asserts that, "The record justifies the conclusion that Parker desired publicity for his infamous charges and that in furtherance of that desire he filed the pleading and documents, so that the records of the courts would contain his charges. In the documents and pleading filed by Parker he is pictured as a man of great ability and force." Also we are obliged to presume that Parker was of sound mind when he committed the contempt of court for which he was punished."

"Parker contends that the charges contained in the documents filed were made by the Puritan Church and that he cannot be held responsible for the acts of that church."

Prior court records were then introduced, "Said Parker has stated under oath that said so-called 'Puritan Church' have made plans to hang and murder numerous citizens and public officials, including the Governor of Illinois, several judges of the Supreme Court of Illinois, the Appellate Court of Illinois, and the Circuit and Superior Courts. Said Parker, in his deposition heretofore taken, identified letters he had written threatening to commit the abovementioned murders, which letters he had signed 'Puritan Church- by Harrison Parker. '"

"Parker's answer to the petition takes up a great many pages of the record. After the answer had been filed the trial court entered the following judgment order:

"It is further ordered and adjudged that said Harrison Parker stand committed to and be confined in the County Jail in said County of cook and State of Illinois for ninety days."

PEOPLE V. PARKER SUPREME COURT OF ILLINOIS MAY 22, 1947

"He (Harrison) denied that the letter was contemptuous and insisted that it was composed by the Puritan Church and deposited in the mails in the furtherance of church duties, and in the exercise of the constitutional rights of freedom of speech and freedom of religion."

The court upheld, again, the lower courts rulings and sentence for contempt of court. The cause for which he had railed around and the court case against the Chicago Tribune died a slow and agonizing death after twenty-five years, and Harrison Parker would never be the same. From Bealuh's letter of November 12th; "After the suit was over, he was a changed man. He got himself ordained as a minister and founded the Puritan Church which, I am happy to say, died when he did. He tried to involve my mother and all his children in it, and named us as trustees, but none of the children wanted anything to do with it and resigned immediately." Starting the Puritan Church may have been the start of a new life for Harrison, but his troubles were far from over, as he would spend the rest of his life in and out of courtrooms, and at least once in jail.

Man in $500 Cutaway Argues Own Case in Supreme Court by George Kennedy

"Regardless of the outcome of the case of "Parker versus Illinois," Harrison Parker achieved one thing. He had his day in court yesterday.

Because he pleaded his own case without counsel, something that hasn't happened in the Supreme Court for more than 20 years, he had the nine justices of the court inquiring into the circumstances under which he was sentenced to 90 days in jail for contempt.

And his opponent, Illinois Assistant Attorney General William C. Wines, was put at a disadvantage. While Mr. Parker, who is 70, glibly cited cases, the justices wanted to know from a lawyer just what had happened in the case in the courts of Illinois. And Mr. Wines was the only lawyer before the bench.

Filing of Papers Involved

It developed that Mr. Parker was sentenced for contempt because of some papers he had filed with the clerk of the Circuit Court of Cook County in response to a show cause order while he was suing a man for slander.

"If he had been ordered to produce the papers, would he have been in danger of contempt under the laws of Illinois?" asked Justice Rutledge.

"No sir," said Mr. Wines. "but there wasn't a word in this order directing him to file the papers. This was in order for him to show cause why he did not produce the papers."

That will give you an idea of the legal questions involved.

Mr. Parker seized the point in rebuttal. "Your honors," he asked, "is justice such a maze, are the courts a trap for the, unwary?"

Mr. Parker had another advantage, Mr. Wines. Mr. Wines wore a slack suit and Mr. Parker did justice to a beautiful cutaway coat and striped trousers.

Coat Cost $500

The first thing he did when he learned he Supreme Court would hear his appeal was to take a train from Chicago to New York to have Wetzel, the famed Fifth Avenue tailor, measure him for the morning clothes. That meant another trip for a fitting. The coat cost him $500 and he figures it was well worth it.

Mr. Parker is a former newspaper executive. He gives his background as business manager of the old Philadelphia North American before 1905; business manager of the Chicago Tribune 1905–1909, president of Hearst Chicago American from 1910 to 1917. Thereafter he became interested in investments and retired in 1931 with a considerable competency.

He began to read history. He spent five years finding out why Cicero was murdered, among other things. He realized that religion is a great force in history. He also became interested in the Puritan church. Although he has a marked Irish accent from an immigrant grandmother, he is the 10th in direct line from a Parker who started the church in Reading, Massachusetts, in 1635. He preaches Sundays to a congregation of about 75 in Lagrange, Illinois, a suburb of Chicago.

He also became obsessed with the idea that his old employer, the Chicago Tribune, owes $100,000,000 in back taxes. As he explained to the court, he seems to arrive at the figure by saying the company failed to pay a tax on distribution of $28,000,000 in cash dividends over a number of years. With the money that should have been paid in taxes, he says, the company started the New York Daily News, which is now worth $100,000,000. He has started taxpayer suits to recover that sum for Illinois.

Justices Interested

The papers he filed with the court in response to the show cause order were resolutions of the "Ecumenical (worldwide) Counsel of the Puritan Church, signed by himself.

His sentence for contempt was upheld by the appellate court and the Supreme Court of Illinois. He also was sentenced to six months in jail for sending letters to a grand jury. He is appealing that, too.

Court attaches said yesterday they had seldom seen the justices so interested in asking questions. They were patient while Mr. Parker went 10 minutes over his time. He finished with a peroration tracing justice from the tablets from Mount Sinai, the Sermon on the Mount, the Justinian code, Spinoza Voltaire, the Declaration of Independence; he cited wash machines and penicillin is evidence of advancement and Bridges vs. California as precedent. In that case the court reversed the contempt sentence against the West Coast labor leader.

Then he said:

"Your honors, if you wish to ask any legal questions about the trial in which the alleged contempt occurred, the lawyer who represented me in that trial is right here behind me. There was no one standing behind him, for he represented himself in that case.

From the Star (Washington DC) February 14, 1948

From an article dated March 6, 1948

Church Needs no Congregation

Parker Mail Case Hearing

told by George Kennedy

When is a Church Not a Church? That is one of the questions post office hearing examiner Daniel J. Kelly has under consideration today in the department's allegation of fraud against Mr. Parker.

Mr. Parker is a 70-year-old gentleman from Chicago who pleaded his own appeal from a contempt citation before the Supreme Court last month. He is still remembered at the court not only for the vehemence of his pleading but for the beautiful cutaway coat which cost him $500.

He was wearing a dark business suit yesterday and a bright bowtie and enjoying the relative informality of the hearing by smoking a Havana cigar. And he had a lawyer.

Calls Lawyer 'Wonderful"

"I've brought a wonderful lawyer with me this time," Mr. Parker said. "At 39, he is the acknowledged leader of the Chicago Bar." His name is Alan Bloch. Wait till you hear him answer the government's arguments. It will be an intellectual treat. "I always enjoy the show he puts on. His digestion of the facts is like hay going through a cow."

William O'Brien of the Post Office Solicitors staff was finishing his summation of the case against Mr. Parker as Chancellor of the Puritan Church of Lagrange, Illinois. On February 24 when postal inspectors obtained a temporary stop order on his mail, the church was getting 4,000 letters a day, all of them containing money, Mr. O'Brien said.

The contributions have been stimulated, Mr. O'Brien explain, but a puzzle contest for a $250 prize. First prize was easy and free. Those who send in solutions got back a letter offering them an opportunity to get into a contest for $3,500 in cash for a $12 contribution to the Puritan church.

Couldn't find church.

Inspectors couldn't find the church, Mr. O'Brien emphasized. They couldn't find anyone in Lagrange who had ever heard of the Puritan Church. They found people who said Mr. Parker did not go to church on Sundays.

They did find an office entitled the Puritan Church above a drugstore where girls were opening mail. On checking the bank account of the church at the Farmers State Bank in Montague, Michigan, they found that more than $230,000 had been deposited in the four months since the contest started – that there had been $166,603 in withdrawals and that there was a balance of $63,970.

What happened to the money? Mr. O'Brien wanted to know.

Mr. Bloch said the withdrawals represented the expenses of the contest.

Why did the church have $63,000 in its account? To put up a structure with, Mr. Bloch said.

"It is been emphasized," said the lawyer that Mr. Parker had no congregation. It is not necessary to have a congregation to build a church. Churches have been built first and the congregation enlisted after their opening.

March 8, 1948

High Court Upholds Parker Conviction

by the Associated Press

"The Supreme Court yesterday affirmed by 4–4 vote the conviction of Harrison Parker, a Chicago church – man, on

Man in $500 Cutaway Argues Own Case in Supreme Court

a contempt charge made after he sent a letter to a Cook County grand jury.

Parker said he sent the letter in his capacity as chancellor of the Puritan Church. The State told the Supreme Court that communications to a grand jury violate the public policy of Illinois and are punishable as for contempt. Parker was sentenced to six months in jail.

The Supreme Court in a 6 to 3 decision last April 5 upheld another Illinois contempt conviction against Parker. In that case he was sentenced to 90 days in jail for filing a "scurrilous affidavit and exhibits" in the office of the clerk of the Cook County Circuit Court.

The letter to the grand jury related that the Puritan Church had documents to support its assertion that the Chicago Tribune had avoided payment of $100,000,000 in taxes and tax penalties."

After all the problems Harrison experienced in Illinois, in 1948 he moved to Washington D. C. in an attempt to start again. Even this move didn't stem the tide of notoriety that seemed to follow close behind. These articles appeared in the Washington D. C. Star newspaper.

SEPTEMBER 25, 1948

CONTEST PROMOTER BUYS $35,000 SITE TO BUILD CHURCH HERE

"Harrison Parker of Chicago announced today that he has purchased property at Tilden Street N.W., and Rock Creek Park for the construction of the Puritan Church.

A representative of the real estate firm handling the transaction said Mr. Parker had paid $35,000 cash for the property and that Harvey Wiley Corbett, associate architect in the designing of Rockeffler Center, had been here with preliminary plans for the church. It will have a radio station in the tower and an open-air amphitheater on the property.

SITE BEING CLEARED

Mr. Parker, who is staying at the Hotel Claridge, said clearing of the property has started and that construction will begin in three months.

There will be no resumption of the puzzle contest he originally used to raise funds for the construction of a church, Mr. Parker said:

"There was nothing wrong with the contest," Mr. Parker said, "but why go on against such opposition."

ORDER STOPPED MAIL

The Post Office Department issued a fraud order against Mr. Parker in April, after putting a stop to his receipt of mail in February at La Grange, Illinois when he was receiving 4,000 letters a day in an office above a drug store from a puzzle contest. Most of the letters contained money. The department found he had deposited $230,000 in a Montague, Michigan bank in the four months the contest had been operating.

Mr. Parker attracted attention in the same month when, although not a lawyer, he pleaded his own appeal before the United States Supreme Court from an Illinois contempt of court sentence of 90 days. A majority of the court turned down his appeal without passing on its merits, holding that, under the legal circumstances, an appeal could not go beyond the courts of Illinois."

OCTOBER 25, 1948

HARRISON PARKER JAILED 90 DAYS FOR CONTEMPT

BY THE ASSOCIATED PRESS

CHICAGO, October 15 - Harrison Parker, 71, self-styled chancellor of the "Puritan Church of America," was jailed last night to begin serving a 90-day sentence for contempt of court.

The jail sentence has been hanging over Parker, a promoter of various business enterprises since 1945. It resulted from his filing an affidavit in the Circuit Court of Cook County in which he branded all llinois Courts as "crooked."

Parker forfeited $1,000 bond in July when he failed to appear in Circuit Court in connection with the contempt charge. The United States Supreme Court upheld the sentence April 6, 1948.

He was taken into custody by two deputy sheriffs as he left the courthouse. Parker had appeared before a Federal grand jury investigating charges that he had defrauded $230,000 from entrants in a puzzle contest promoting his church.

Parker also is under a sentence of six months for contempt. That sentence was upheld by the United States Supreme Court in May."

CHURCH FIGURE FIGHTS EXTRADITION TO ILLINOIS

"A legal battle got under way in District Court yesterday over the question of returning Harrison Parker, 75, active figure in the "Puritan Church," to Chicago to face mail fraud charges contained in a 1949 indictment.

Judge Burnita Shelton Matthews ordered him returned to Illinois, but attorneys for Parker, who calls himself chancellor of the Puritan Church of America, immediately filed a habeas corpus petition. A writ was issued by Judge Walter M. Bastain, who set Thursday for a hearing.

The mail fraud charges grew out of a puzzle contest, which the indictment says, was operated in the name of "The Puritans"and the Puritan Church of La Grange, Illinois.

Parker, a resident here for the last two years, was at one time a newspaper executive for the late William Randolph Hearst. His present address is 820 Connecticut Avenue N.W.

Parker's bond was set at $2,000, pending next week's hearing. August 16, 1952"

August 22, 1952

'Puritan Church' Aide Wins Round in Fight in Mail Fraud Case

"Harrison Parker, 75, an active figure in the "Puritan Church," yesterday won a round in District Court to prevent his return to Chicago to face mail fraud charges, contained in a 1949 indictment.

Judge Walter M. Bastain ruled that an arrest warrant recently served on the defendant was defective. The defect apparently was a clerical error made by a Chicago deputy court clerk.

It appears that a new arrest warrant will have to be issued by the Chicago court to return Parker to that city.

Parker had been out on bond since he was arrested."

May 12, 1953

Chicago Judge Criticizes Court Here for Dismissal

"Federal Judge J. Sam Perry of Chicago yesterday criticized Chief Judge Bolitha J. Laws of the U. S. District Court for the District of Columbia for refusal to surrender a defendant.

Judge Perry's bench warrant for Harrison Parker, 75, self-styled chancellor of the "Puritan Church" of La Grange,' Illinois wanted on a mail fraud charge, was dismissed here. Chief Judge Laws advised the defendant already has appeared in Chicago 11 times, with no trial date set.

Yesterday the Chicago jurist putting the case on trial call, said: "It's strange to me that the District Court of the District of Columbia would hinder the administration of justice of this court."

••• IT'S TIME WE GET PARKER TO TRIAL."

On April 2 Chief Judge Laws dismissed Judge Perry's warrant calling for Mr. Parker to return to Chicago for a psychiatric examination. Mr. Parker and five other persons were indicted in Chicago in 1949 on charges of mail fraud and conspiracy to defraud in connection with a puzzle contest promotion.

$39,184 TAX LIEN FILED AGAINST PURITAN CHURCH

An income tax lien for $39, 184.24 was filed today in District Court against the Puritan Church for taxes allegedly due on the church's income between 1945 and 1948.

The lien is the latest of a series of actions against the church and its chancellor, Harrison Parker, formerly of Chicago. Mr. Parker, who is 73, promoted a number of puzzle contests to finance his church.

The Post Office Department put a stop to his mail in 1949. Postal inspectors found that $230,000 had been deposited for the church in a Michigan bank and that 166,000 had been withdrawn."

OCTOBER 6, 1954

PROMOTER OF CHURCH CONTEST BALKED IN TAX LIEN FIGHT

"Judge John W. Kern of the United States Tax Court today ruled Harrison Parker, 78-year-old contest promoter, out of order when he attempted to make an oral motion concerning the impending sale of real estate to satisfy a tax lien.

Mr. Parker appeared in the court with an architectural model of his Puritan Church under his arm. The church has not been built. It is the property he purchased in 1948 for its construction at Tilden A venue and Rock Creek Park that is to be sold on October 21 on a Federal income tax lien for $39,184. The money came from a puzzle contest for the church which brought in $230,000 before the postal inspectors put a stop order on his mail.

When Mr. Parker asked for 10 minutes to make an argument during the motion sessions of the court this morning, Judge Kern ruled that he had no motion before the court. Motions have to be submitted in writing, he pointed out.

Before he was silenced Mr. Parker did manage to say that the property will not be sold; that the Government was bluffing. If the property were sold, he said, "the very stones in the street will rise." No one's property would be safe, he declared.

The law was so bad, he said, that all the Government has to do to take over the title on any property was to serve a lien.

"The Government owns that church," he said pointing to the model of the un-built structure. "Now it wants to sell it to get money to buy bullets to send overseas." Mr. Parker has consistently held, with little success in the courts, that the money from the contest was not subject to income tax because it was church money."

OCTOBER 23, 1954

U. S. SEIZES LAND FOR BACK TAXES

"A tract of land owned by the "Puritan Church" at Tilden Street and Broad Branch Road N. W. has been taken over by the United States Government for nonpayment of taxes.

The property was sold for $17,500 minimum fixed price, when none of the approximately 30 persons attending the auction Thursday bid above this figure. Internal Revenue Service officials explained that the sum, less expenses for the sale, will be credited to the tax debt of the organization. Officials stated that it owes the Government $69,352.71 in taxes and interest for the period 1945-48.

The group has the right of redemption for one year, after which the property can be sold.

Slightly over 1.6 acres are included in the tract, which was bought by Harrison Parker, 78-year-old contest promoter, as the site for his "Puritan Church."

The Internal Revenue Service alleges that money for the proposed construction was obtained from a puzzle contest which brought in $230,000 before postal inspectors stopped Mr. Parker's mail.

Mr. Parker has contended in a long series of court litigation that the money from the contest is not subject to income tax ."

APRIL 3, 1956

CHURCH LEADER WINS ROUND IN MAIL FRAUD CASE HERE

"Another effort to remove Harrison Parker to Chicago for trial on mail fraud charges was rejected in Federal Court yesterday after proof that the 76-year-old figure in the "Puritan Church" already had appeared in Chicago 11 time previously.

Chief Judge Bolitha J. Laws of the U. S. District Court for the District of Columbia was told that the trial had been continued 11 times.

Parker is charged with furthering a fraudulent map puzzle contest. He was indicted more than four years ago and since has become a familiar figure at hearings in Federal Court and before the Supreme Court.

ORDERED TO HOSPITAL

Last year he was ordered to present himself at a Downey, Illinois hospital for mental examination. A month later a bench warrant was issued for his arrest. The proceedings were dismissed when Parker presented himself before the District Court in Chicago. But no witnesses were present and the United States Attorney there was not prepared for trial. The defendant was told he was to take a mental examination.

The commitment order was postponed and the defendant freed on personal bond pending appeal.

When he failed to perfect his appeal, his bond was forfeited on a bench warrant issued for his arrest. It was a result of this that Federal authorities in Chicago sought his removal.

JUDGE OUTLINES DECISION

In rejecting the removal application, Judge Laws declared; "No trial date has been set nor, apparently, is one contemplated at this time. There is no indication that trial will be had forthwith or at any early date if defendant is found of sound mind. Defendant's appearance before this court on removal proceedings gave no indication of insanity or other inability to stand trial.

"On the present record it appears defendant has not in anywise attempted to frustrate prosecution ... but has been willing to appear for trial at all times. Indeed he now asserts he is willing to appear for trial w hen one is assured. On the present record, this court, being advised the prosecution even at this late date, four years after indictment, simply seeks to determine defendant's mental ability to stand trial without any assurance of early trial, and being of opinion that under these circumstances the defendant would be unduly harassed, the application for warrant of removal will be denied."

SEPTEMBER 18, 1960

D. C. MAN LABELED Top ANTI-CATHOLIC BY ROBERT E. CLARK, STAR STAFF WRITER

"An 82-year-old Washington "minister" has been singled out by the Democratic National Committee as one of the leading anti-Catholic agitators in the United States.

The name of the Rev. Harrison Parker, once the subject of a Federal grand jury investigation into a church-promotion puzzle contest which raised $230,000 is being circulated among Democratic Party workers seeking to stem the tide of antiCatholic campaign literature.

The national committee's office of community relations, set up to deal with the religious issue, obtained Mr. Parker's name from an article in "Facts," published by the Anti-Defamation League of "B 'nai B'rith, a Jewish organization. Excerpts from the article are being distributed to Democratic workers, the national committee said.

FOUR NAMED

A committee memorandum quotes "Facts" as saying the four major anti-Catholics operating in the presidential campaign are Mr. Parker, the Rev. Harvey Springer of Englewood, Colorado, the Rev. Carl McIntire of Collingswood, New Jersey, and Brig. Gen. (retired) Herbert C. Holdridge of California.

Quoting from "Facts," the Democratic memorandum says: "In Washington, D. C., Rev. Parker operates with tax exemption as the 'Puritan Church. ' He has been for some years one of the most active professional anti-Catholic agitators in the United States. He holds the title of 'chancellor' of the 'Puritan Church - the Church of America.'"

Mr. Parker, who lives at 1868 Columbia Road N.W., could not be reached for comment yesterday."

from the Star 9/18/1960

SEPTEMBER 22, 1960

U. S. CALLED POWERLESS To BAR PARKER LITERATURE

BY ROBERT E. CLARK

"The Post Office Department said today it is powerless to halt the mailing of antiCatholic literature such as that being sent to thousands of persons throughout the country by the Rev. Harrison Parker of Washington.

The 83-year-old, who list himself as the chancellor of the Puritan Church of America, has been named by the Democratic National Committee as one of the four leading anti-Catholic agitators in the United States.

Mr. Parker, who has had no church nor congregation since he came here 12 years ago, said in an interview that he has mailed out about 100,000 packets of literature attacking the presidential candidacy of Senator Kennedy.

Cost of the operation thus far has been approximately $25,000, he said. He refused to identify other members of his church whom he said had helped with the mailing operation and contributed to the cost.

LEAFLET SAMPLES

"Rum, Romanism and riot hooligans are now prepared and ready to close all churches of the Protestant and all synagogues of the Jews in the U.S.A. as they have in Spain and other Catholic ruled nations," reads one of the leaflets signed by Mr. Parker.

Another, aimed at Senator Kennedy's father, says:

"Civil War is possible in the U.S.A. because the UnAmerican 'Catholic Party' is being formed with Joe Kennedy, the Roman Catholic Millionaire Whiskey Merchant, as 'Boss.'"

CAN'T LEGALLY STOP IT

Leo G. Knoll, deputy general counsel of the Post Office Department, said there is nothing that can be done legally to stop Mr. Parker or others who send out "hate literature" in other parts of the country.

Materials which incites to arson, murder or assassination is unmailable under Federal Law. But the anti-Catholic literature stops short of any legal offense say postal authorities, who have been watching the situation closely.

"There is no law which states we can declare unmailable any article or publication which attacks a religious group as a whole," Mr. Knoll explained.

SOUGHT TIE-UP

Mr. Parker, it was learned made an effort this week to ally his anti-Catholic campaign with the Citizens for Religious Freedom, sponsors of the controversial meeting here earlier this month which was attended by Dr. Norman Vincent Peale and some 150 other Protestant leaders. Dr. Peale has since withdrawn from the group.

Mr. Parker called at the Raleigh Hotel headquarters of Citizens for Religious Freedom and talked with its executive director, Dr. Donald Gill. Dr. Gill said later that his group had "no connection whatsoever" with Rev. Parker and wanted none.

"He was trying to get us to follow some of th.e ideas he has put out in his material, which we would have nothing to do with whatsoever," Dr. Gill said. "We had not invited him to our office, and we ushered him out as quickly as possible."

Citizens for Religious Freedom holds that Senator Kennedy's religion is a valid campaign issue which should be discussed openly rather than disregarded. It has denounced anti -Catholic bigotry.

Mr. Parker, of 1868 Columbia Road N. W. , said his mailing list is made up mainly of the "communicants" of his church, whom he said number about 200,000. He said he was ordained a minister in 1943 in the Masonic Temple in Chicago and prior to 1948 preached at a Puritan church in La Grange, Illinois.

"I am not anti-Catholic, I am proAmerican," he declared. The message is repeated in his literature, which is mailed under a postage paid permit from Arlington.

ENVELOPE FOR DONATIONS

The literature being mailed out by Mr. Parker includes an envelope in which the addressee may mail a contribution to the Puritan Church. Donations are tax-deductible, the invitation advises.

The contribution envelope contains space for the addressees to write in the names of others they would like to have receive the anti-Catholic literature. They may also order additional copies themselves at the rate of 40 packets for each $10 donated.

Mr. Parker said contributions are beginning to come in , but declined to say how much money had been raised in this way."

paper, Star - September 22, 1960

CHURCH TAX SALE COMPLAINT LOSES

"District Court Judge Edward A. Tamm yesterday dismissed a Washington minister's complaint seeking to set aside a tax sale of property he claims belonged to his church.

Judge Tamm dismissed the complaint of the Rev. Harrison Parker, he said, because of the court is without jurisdiction to try the casc.

The Internal Revenue Service seized the property at Tilden Street and Broad Branch Road N.W. in 1954 to satisfy a $39,000 tax lien.

No church building has ever been erected in the District and Mr. Parker has not had a congregation since coming to Washington 12 years ago, court records show."

Harrison, who as just stated, lost his last court appeal November 17th, 1960, would again suffer another loss. On December 16th, Edith, his wife of 59 years died at their home at the age of 84. Six months and twenty-six days later, Harrison would also die after a month-long hospital stay. Both of the remains of Harrison and Edith were cremated and interred at the Stubbs family plot in Ashland, Ohio.

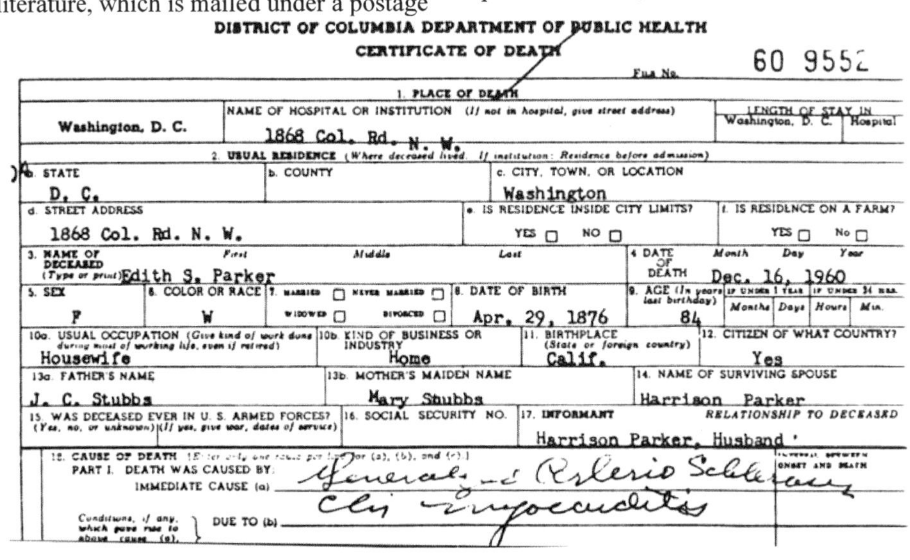

DISTRICT OF COLUMBIA DEPARTMENT OF PUBLIC HEALTH
CERTIFICATE OF DEATH

File No. 60 9552

1. PLACE OF DEATH: Washington, D. C. — NAME OF HOSPITAL OR INSTITUTION: 1868 Col. Rd. N. W. — LENGTH OF STAY IN Washington, D. C. / Hospital

2. USUAL RESIDENCE: a. STATE D. C. — b. COUNTY — c. CITY, TOWN, OR LOCATION Washington — d. STREET ADDRESS 1868 Col. Rd. N. W. — e. IS RESIDENCE INSIDE CITY LIMITS? YES / NO — f. IS RESIDENCE ON A FARM? YES / NO

3. NAME OF DECEASED: Edith S. Parker — 4. DATE OF DEATH: Dec. 16, 1960

5. SEX: F — 6. COLOR OR RACE: W — 7. MARRIED / NEVER MARRIED / WIDOWED / DIVORCED — 8. DATE OF BIRTH: Apr. 29, 1876 — 9. AGE (In years last birthday): 84

10a. USUAL OCCUPATION: Housewife — 10b. KIND OF BUSINESS OR INDUSTRY: Home — 11. BIRTHPLACE: Calif. — 12. CITIZEN OF WHAT COUNTRY? Yes

13a. FATHER'S NAME: J. C. Stubbs — 13b. MOTHER'S MAIDEN NAME: Mary Stubbs — 14. NAME OF SURVIVING SPOUSE: Harrison Parker

15. WAS DECEASED EVER IN U. S. ARMED FORCES? — 16. SOCIAL SECURITY NO. — 17. INFORMANT / RELATIONSHIP TO DECEASED: Harrison Parker, Husband

18. CAUSE OF DEATH — PART I. DEATH WAS CAUSED BY: IMMEDIATE CAUSE (a) Generalized Arteriosclerosis — DUE TO (b) Cly [illegible]

The Oil Years

THE OIL YEARS

As a very large two color poster states, Oil Makes Millionaires! Thus is born oil fever at Fruitvale.

Further south in Muskegon County, approx. 10 to 12 miles, a major oil field was opened, and hit a feverish pitch by the end of 1928 with headlines reporting major flows and untold wealth.

Not knowing for sure how far north the field may range, two groups were formed to explore for oil in Fruitvale. As reported in the Grand Rapids publication, the Tradesman, Harrison Parker under the name of the Better Business Bureau, devised a plan to fleece Fruitvale property owners out of their money for oil exploration. What is known, is that land owners for a fee of $1. 00 per lot, could be an investor and take a share of the profits equal to the percentage of the investment. If every lot owner bought into the well, the total received by the drillers would be about $35,000. The lot and land owners were thus contacted with the opportunity to buy into the Fruitvale oil field.

Today, how much wealth if any was promised to the Fruitvalers if they joined is unknown, but the results of their endeavors are.

The Fruitvale Resort Well #1 was drilled in Blue Lake Township, Muskegon County, south and west of the Rochdale Inn. The drilling commenced on October 18, 1929 and was drilled to a depth of 2245 feet. A trace of gas was reported at a depth of 2226 to 2229 feet, but for oil, the well was dry. Drilling ended December 12, 1929 and the hole plugged. It was over a year before the next well was drilled by the Fruitvale Land and Lot Owners, in Section 20, Otto Township, Oceana County. Although the record indicates that oil was located, it only produced a small amount.

As the chart shows, a total of 33 recorded wells were drilled in the Fruitvale lands between 1929 and 1981 with only the two by organizations ofFruitvaler's. While the total oil production reported was a mere 4334 barrels, just a drop in the bucket by todays standards. Even with the poor showing, the Fruitvale lands continue to see seismic testing by major oil companies, with some signs of promise.

ANOTHER WELL AT FRUITVALE

"Plans for drilling another well in the vicinity of the Fruitvale Land and Lot Owners No. 1 C. J. Sipple well in Otto Township, Oceana County were announced. T. L. Brown, chairman of the executive committee and propreitor of Rochdale Inn, arrived here. Adolph Anderson, president of the Farmers State Bank, of Montague, has agreed to act as trustee for a subscription fund to be raised among Fruitvale lot owners for the second well. Exact location of the well has not been announced. L. M. Strauss, another member of the committee who has interest in large acreage near the well, also is said to be negotiating for the purchase of a rig preparatory to drilling a third well in the vicinity."

OIL INCREASES IN FRUITVALE WELL

Drilling operations at the Fruitvale oil well were resumed this week and is proceeding cautiously to avoid striking salt water. There has been an increase of oil as the drill penetrates the pay sands in the Traverse formation and it is estimated that they have at this time a 50 barrel well. It is hoped to strike a larger production of oil at a lower depth. At a meeting of the stockholders of the Fruitvale Land and Lot Owners company at Chicago last week, at which about 250 were present, the executive committee was increased from three to five members. Thomas L. Brown, of the firm of John R. Robertson, prominent Chicago Realtor, and C. J. Sipple, drilling contractor on the well were added to the committee comprised of Louis M. Strauss, D. J. DeWolfe and Gustave Kopp. It is said that a wild cat oil well will be put down on the old pilgrim place west of this village by Hjalmer Nelson, this coming spring. He has secured leases on considerable land in that vicinity."

FRUITV ALE WELL SHOT

"The Fruitvale Lot and Landowners well No.1, near the Riverside Inn, shot Monday afternoon at a depth of approximately 1990 feet int he Upper Traverse sands, made showings of gas and oil. Although oil men, including C. J. Sipple, driller and promoter of the well, were unable to predict what the outcome of the showings would be, considerable optimism was expressed when natural gas raised the 1900 foot water column and bubbled out near the top of the drive pipe. The well, shot with a nitro-glycerin charge shortly after 4 p.m., was bailing oil and water 20 mintues later, following bailing operations. Only a few people were on hand to watch the well shot in. Further cleaning work began this morning, and at noon six men were to have run casing with packer, following which the well was to have been pumped out to make a test.

The well was plugged more than a year ago, it was said, but due to continuous seeping of gas it was decided last December to continue drilling. Hence the well was drilled into the Dundee sand and then plugged up to 1930 feet, when it was believed the best showings would result in a 10-foot section from 1890 to 1900 feet."

WHITE LAKE YACHT CLUB NEWS
OIL AT FRUITVALE

During operations of the last month there is every indication that the Fruitvale community is destined to become a thriving oil center. Early in the month a good pumper was brought in by the Fruitvale Land and Lot Owners well located on Otto Township. The gas flow was estimated at 20,000 cubic feet per day and at present a portion of this being used in pumping the crude. A new rig was set up in Fruitland Township, Section 1, near U. S. 31 about halfway between Muskegon and Whitehall on February 20th. According to operators in the Fruitvale field they fully expect to open up a new Western Michigan pool.

Mr. Hugh Frye, who has been in some way connected with many of the big fields in the United States for the past twenty years, is very optimistic of the Fruitvale field's future. He is preparing for the press a report which will be mailed to some ten thousand lot owners in the Fruitvale district each month. In this report he will give detailed information of all operations as they proceed in this Field. Anyone interested in receiving this monthly report can obtain information by writing Hugh Frye, Colonial Inn, Whitehall, Michigan.

OCTOBER 31, 1929
FRUITVALE WELL DRY IN TRAVERSE

"The Fruitvale wildcat, well, which is being drilled with funds raised among lot owners of one or more lots near Rochdale Inn, was dry in the upper Traverse formation yesterday striking water at 1,815 feet. The well is located in the southwest quarter of the southeast quarter of Section 6-12-16, Blue Lake Township, and is one of two present drilling wells in Muskegon County outside the proven field. It is drilling toward the lower Traverse and Dunday at about 1860 feet.

FRUITVALE WELL SHOWS INCREASE

Twenty-two barrels of oil were pumped

OIL WELL DRILLING RECORD

Otto Township - Fruitvale Plat's

Date	Sec.	Location	Owner	Fd.	Driller
1/15/31	20	SW-SW	Fruitvale Land & Lot Owners	Oil	C. J. Sipple
12/30/32	35	NW-NW	Freedman and Strauss #1	Dry	C. J. Sipple
5/17/34	16	SW-SE-SW	William B. Lidke #1	Dry	Reed Oil Co.
6/09/34	13	SW-SW-NW	Brinnen #1	Dry	Reed Oil Co.
10/31/34	23	SW-SW-NW	John R. Robertson #1	Dry	Reed Oil Co.
8/08/39	27	NE-SE-NW	W. River Land Co. Tract #1	Dry	Reed Oil Co.
2/13/41	23	NE-SW-SE	E. R. Swett #1	Dry	Musk. Dev. Co.
8/13/51	32	SE-SE-SE	State - Otto #1	Oil	C. B. Miller
9/13/51	18	SE-NW-SW	R. J. Skala #1	Dry	Turner Drilling
1/07/51	19	SW-SW-NW	G. Peters et at #1	Dry	Turner Drilling
9/23/54	20	SW-SW-SE	State - Otto #1	Dry	Miller Bros.
8/09/55	29	NW-NW-NW	Ed Burke - F. Horton #1	Dry	Norocko Oil
10/11/55	30	SW-NE-NE	Ruben W. Westberg et at #	Oil	Flory Drilling
12/02/55	30	SW-NW-NE	Moses J. Jones #1	Dry	Flory Drilling
&1/19/56	29	NE-SW-NW	State - Jenson # 1	Dry	Musk. Dev. Co.
6/15/56	20	SW-SW-NE	Ken Eggerton # 1	Dry	McClure Drill.
7/12/56	30	NE-NW-SE	Fred W. Baasch - State #1	Dry	Flory Drilling
7/13/56	19	SW-SE-SE	Melvin Phillips #1	Dry	Flory Drilling
10/29/56	30	SW-NW-SW	Roach - State et al #1	Dry	Flory Drilling
11/10/58	24	SE-SE-NE	Alma F. Plank #1	Dry	Flory Drilling
7/13/59	24	SE-SW-SE	State - Otto #1	Dry	Flory Drilling
12/04/64	20	SW-SW-NW	Dale Holbert	Dry	Flory Drilling
12/07/65	20	NE-SE-SE	State - Otto #2	Dry	Flory Drilling
6/02/69	20	SW-SW-SW	State - Otto #2	Dry	Miller Bros.

Total production of Otto Township Wells - 4,308 barrels

Blue Lake Township – Fruitvale Plat's

Date	Sec.	Location	Owner	Fd.	Driller
12/12/29	6	SW-SE	Fruitvale Resort #1	Dry	C. J. Sipple
11/23/40	5	SW-SW-NW	Thomas Cussen # 1	Oil	Welsh Oil Co.
7/31/40	5	SW-SW-SW	Thomas Cussen # 1	Dry	Voorhess Drill.
7/28/53	9	NE-SE-SW	Sweet-Ames-Lidke #1	Dry	McClure Drill.
2/25/54	16	NW-NE-SW	Sweet-Ames-Lidke #2	Dry	Fen-Par Exp. Co.
11/13/54	15	NE-NE-NW	Sweet-Ames-Lidke #3	Dry	Busk-Ormiston
1/05/61	6	NE-SW-SE	Oveta Duerringer #1	Dry	Clapsaddle
12/27/61	8	SW-SE-NW	William Eilers	Dry	Flory Drilling
3/10/81	6	SW-NE-SE	Anchor Oil-Johnson Dee Oil	-	Anchor Oil

Total production of Blue Lake Township Wells - 26 barrels?

from the Fruitvale Land and Lot Owners' well, located in Otto Township, Oceana County, in six hours, one day this week, according to officials of the syndicate gas flow was estimated to be about 20,000 cubic feet a day, a comparatively small amount but the best showing of any of the four wells drilled during the past two years in the vicinity of the Rochdale Inn, Fruitvale. The well broke down after pumping this record amount of oil in a few hours and has been repaired ready to go on the pump again. A meeting of the shareholders of the well will be held in Chicago within the next 10 days to raise money for a second well to be drilled about a half mile east of the No. 1. Buchanan and Frye, independent operators, are cleaning out their No. I Fruitvale well in Section 6 of Blue Lake Township and have reached a depth of about 600 feet in their renewed operations. This well has been seeping a small amount of oil and gas for the past six months since it was plugged and temporarily abandoned as an unprofitable hole. Operators hope to make it a producer. There is considerable lease activity in the vicinity of these wells as several other drilling projects are in the wind and operators are hoping to open a new western Michigan pool."

A NEW OIL FIELD—that gives opport[u...] own land, lots or leases i[n...]

The genuine profits that have actually made most of the millionaires ha[ve...] or by the shrewd lease buyer who has been wise enough to bu[y...]

Muskegon is Attracting the Largest Oil Operators—Both Producers and Refiners

Michigan Oil is of Fine Quality. The Fields are Centrally Located and Expenses Nominal. Many Refiners are Bidding for this Oil.

MUSKEGON CHRONICLE, MONDAY, JUNE 24, 1929

CRUDE OIL SHIPPED TO TOLEDO REFINERY

22 Tank Cars Loaded at New Rack on Giles Lease

MUSKEGON, MICHIGAN, TUESDAY, JUNE 25, 1929

CHICAGO COMPANY PURCHASES CONTROL OF REFINERY HERE

Contracts Closed for 2,500 Barrels of Oil Daily from Field

GROUND IS BROKEN FOR THIRD REFINERY

Naphtha Will Be Chief Product of Plant to Be Built East of City

DIXIE TO BUILD NEW TANKS FOR OIL FLOW HERE

Size of Collection Pipes Through Field to be Doubled

WORK TO BE RUSHED

Tankage for 80,000 Barrels of Oil to be Available in Near Future

MUSKEGON CHRONICLE, WEDNESDAY, JUNE 26, 1929

STANDARD RAISES OFFER FOR CRUDE

Paying $1.25 Per Barrel for Dundee Oil in Muskegon Field

OIL SHIPMENTS TO REACH NEW MARK

Nearly 150,000 Barrels of Crude to Leave Here This Week

Oil Companies Spending Millions—Pipe Lines—Tank Farms—New Refineries

Pure Oil Co., Dixie Oil Co., Shell Oil Co., East Ohio Gas Co., Benedum-Trees Co., Sun Oil Co., Texas Co., and Local Companies are Very Active Throughout the State.

That the Michigan oil fields are permanent is evidenced by the amount of money being spent and the development work now going on by the large oil companies.

In the Mt. Pleasant field the Pure Oil company has a large force of men laying pipe lines and erecting large storage tanks on their 300-acre tank farm. It is reported that they intend to build a 6-inch pipe line to tide water at Bay City.

The Pure Oil company are erecting 18 steel derricks along the Mt. Pleasant-Midland highway, and other companies are putting up as many more over the field.

The Ohio Producing and Refining company are building gathering lines, as well as carrier lines to take care of their own production and other independents who wish to sell their oil. This company will no doubt erect a refinery in the near future.

In the Muskegon district, the Standard raised the price 15 cents, and some of the bidders are now paying a premium for the crude. Four refineries are in course of erection, and there are five pipe lines bidding for the oil.

During the past week some 150,000 barrels of oil have been shipped; as soon as the checks for this oil, and the oil that is now being sold every day, reaches the treasury of the individual oil companies and is distributed to its stockholders, they in turn will feel cheerful and the doubters and knockers will wish they were riding along with the Golden Liquid.

One does not realize the money that is now coming into this state unless one sees the big Standard and Shell Oil tankers sailing out of the harbor and the Pere Marquette R. R. hauling trainload after trainload of oil to refining points in Ohio, Illinois and Indiana.

No other mineral is as far reaching in its benefits as oil—everyone gets a percentage of the money, the merchant, hotel keeper, real estate owner, manufacturer, lease owner, stockholders, drillers and oil companies.

Michigan Oil & Mining News—July 3rd, 1929.

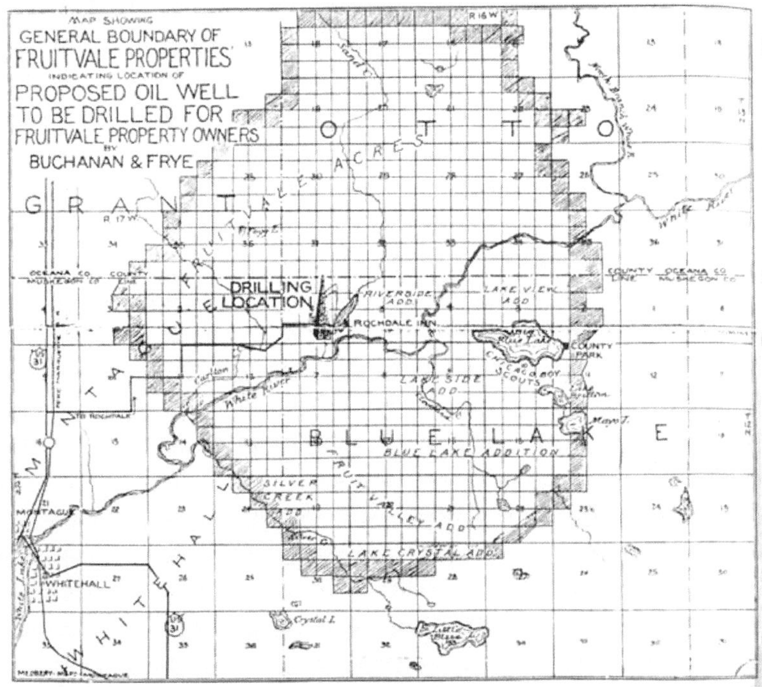

Fruitvale Offers a Wonderful Opportunity—The Proposed Location is Well Selected

A few miles to the south the great Muskegon Field has changed cheap unsalable lands into properties of great value and readily converted into cash.

Record Well Here Sunk On One Acre Tract

Mr. and Mrs. Joseph Trent of Laketon Worked in Factories Here to Pay for Small Farm.

MUSKEGON CHRONICLE, FRIDAY, JUNE 28, 1929

MT. PLEASANT WELL FLOWS 350 BARRELS

Several Others Are Nearing Completion in Dundee Pay Sands

MUSKEGON CHRONICLE, FRIDAY, JUNE 28, 1929

UNITED PETROLEUM BUYS LAKETON LEASE

Detroit Firm Obtains Oil and Gas Rights on 8.5 Acres

C. M. C. SAVING IS $500,000 A YEAR WITH GAS

Supply Here to Last 30 Years, ...ration Engineers Say

MUCH WORK ELIMINATED

Product Being Taken From One of Three Wells Under Contract

OIL WORKS MAGIC IN MICHIGAN SAND

"Black Gold" Rewards Lives of Drab Toil on Muskegon Bad Lands.

BY JOHN S. STONE.

Two Wells Paying.

How Three Families Triumphed.

Michigan Oil Wealth has made many independently wealthy and it is just an infant as an Oil State. Fruitvale may be the next great oil field.

Fruitvale Should Be Tested

A 20 Acre Lease in Fruitvale Together With a Good Producing Well Would Be Worth a Lot of Money.

tunity to make money to the persons who
in proven areas—Michigan

ve been found by the farmers on whose property oil has been discovered, uy land near a drilling well whose prospects looked encouraging.

Oil Takes Many Owners of Lands and Leases From Poverty to Affluence. Great Fortunes are Made Over Night if Oil is Discovered. Test Wells are Important. If You Own Land Well Located in Michigan You Should do Everything Possible to Have a Well Drilled at Once. You May be the Next to Reap the Great Profits.

Land Once Worthless Gives Up Oil and Now is Worth Millions

RANGER, Texas, Jan. 3.—Drop back into Eastland County, Texas, in the year 1898. It was a rough, wild, thinly settled country twenty years ago, with plenty of land to be had for 10 cents an acre. Today valuations in that county alone are said to have appreciated one billion dollars as a result of the 1917 October discovery of oil in the McClesky well near Ranger.

To cite a specific case, take that of Thomas Tinsley, who held 3,182 acres, mortgaged. The property did not yield enough to pay the interest, and suit in foreclosure was instituted. From the resultant forced sale exactly $25 was obtained. Of that, $21.50 was levied on to satisfy court costs and sheriff's fees.

The 3,182 acres brought then $3.50, or a little more than a tenth of a cent per acre. That was in 1899.

A few weeks ago one hundred and twenty-five acres of that same land sold to the Magnolia Petroleum Co. for $154,000, or $1,232 an acre. Such is the difference in 20 years, combined with oil.

But Thomas Tinsley, if he still lives, does not rejoice. A great landowner once, he lost everyfoot, the records say.

FORMER STAGE DRIVER NOW HAS INCOME OF MILLIONS

FORT WORTH, Texas, Dec. 20.—Fifteen years ago, Breck Walker was a stage driver in Texas, but he was not one of those typical teamsters who hauled people over the prairies in the early days. Walker had an eye to business. He saved his money and finally became identified with banking enterprises.

Eight years ago he acquired large acreage in Stephens county, Texas, where gas was struck in the drilling of a water well. Last week a 50,000,000-foot gas well was struck three miles south of Breckenridge by the Walker-Caldwell Company—the Walker named in the firm's title being the former stage driver. His income is now estimated at several million dollars a year.

The gasser south of Breckenridge is expected to lead to the opening of a gusher pool. Negotiations are under way whereby the Lone Star Gas company, of Dallas, is to connect its lines with the new well.

So runs the story of Breck Walker. And so it is demonstrated, beyond the well known "shadow of a doubt," that it pays to have an eye to business.

$100,000 PAID FOR ONE ACRE

Eastland Company Gets Record Price For Burkburnett Land.

Wichita Falls, Texas, Nov. 21.—A record breaking deal was closed several days ago when the Eastland Oil and Refining company received more than $100,000 for one acre of land in block 88 of the Burkburnett field. This tract was sold to New York parties with the understanding that a well drilled in on it must make 500 barrels of oil per day.

The Eastland Oil and Refining company owns considerable acreage in the Burkburnett field. It has four wells producing oil on its lot 31 in block 88, Evans survey, which are making an approximate production of 6000 barrels per day.

This company has put its new refinery, situated at Dallas into operation. A line is now being laid from the refinery plant to several industrial concerns in Dallas who have contracted for fuel oil. The company will deliver [illegible] barrels or [illegible] trainloads of this oil to Dallas concerns. The company has contracts for enormous quantities of oil from eastern concerns, too.

TUMULTY BUYS OIL LEASE.

[illegible], Texas, Nov. 24.—Joseph P. Tumulty, secretary to president Wilson, has purchased an oil lease in this vicinity.

Former Baseball Player Now Is Millionaire From Oil Investment

NEW YORK, Jan. 3.—Fortune is puttin' over easy ones that are splittin' the pan for Rebel Oakes.

The former major league outfielder, later manager of the Pittsburgh Feds and more recently the boss of the Denver ball club, is now Mister Oakes, oil magnate, close to a millionaire and a baseball magnate-about-to-be.

Rebel has made a big hit. A little farm of his down in Louisiana took a notion to churn up some oil, and while it continues to gush around about $15,000 will be rung up daily on his cash register.

With more money than he knows what to do with, the Rebel has an ambition to get back into baseball in one of the few roles that he has never filled—an owner.

Recently he sauntered into the office of Barney Dreyfuss, in Pittsburgh and casually asked the Pirate chief what he would take for his ball club.

The Smoky City magnate was inclined to consider it a good joke, until Oakes produced a roll the size of a truck tire and convinced his hearer that he meant business.

Rebel saved a nice pile while he was going good in the gardens of the major league. He invested the money in a plantation near Homer, La.

Oil drillers prevailed on him to allow them to go down on his land. They found three gushers that are producing 20,000 to 30,000 barrels daily and the owner's royalty is 12 barrels to every 100. There are indications of other wells on the tract.

The Rebel muffed few good ones in the field in his day, and it looks as if he didn't misjudge the latest fly that fortune sent into his territory.

FROM $1.00 PER ACRE TO $3,000 IN ONE YEAR

COMANCHE, Texas, Nov. 29.—Comanche county mineral leases that two years ago could have been had from 25 cents to $1 per acre have advanced to $20, $50, $100 and up to $3,000 per acre and still soaring.

FARMER GIVEN $140,000 FOR 35-ACRE LEASE

SPRING VALLEY, Okla., Dec. 31.—H. N. Owen, a farmer here, disposed of an oil lease on 35 acres of land in Tillman county, near Red river, for $140,000, and A. E. Hashuka leased a tract of his land for $155 an acre. It will be seen by these transactions that the list of plutocrats among Tillman county's farmers is growing apace.

There is no oil on this lease and the price indicates the wonderful advances in the prices of oil leases in the southwest. The value of the lease is many times the value of the land.

CHICAGO, TUESDAY, MARCH 23.

Chicago American

Office Boy Puts $400 in Oil Lease; Now It's Worth $10,000

You've heard about the dusty hobo rambling through Texas who slipped in a greasy puddle and rose cursing the tourist whose automobile had dribbled oil all over the road—only to find that he'd plopped into an oil spring. They say that hobo is worth a few million now and has his own automobile to dribble oil over country roads.

Well, the story of 17-year-old Benny Hirschfeld, the "handy boy" in a La Salle st. broker's office at 227 S. La Salle st., is like that.

When Benny sold his $400 worth of Liberty bonds some time ago and bought an oil lease from his employer, he thought it'd be pretty fine to "clean up" a hundred or so on that lease. Geysers of oil were [illegible] wouldn't his lease—

It did.

"I was offered $10,000 for that there lease yesterday," Benny said [illegible]. "But I guess I'll hold onto the thing. I sort of imagine there's oil on that land."

WESTERN OIL

Delivery Boy Gets Fortune In Oil Leases

SHREVEPORT, La., Nov. 1.—All price records for undeveloped acreage in the north Louisiana fields were smashed when N. N. Kronenberg, of Shreveport, sold ten acres in the northeast quarter of section 22-21-7, northwest quarter, for $100,000, to F. B. Kistler of Denver, Colo.

The acreage lies directly opposite holdings of Homer Chief Oil company, on which a well is being drilled. A few years ago Mr. Kronenberg was in delivery business in Shreveport, but branched into the oil game, in which he has amassed a fortune.

Girl Makes $20,000 on Oil Lease

KANSAS CITY, Mo., Feb. 26.—About a year ago a "friend of the family" whispered in the ear of Miss Laura Dodson, a manicurist, that big things were "bound to happen" in the section near San Antonio.

Miss Dodson took advantage of the "tip" and purchased a lease on forty acres of land for $1,000. Today it became known she has "cashed in" for $21,000 on the lease.

CHICAGO DAILY TRIBUNE: TUESDA

MULE DRIVER GETS 40 MILLION FOR OIL WELLS

Kansas City, Mo., March 18.—[Special.]—Thomas B. Slick of Oklahoma City has sold his oil properties in the midcontinent field to the Prairie Oil and Gas company. The price is believed to be about $40,000,000.

Slick, who started life as a mule driver, came to Oklahoma 20 years ago from Clarion, Pa., where he had started in the oil business with his father.

He became the world's "greatest wildcatter," spending millions in acquiring leases in districts remote from production and then startling the industry by bringing in discovery wells.

Negro Farmers Rich From Oil

SHREVEPORT, La., Nov. 25.—While most of the negro farmers in Claiborne parish are tenants, some of them own land and these have shared in the tidal wave of good fortune. Among them are Will Chatman and C. J. Jackson. Chatman's [illegible] acres is in section 31, where some of the gushers have been brought in, and while production is at a minimum in the field now, his monthly royalty checks average $[illegible]—more than the market price of his holdings a year ago. Jackson has less production than Chatman, but his land lies [illegible] and comprises 200 acres. Their market price a year ago was $10 an acre. They are worth $[illegible],000,000 now. Jackson has sold parts of his royalties and has realized about $15,000 in cash from such sales.

Land Once Cheap is Sold to Oil Company For $4,000,000

SHREVEPORT, La., Feb. 14.—The value of the sage advice given every young man to invest in land has never been more emphasized than in the recent record sale by Dr. G. T. Shaw, whereby he transferred his royalty interests in Claiborne Parish, Louisiana, property to Dominion Oil Co. for $4,000,000.

Some of the largest wells in the country have been brought in on Dr. Shaw's land, but he never drilled a one nor spent a dollar to produce the potential 150,000 to 200,000 barrels of oil a day of which it is estimated his property is capable.

To Dr. Shaw accrues one-eighth of that production by virtue of his ownership of the land. It is that royalty that makes him a multi-millionaire. Nine months ago there were no wells there; that property was worth hundreds then where it is worth millions now.

Study the Fruitvale Map

NOTE—Location is in a District that is Attracting Much Attention.

Would Be Worth a Lot of Money.

Club Lake Wolverine

Club Lake Wolverine

Since its inception in 1911, the Fruitvale lots that were given away were gradually bought back from unhappy Fruitvalers until by the early 1940s, Gus Kopp had repurchased thousands, mostly in the outline subdivisions. After the closing of the Rochdale Inn in 1941, the small amount of income that Gus had was not nearly enough to pay the taxes on the nearly 2,500 acres of land and it reverted back to the State of Michigan. About three years later, the property was sold by the State to an investor from Chicago the name of Robert Lewis Ames. In 1947 William B. Lidke who had prior ties to Fruitvale as a board member, acquired this part of Fruitvale. With him in this project were his wife Johanna, son William G. Lidke and wife Gertie, along with daughter Dolores Lidke. It was Mr. Lidke's intention to form a club for members only, for hunting, fishing, and relaxation.

Constructing a dam on Cleveland Creek in Blue Lake Township, Muskegon County, Lake Wolverine was created as the club's centerpiece. Called Club Lake Wolverine, it offered the unrestricted use of over 2,400 acres of; "virgin, timbered, pictureqe land, with hills and valleys, miles of trout streams – a clear water spring – fed lake, three miles and more long, a mile wide, surrounded by large and small bayous, hilly and flat timbered shores that provide ideal locations for summer cottages or permanent homes." In addition to the lake and waterfall that was created, an administration building with lunchroom and grocery store, and a gasoline station was provided. Also planned was a "68 acre flying and landing field for aeroplanes," and a 50' x 160' clubhouse with dining room, card rooms and library.

Memberships were sold the sportsman from Muskegon, Rothbury and Ludington, Michigan. All seem to be going well till October 14, 1953 when the dam went out and drained Lake Wolverine. The news report of the event is as follows:

Resort Operator Tells of Threats

"Floodwaters in Blue Lake Township were receding today as investigators sought to determine the cause of the sudden collapse of the dam holding back the 16 foot waters of Lake Wolverine at Russell Road.

Threatening letters received by owners of Club Lake Wolverine – consistent trouble with poachers and hoodlums and recent evidence of sabotage at the dam tended to support the theory that an explosion wrecked the $25,000 dam at midmorning yesterday.

But many persons, including some sheriff officers, clung to the belief that muskrats had weakened the wooden and concrete dam. Others said water seepage on either side caused the breaks which released tons of water from the man-made lake extending back three miles along Cleveland Creek.

A loud explosion was heard shortly after 10 a. m. Two large breaches developed on either side of the dam, over which extended a private roadway leading to cottages on the lake. Floodwaters swept downstream, carried away the Russell road bridge 500 feet west of the dam and flooding the roadway. Water covered marshy areas of Cleveland Creek valley to the White River, but it did no further damage downstream.

"It never would have gone out by itself," declared William Lidke, former Army engineer who created Lake Wolverine as a private resort in 1947 by damning the waters of Cleveland creek. He said he and other workmen heard a "boom," and some saw portions of the dam appear to rise up as tons of water surged through widening breaches.

Mr. Lidke said he found a large hole in the dam approaches two weeks ago. It appeared as if an explosion of some sort had occurred.

A month ago he received another threatening letter which read: "It (the dam) will blow up just like the Rochdale Inn. There was no signature on the penciled letter. The Inn was destroyed by fire a number of years ago. The club owner said he had received other crank letters in recent years.

Some persons objected when Cleveland Creek was dammed in 1947 by Mr. Lidke, who created Lake Wolverine as a private lake and game preserve for club members who leased property and built cottages. The club owns 2,600 acres in Blue Lake Township.

"We have had constant trouble with poachers and hoodlums who kept breaking in. I can't accuse anyone, but I'm sure the dam to do not go out by itself," declared Mr. Litke.

As was the case with Fruitvale, after the club development was started with investor's money, the needed working capital to keep it going year after year dwindled. Records show that during its existence, 58 memberships were sold. Of this total, only 17 members build cottages on their sites. Original memberships cost from between $100 and $500 each, with everyone paying yearly dues. During 1957 and 1958 the property was sold to video wasabi scout camp. The club sold all of its holdings, while each member worked out their best deal with the scouts. The prices realized by the members, ranged from $150 for ones membership, up to $10,625 for one of the better cottages. One member was able to negotiate the right to fish Cleveland Creek for one year.

Andy Anderson

Just For Fun

Hal Chase and His Ramblers

Just For Fun

As close as can be determined, only about 150 cottages were ever built in Fruitvale during the period from 1912 to 1942. So what did the other thousands of visitors do during their summer vacations? Those who came as visitors from seeing newspaper ads and promotional brochures were mostly from the states of Wisconsin, Minnesota, Illinois, Indiana, and Ohio. These vacationers came by buses, trains, and the Goodrich steamers. As they arrived in Muskegon or in the Whitehall Montague area, Rochdale buses, private run bus services such as the one operated by Tom King, or in the early days horse-drawn carriages greeted travelers for the final leg of the trip. Many who came stayed at the Inn, and as evidence to its popularity, saw almost yearly additions to increase the size. Regular yearly guest would usually try to book one of many cottages within a short distance from the Inn. Just south of the falls, in an area that once was the home of the Fruitvale Poultry Farm, in later years would be the location of five cabins for visitors. Just to the north of the Inn in the early years was a tent city for the hundreds that came to see their lots. After the initial onslaught of Fruitvalers, more permanent shelter was provided with wooden tents, called igloos, plus four more small cottages.

It seems that the features that attracted vacationers, some coming year after year, may also have contributed to the short season, and the Inns financial troubles.

Fruitvale and in particular Rochdale Inn, offered a simple carefree time, yet a day so full of activity's, the only time the guest spent in their room was to either change clothing or sleep. Of course for times of leisure, there was just lounging around on the beach under a cool shade tree with a gentle breeze, or sitting on the veranda overlooking the pond and occasional bathing beauty. Some of the ladies, a game of bridge was in order and often it listed the summer. Few children accompanied their parents to Fruitvale, for those that came during the early years, a playground area next to where the clubhouse would be built, provided much entertainment. This playground provided swings, a slide, trails and a picnic area along with benches for the parents and a horseshoe court. Due to the small number of children attending, after a few years the area became overgrown with brush and saw little use. In the late twenties, most of the trees were removed for a house and garden, and only the memories of children laughing remain today.

Numerous other activities offered at one time or another included:

Walking Trips

Usually not more than 2 miles in length, they took in such places as the old Pe-Ta-Ka Lodge, Andy Anderson's house, the grave of the unknown, and the fire tower. Pe-Ta-Ka Lodge was located about 1 mile west and a little south of the Inn near the White River, a large two story building used as a hunting lodge and decorated with trophies from faraway places, made an interesting place to visit. In later years the Lodge was abandoned, and thus provided an even more intriguing location, as stories of wild parties and gambling were told to those who came.

Andy's house was about a mile north

Tom King (standing on R.) and the Rochdale bus taking swimmers to Blue Lake in 1929

of the Inn down a dirt to track road, as it is today. Andy came from the Chicago area with his wife and purchased two of the 5 acre fruit and poultry garden parcels in Otto Township. Upon retiring from the Chicago transit system, he moved here full-time. The Anderson's have an attractive home surrounded by a cedar lined circle drive, chicken houses, and a unique word work shed. Find the house the next to the drive was Andy's special place, the building about 10 feet square with a low ceiling and no windows. Inside, the walls and ceiling were completely covered with playing cards and astrology materials. As a hobby and for some extra income, and he would perform card tricks for the Rochdale Inn for guest and predict their future for one dollar. Story is that Andy's wife who was not feeling the best, never left the house for over seven years, while Andy on the other hand became the Inn's mascot and was liked by everyone.

Seeming to be everywhere when needed, and he also helped carry baggage and other odd jobs. As a tribute to his kind heart, he can be seen in many of the group photos that were taken at the end of each week. Outlasting his wife, Andy sold his house and moved to Muskegon and near the end the City Rescue Mission.

Dead Man's Rollaway

A short distance from the county line bridge on the bank of White River, was the grave of the unknown. Here many Fruitvalers would come to place flowers at the grave site. Dating back to the mid to late 1800s a group of lumber jacks came to this location on the White River to prepare logs for rolling into the river and then downstream to the sawmill. When the men arrived they found the body of a male lying on the ground. None of the men recognized him, nor were their reports on anyone missing. Not being able to tell whether he was Indian or white, they move the body out of the way, dug a grave and placed a marker at the head. In later years owners of the property maintained the site and erected a white picket fence and large cross in his memory.

The Fire Tower

After visiting the grave, the bravest and most adventurous, would then continue about another 1/2 mile south and up the hill along Russell road to the fire tower. At a height of nearly 65 feet and located on the highest hill in the area, the tower was appropriately nicknamed Pikes Peak. Although many came only those with nerves of steel would climb to the top, for the spectacular view of all of Fruitvale.

Meanwhile back at the Inn, a whole host of activities were offered for those who weren't into hiking.

A Game of Baseball

During the late 1920s and into the 1930s, baseball was often the game of choice for the athletic. Played in a field across the street from the Inn, weekend games were organized between the

Fruitvalers (home team), and the boys from Whitehall and Montague (the visitors). Although just for fun, the games and the friendships that developed are still remembered today by local residents.

Swimming

Created from the damming up of a spring fed creek, the waters of Brown's Pond only entice the heartiest of souls. A beach was created on the pond and a large dock with diving board was added in later years, but few would find the waters enjoyable for swimming. One past visitor tells of a man who became inebriated and was promptly tossed into the pond, and promptly came out sober!

As one of the most famous attractions of the Inn, the waterfalls just below the dam on the other hand, did attract numerous guest. Few people felt that their vacation was complete without a dip in the falls. Even though this was the same water as the pond, the great force of the water rushing over their bodies, seemed to invigorate all those who came.

For anyone wishing to go swimming, the Rochdale buses ran regular trips down the bumpy sand roads to Blue Lake about a mile away.

Boating

In some of the early postcards from Rochdale, happy vacationers are pictured boating on Brown's pond. But not long after that, on the back on one of these cards, a guest writes "Dear Mom; We arrived here about seven – in time for lunch. It was an ideal day to drive. They must have borrowed some boats for this picture, as we have only seen one so far. Love Mildred, July 19, 1937".

Story Telling

Although the gentlemen I talked to, was too young to attend at the time, the adults would often gather together each night for storytelling. Just across the pond from the Inn was an area known as the pit. Created earlier when sand was removed while constructing the dam, this area provided a natural arena for a late-night gathering. Vacationers would sit on the edge, huddled together for warmth, while the storytellers sat next

to a large fire and told stories of mystery and adventure.

Horseback Riding

Behind where the dance hall was located, was the horse barn. Although not large in number, horses were kept, apx. 8 in all, and were available for a small rental fee.

In the 1930s Rochdale even entertained the guests with a rodeo. Put on about once a month during the season, they consisted mainly of daring horseback riding and rope tricks, but was well done and liked by all.

Tennis Anyone?

As in any good business, keeping up with the latest trends is important

fortunately for Rochdale, most of the time the money needed, wasn't there. Somehow though Gus Kopp was able to have a cement tennis court installed behind the Inn and next to the Annex. With a spirit of competition, a few local tournaments were held, and trophies awarded. Somewhere in someone's attic may lay the tribute to the first place in tennis, Rochdale Inn 1939. A couple of years after the first court was installed, a second one was added for tennis or volleyball. This one though was rarely used, for it was completely in the sun, while the first was mostly shaded. These two courts, with weeds growing up between the sections, is the only part other than the dam, that remains almost intact today.

Starting in the 1930s under the supervision of Gus Kopp, most of the physical activities that were offered above, came under the direction of the Recreational Director and his assistant. The directors were youthful athletic men, some with a professional background, such as Bill Makie, while others like 'XYZ' was only 18 but looked in his mid-20s. Although activities were available as listed above, these men were more a hit with the young ladies and their lonely hearts. There was on at least one occasion, a female assistant to the director by the name of Katherine Schreiber. Katherine offered exercise classes for the ladies by using the tennis courts in place of a gym.

Boating on Brown's Pond.

ROCHDALE INN
MONTAGUE, MICH.

DANCING

EVERY NIGHT

To The Music Of

Buddy Friend

And His Orchestra

at

ROCHDALE INN'S

BEAUTIFUL CLUBHOUSE

Dinner Concert 6 to 7 P. M. Daily

Buddy Friend and His University of Michigan Band.

Art Noey and his boys

Breaking All Records!

JOE GERKEN

AND HIS

ORCHESTRA

Dancing Every Nite

– at –

Rochdale Inn

Let's Dance

Music always played a big part in the entertainment of guest at the Inn from the beginning of Fruitvale and until the Inn closed. The earliest reference was a piano owned by the Parkers, and played at social gatherings and the World War I fundraiser that Edith Parker had. As the Inn became the most prominent part of Fruitvale and the center of activity, orchestras were brought in to entertain the guests. These included; Hal Chase and his Orchestra, Ivan Combe and his Orchestra, Metta Craig and her all girl band, 'Smiling' Joe Gerkin and his band, Harrison 'Buddy' Friend and his Orchestra, the last one to play before the Inn closed, Hal Wasson and his Ramblers.

Buddy Friend recalls just returning to Muskegon from down south, when the secretary of the local music union called saying, "Gus Kopp from the Rochdale Inn is in my office and they need a sax player right now, can you do it?" Buddy played the rest of that season before going off to school at the University of Michigan. A couple of years later, Gus came to the University to audition bands, and wound up choosing Buddy Friend and his University of Michigan band. The pay was good for the time, as Buddy received $50 per week and his sidemen

each received $35. Lodging was included as were meals, and cottage they had was the furthest from the Inn and guest, due to their occasional 'wild' parties and late hours they kept. The bands or orchestras would play seven days a week, starting at dinner they would play until about 7 p. m., then pack up their instruments and go across the street to the dance hall. There they were played until about 1 a. m. Whenever a special event, such as a bathing beauty contest was offered at the beach they would play for it. The dance hall contained a piano as did the dining room, so they didn't have to carry that!

And The Winner is...

Not all of the entertainment of the Rochdale Inn required each guest to participate, some were just fun to watch. One such big hit was a bathing beauty contest. As seen in the photo, all the girls were winners. The last three on the right were; Miss. Detroit, Miss. Miami, and the winner on the end, Miss. Rochdale.

Another activity that was well received, was the costume parties that were often held. These usually occurred in the recreation room, located in the lower level of the Inn.

Party goers at Fruitvale

(R to L) Miss Rochdale, Miss Miami, Miss Detroit, Miss Chicago

Chief Owasippe and His Scouts

YOUR LOT AND $95.00
WILL BUY A NICELY WOODED
5 ACRE TRACT

Situated within the area embracing Western Michigan's beautiful MANISTEE NATIONAL FOREST. An ideal location for a summer home or camp site. Convenient to lakes and trout streams. Hunting and fishing. A good investment. For terms and further details call or write to the office of The Improvement Club, Room 318, No. 431 So. Dearborn St., Chicago 5, Illinois.

Date of this BILL, APR. 1, 1955
No Discount Allowed
After May 15th, 1955

Gross Bill	$	.75
Cash dis.	$	.15
Net . . .	$	.60

28975

FRUITVALE IMPROVEMENT CLUB
431 S. DEARBORN ST., CHICAGO 5, ILL.
Telephone HArrison 7-2037

Mr. Geo. E. Scholey
135 West Maple Street
Clyde, Ohio

Chief Owasippe And His Scouts
The Story of Chief Owasippe

In the year of 1887, and a place on the bank of the White River, south of a location called the Trading Post, begins the legend of Chief Owasippe. On a warm summer's day, several local boys while fishing with stick poles and worms, discovered the remains of an old dugout canoe protruding from the bank of the river,. Seeking help, the boys returned to Whitehall a few miles away to get their parents and friends. Upon returning, the group of citizens unearthed the treasure. What they found was, two canoes, and the skeletons of two men, along with a copper kettle, arrowheads, and some beads. It was believed that these two bodies, were those of Chief Owasippe's sons.

As reported in an August 7, 1924 newspaper article, the story of Chief Owasippe is as follows: "In this locality there lived an old Indian chief, Owasippe IV or V, who had two sons, the apple of his eye, and the favorites of the tribe. They were known as Big Bear and Little Bear, being named after the constellations and the heavens. Now as you probably know, it was the custom of the Indians to send their young man upon an ordeal, when they reached the age of manhood. So Chief Owasippe called the tribe together for a farewell council fire. The sons danced for the people and the tribesmen in their turn honored their young princes. The old Chief gave them good advice, and warned them of their dangers, whereupon the boys left for the journey down the White River, into White Lake and into Lake Michigan. They were to return upon the second night."

"On the afternoon of the second day, a dreadful storm broke forth, one of the most severe the country has ever known, and the sons did not return at the appointed time. The Chief became anxious. Every morning and evening, he went to the crest of the hill and watched the land of the setting sun. It became later, that he spent all this time upon the lookout, and one day his people found him dead at his post under a pine, looking out over the country he ruled."

"The sons never returned, although the Chief had sent out scouts and runners, and what became of them was never known until the people found the canoes at Burying Ground Point."

"The supplement was at the sons were returning and were just off of the point, when the storm overtook them. They landed and turn their canoes over for shelter, and went to sleep underneath. During the night a landslide buried the princes, and they were never heard from until the river washed the sand from off their resting places. The Chief was buried at his lookout, between two pines, as was the Indian custom.

With the burial site of Chief Owasippe and his two sons, both near where the boy scouts would start their camp, it was a natural name to pick, and an exciting story to tell the scouts that would come each season.

Both Fruitvale and Owasippe, were started in the same year, that being 1911, and the decline of one gave rise to the other. Although not connected in any way, other than the employment of Gustave (Gus) Kopp, the boy scouts would eventually acquire a large portion of the Fruitvale properties.

Starting with the gift of 40 acres near Crystal Lake, from the Whitehall Chamber of Commerce, the Chicago Area Council, Boy Scouts of America would prove to be a great asset to the community.

As with the Fruitvalers, the scouts traveled to their camps from Chicago, by way of Goodrich steamer to the docks of Whitehall. But that was where luxury ended and for the scouts, a high adventure began. The Fruitvalers were picked up by bus for their journey, while the scouts, being rugged is they are, hiked the more than 3 miles with packs and all supplies to the camp. For most scouts, this was her first wilderness trip from their Chicago homes. Unlike today, the lands comprising Fruitvale and just to the southwest, Owasippe, was not always a friendly place to visit. There were many more wild animals at that time, such as bear, and your neighbors were often miles away. This did not deter the scouts in any way though, each season the camp prospered and new buildings were constructed to service their needs. In the first few years, a water well was dug, a dock on Crystal Lake was erected, and an administration building was constructed of lumber from 'deadheads.' During World War I, as was the case with Fruitvale, a decline in activity came about due to the number of men going into the service. This effected the scouts, in that there was a shortage of scout leaders to accompany the boys to Owasippe. Even with a shortage of leaders, there was no shortage of willing scouts. Year after year new camps were added, Camp West, Camp McDonald, Camp Dan Beard, in an effort to accommodate increasing use by the Chicago councils.

In 1924, the Exchangites of Whitehall, donated another 40 acres of land to the camp, to show again, the local support of the scouts. Almost in every issue of the local Whitehall paper, 'news' from Owasippe is reported; "500 Boys Scouts at Camp," "Great Boy Scout Circus – Annual Event to be Larger and Better Than Ever," "Camp is Made Postal Station," "Boy Scouts Are Coming – Annual Winter Campers to Visit Owasippe Sites.

With financial trouble looming over Fruitvale, in 1925 Gus Kopp, will sell to the scouts 280 acres on the south side of Big Blue Lake for expansion. This land contained more than one and one half miles of water frontage and was purchased for $35,000. The following year the scouts will purchase the Point Comfort Inn on the west side of the lake, being last commercial resort property on the entire lake at the time. The old inn was used by the scouts as the Camp Checagau dining hall until it burned down in 1935.

By the mid 1920's, the Owasippe Reservation had expanded to six camp's, in addition to the ones mentioned earlier, they included; Camp of Black Hawk, and Camp Checagau on Big Blue Lake and Camp Bel–nap, located between lakes O-jiib-way and Wat-i-see.

The camps were always well-maintained and supervised by very capable leadership from the Chicago area. In addition to the normal scouting activities that the boys worked on, occasionally they would have a very important special guest. During July of 1926 the camp was host to an Indian chief. Mr. F. G. Smart, was a full-blooded Chippewa Indian, and went under the Indian name of Chief Go–Smiling–Home–Once–In–A–While. Chief Smart had a college degree from Georgetown University, and was highly recommended from the Secretary of the Interior. While at Owasippe, he provided the scouts with many stories, and his Indian craft skills. Another early visitor of the camps was a Mr. Mills. As a member of the Anti-Smoking and Drinking Club, Mr. Mills was on a nationwide tour expounding the virtues of his group. "His talk did a world of good, it will prevent a number of boys from ruining their lives; the scouts will carry the news to others who are less fortunate in learning about the actual harm these vices will commit upon the approaching generation."

During this same time period, Owasippe also set up a camp for the 'colored scouts.' With its own director and full staff, the camp provided all of the activities available to the other scouts at Owasippe.

In 1934, on a hill overlooking the White River a group of scouts found a curious indentation in the ground and started digging. What they found were bones, human or animal, no one knew for sure! Thinking that they may be those of Chief Owasippe, the scouts each contributed to the purchase of a granite marker for the site. Over the years it was tradition among those at camp, that one of their many hikes taken while at camp, would be to the grave of Chief Owasippe, to pay their respects. Years later, in 1958, it was reported that, "Two Eagle Scouts of that era discovered a gravestone which read OUAC I PI X I VI, Mike Baldwin and Bill Petrosi reported their find and all staff members who inspected it agreed it was old. The location of the stone slab fit the description of Owasippe's burial site, much as the 1934 gravestone did. Thus a new location was honored as being the burial site of the old chief.

With the purchase of the Club Lake Wolverine properties the scouts acquired not only a vast tract of land, a lake of over 2 miles in length, and several buildings and cottages, but a place to finally call home base. At the intersection of Russell and Silver Creek roads, in a clearing that was a large farm in the late 1930s, as the new location for the camp headquarters, it was an ideal location. At a cost of nearly $3 million dollars, a new administration center, which included a 14 bed hospital, maintenance building, two ranger residences, trading post, central lodge, and chapel were built. Other buildings were constructed at the family camp.

From the 75th anniversary publication of the scouts in 1986, the dedication of the buildings was made ready; "By mid July of 1965, all of this was ready to be dedicated. Governors, Scout executives, corporate executives, judges and clergy attended the ceremony."

"So did Josephine Hercik McCabe." Like many other places and organizations with long histories, Owasippe has attracted one or two eccentrics."

"Josephine Hercik McCabe grew up on a farm near the camp. She married, but after a while was divorced and moved back to the farm. She lived in a trailer there, across the road from the farmhouse, and became a non-official camper."

During the 40s Whit Lloyd recalls, "The order of the Aero had a banquet after each ordeal session. Josephine got wind of these proceedings and after the cooks had gone to bed – but before the Aeromen got the mess hall – she would 'borrow' some of the sandwiches, cake and bug juice. She also had a habit of raiding the camp's garbage dumps."

"The campers and staff looked after Josephine through the years. They took her into town when necessary and when she could no longer care for herself, they made sure she was settled into a good nursing home."

"When she grew older, Josephine took to wearing a hearing aid, but she never put any batteries in it. So if you went over to discuss anything with her, you brought your own batteries and plugged her in. When the conversation was over, you took the batteries with you for the next time."

"One wonders how this procedure worked the day a staffer drove by and spotted Josephine repairing the trailer roof in the rain with no clothes on. She managed to let him know she saw no point in getting their clothes wet, too."

The scouts decided to make an offer for the Herrick farm, the deal allowed that Josephine could stay on the property. She agreed, with two stipulations: "First a sign reading this property protected by BSA" was to be placed near her home; second, the several thousand dollar price was to be paid to her in cash all in $1 bills."

"The bank provided space for her to count the money." gossip added that she buried the bills.

Gus and the scouts

After most interested in Fruitvale ended, and the Rochdale Inn closed, Gus was hired by the Boy Scouts. In a complete reversal of his former job of selling Fruitvale lots, it was now Gus's job to repurchase the land for the Owasippe Scout Reservation. At the time, the scouts and set a purchase price of $10 per 25 x 100' lot, that they would allow Gus to spend. Any lot that Gus was able to purchase for less than that amount, he was to receive one half of the difference. So if he could get the owner of the lot to donate it to the scouts, they saved $10, and would thus pay Gus $5. Gus would work closely with the scouts and the land purchase until his death in 1968.

Today, the few remaining lots scattered throughout the Owasippe Scout Reservation, carry a value from $50 and up, depending on their location.

With Gus's help, and that of others who would come after, the reservation would grow in size to comprise over 8,000 acres, then in 1977, with rising real estate taxes and maintenance cost, the 'core concept' was developed. The scouts had more real estate than was needed to service the summer campers. With this in mind, 3,935 acres of land was put up for sale, while the reservation concentrated on acquiring land within its core, 9 square miles surrounding the headquarters.

Today the Owasippe Scout Reservation is a major asset not only to the preservation of the land, but also to the local communities. Most of the supplies needed to operate the camps, are purchased locally, some of the year-round staff are active in local politics, and at times, the reservation is open to hunting and outdoor recreation for local residents.

Kenwood 6080 **4306 Calumet Avenue**

JOHN G. HEIM

-REAL ESTATE-

Fruitvale Lots and Tracts. Also Chicago Property

I SPECIALIZE IN FRUITVALE PHOTOGRAPHY.

-Chicago Exposures By Appointment-

COMING TO FRUITVALE?

A problem that plagued Fruitvale from the start, among others, was just getting there.

Most of the early travelers of course came from Chicago where all the lots were given out. Their first leg of the trip to Fruitvale was by Goodrich Steamer from the Chicago River to the Goodrich dock in Whitehall or Montague. In 1919, the fare for one way was $3.25, with a round trip costing just $6.00. After the six hour journey by steamer, the weary passengers were taken by small power boat up the White River to the Fruitvale landing. The Goodrich boats brought thousands of Fruitvalers to Michigan, until the company went out of business in the 1 920s. The trip up the White River, though a scenic voyage of Michigan wilderness, would take as much as two hours to cover a land distance of six miles! In order to establish this river route, the Fruitvale developers went to great expense and time, in opening up the river for usage. The first step was in removing a large wooden bridge across the river at a place called the Trading Post. This created quite a stir with local residents, in that the bridge was widely used and the only bridge for miles in either direction. But as was the case in the early 1900s, those with money and a need, pretty much did as they pleased. After removing the bridge, the dead-heads were next. Created from old trees that have fallen into the river, and pine logs that sunk while being floated to the mills, dead-heads were dangerous to small river craft. Using muscle and a lot of dynamite, these deadheads along with some sand bars were removed. Once at the Fruitvale landing, the passengers walked across a short wooden board-walk, where they were greeted by staff for the final quarter mile journey by buggy to the Inn. Due to the constant 'cleaning' required on the river route, this means of transportation only lasted a few years.

After giving up on the river route, passengers were picked up from the Goodrich docks by private bus service, or by Rochdale Inn buses. Early newspapers articles refer to a time in which a couple of ladies, upon spending a great deal of money on their travel to Fruitvale, were very anxious to see their lots. Picked up by a Tom King in his buggy, only thoughts of paradise in the City of Fruitvale, was the conversation over the bumpy sand road to Fruitvale. On their way home, Tom reported that the ladies cried of disappointment on the way back.

Some land owners braved the long trip, and came by private car. After making it as far as Montague, numerous signs on trees would direct the traveler. A Mrs. Messmore often came with her family to stay at Fruitvale, and enjoyed the drive, almost that is! Only a mile from the Inn, Mrs. Messmore joy would turn to fear, as the bridge over Carlton Creek was very narrow and contained low guard rails. This bridge, located next to today's current bridge, is to small for modem cars and is no longer used.

Another widely used form of transportation was by train. In 1919 a Mr. Hawkinson, "missed the boat July 3rd (Goodrich Boat), so he went by train. On arrival of the train at Muskegon (where they have a chute to fill the tender with coal) the fireman could not close the chute with the result that the entire engine was covered with 'coal and Mr. Hawkinson arrived at Fruitvale several hours late, and also out of sorts."

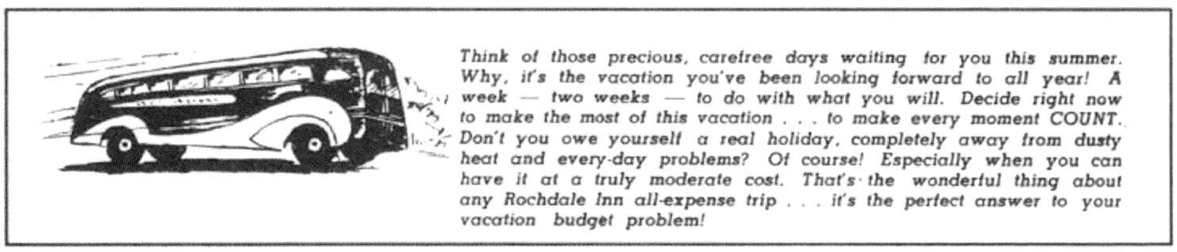

Rochdale brochures were update yearly

Fruitvale The Controversy Continues

Fruitvale - The Controversy Continues ...

During the time that Hugo Ruzicka owned the Rochdale properties, the dance hall and former Parker house burnt down. On the plus side, Hugo did rebuild a smaller structure over the foundation of the Inn that was destroyed by fire in 1944. After Hugos' death in 1955, the Inn site was purchased by Mickelson and King, two real estate investors from the Whitehall/Montague area. It was their intention, as was Mr. Ruzicka's, to reopen the smaller structure as a sportsman's club and possible restaurant. Mickelson and King spent several thousand dollars more, trying to fix up the building. During this time they had a new roof put on, along with extra support beams inside the building. But working against them at almost the same speed, was local groups of kids that found the empty building an ideal place to hang out. Vandalizing the inside, and often setting fires to keep warm, the vandalize won the war. Mickelson and King had the building, and the old annex next door torn down and have since put the land with tennis courts up for sale. Today, only the crumbling foundations of what once supported the in spot for thousands of resorters from the mid-west for over thirty years. In addition to the demise of the Inn, annex, dance hall, and Parker house, between the closing of the hostelry in 1941 and the early 1960s, all of the other buildings, except for a few small cottages that where built by Fruitvale, were torn down! The cottages left standing, are now located at the White River Campground, the area that contained the Fruitvale chicken farm.

The loss of the resort buildings did not result in the death of Fruitvale and the controversy surrounding it though. By the early 1970s, the Muskegon County Road Commission was planning on a new route over Brown's Pond, as the old single lane bridge built in 1920 over the dam, was no longer safe for heavy traffic. As reported in a May 1973 article of The Muskegon Chronicle, Muskegon County had its own "Watergate. "

Township Faces 'Watergate' Problem

by John A. Chisholm

MONTAGUE - "Blue Lake Township has a "watergate" problem of its own - minus the scandals. This watergate concerns the dam under Fruitvale Road, where that highway crosses Sand Creek at Brown's Pond.

The Muskegon County Road Commission has plans for correcting dangerous condition of double curves in the narrow highway at this point, a building a road to the north of the present hazardous highway. A culvert would provide for the flow of Sand Creek.

However, the present bridge will not be disturbed, inasmuch as the watergate dam which impounds waters of Sand Creek to make Brown's Pond is a part of the bridge.

The location of the roadway at this point was dedicated to the county many years ago, said Norman Williams Blue Lake supervisor. As years passed the title was dissolved, but nobody worried about it. Now nobody owns the site, Mr. Williams said.

The county will leave the dam, but will not maintain it, he said. The problem is who will keep the dam repaired if not maintained, some day it will give way, Mr. Williams points out, and the waters of what today is a beautiful little lake, will go tossing down Sand Creek and into the White River a short distance away, leaving a barren muck hole.

Mr. Williams said the township is seeking to interest the State Department of Natural Resources in assuming responsibility for the dam. He pointed out the DNR has planted trout in the pond and should have an interest in its maintenance."

The road commission had during that time, proposed several alternative locations for the new bridge, but most were not to the liking of the local residents.

Bridge Petitions Being Circulated

James Cordray and other property owners affected by the proposed modernization of the crumbling one-lane bridge at Brown's Pond in Blue Lake Township have sent a letter to the Muskegon County Road Commission asking that the matter be placed on the agenda for the next road commission meeting.

Mrs. Cordray told this newspaper that more petitions are also being circulated.

Residents along Fruitvale Road, where it crosses Brown's Pond east of White lake have been unhappy over one of three proposed plans by the road commission to "straighten out" Fruitvale by putting a new modern bridge over the middle of the scenic pond.

Road commission officials presented their latest route to property owners two weeks ago. Instead of crossing the pond, it would veer south just before the bridge and then cross a 10-acre parcel the commission plans to buy, before connecting again with Fruitvale Road some 1,700 feet to the west of the pond.

Road commission officials seem intent on having the latest route accepted in order to get federal funds, while most residents appear ready to fight for the survival of the rustic bridge.

Petitioners Oppose Bridge Plan

by John Swartley

Chronicle White Lake Bureau BLUE LAKE -A troubled bridge over waters in Blue Lake Township has promoted a campaign by local residents to preserve an historical landmark.

The fight moved to Muskegon County Road Commission offices Wednesday as plans for a $200,000 Fruitvale Road - Brown's Pond bridge were revealed.

The citizens group, led by James Cordray and Robert Reed, claims the road commission project may spoil forever the beauty and environment of the Brown's Pond area. They are supported by 150 etitioners.

Road commission officials counter by saying the project is the "best one available" and will leave the pond's historical Rochdale Dam, built in 1910, intact.

County engineers have ruled . that a one-lane bridge over the crumbling dam is unsafe and should be abandoned within a few years. After considering several alternative, the road commission now proposes to re-route Fruitvale Road and the bridge to a site immediately south of Rochdale Dam.

Cost of the project would be $200,000, with $140,000 of that figure paid by the federal government. Construction would mean cutting out sections of a west slope and filling in a portion of the Sand Creek Valley.

Road commission officials say they have an option to purchase 10 acres of land off Fruitvale Road to complete the project.

The road would be designed to carry 50-mile-per-hour traffic, a requirement of federal funding guidelines.

"We think this design is the best in terms of not disturbing any more than we have to of the surrounding properties," explained commission chairman F. Charles Raap.

The present roadway over Rochdale Dam would be closed to allow foot traffic only. Mr. Raap said land adjacent to the dam would be under county ownership and might later be developed into a roadside park.

Citizens at Wednesday's meeting opposed the plan on several counts. Mr. Cordray charged that the county is responsible for the dam's deterioration by allowing heavy truck traffic over it and now is escaping future liability if the structure breaks open.

"One of our main concerns is that we are able to retain the dam in a safe condition," said Mr. Cordray.

"We're afraid that after you get off it, the dam won't be taken care of and then we'll lose it and Brown's Pond both." The issue is complicated by the fact that no legal owners of the dam are now on record. Title to the property disappeared years ago after the county gained right-of-way privileges.

If the dam road is abandoned, road commission officials say they will not be liable for future reconstruction expenses. Chairman Raap did assure the group that if the 10-acre land purchase goes through, "the county will assume our share of the cost along with other riparian property owners for maintenance on the dam."

Traffic hazards encountered by designing a 50-mile-per-hour roadway were cited by Mr. Reed and another property owner, Charles Mickelson.

The current one-lane bridge automatically slows motorists, said Mr. Reed, and no major accidents have occurred since the 1940s. The area receives heavy pedestrian traffic in the summer, he explained, and he feared future mishaps.

Michael Kobza of the commission suggested that a pedestrian walkway might be erected at township and property owner's expense.

Mr. Reed also favored a northern loop route around the pond and, retaining the Brown's Pond bridge as a local road. This was one of three alternatives discussed at a previous public hearing, the other being a bridge crossing directly over the pond.

The current bridge proposal was chosen due to lower cost, according to chairman Raap.

The northern loop route would cost an estimated $270,000 while a renovation of the current one-lane bridge would cost the county $160,000 - $100,000 more than the proposed design.

"We feel we haven't got it (the $100,000), and we can't afford to spend that kind of money," Mr. Raap told the citizens.

"We have 700 miles of county road other than your own that we have to worry about."

Mr. Raap said the only feasible alternative to the one now being considered would be to close the bridge and the Brown's Pond section of Fruitvale Road to through traffic entirely.

A meeting between county engineers and interested property owners is scheduled for Monday at 4 p.m. for a first-hand look at the bridge site.

Only after a great deal of time and money was spent studying all of the alternate routes around the old bridge, did the county decide to by-pass the location, and move the road 3/4 mile north and close the Fruitvale bridge for good.

Fruitvale Still Remains ...

More than 70 years after its inception, the Fruitvale and its sister development, Lakewood, were still making news in the 1980s.

It seems that an out of state land "speculator," was purchasing some of the lots at tax sale, and selling them at an inflated price to unknowing buyers. Sound familiar?

APPENDIX

FRUITVALE PLATS

Lot and acreage counts:

Plat		Lots
Original Town		2,035
Fruitvalley	Addition	9,326
Lakeview	Addition	881
Riverside	Addition	2,053
Silver Creek	Addition	2,202
Lake Crystal	Addition	1,732
Lakeside	Addition	2,765
Blue Lake	Addition	21,072
Country Club	Addition	351
		42,372 lots, average size 25 x 100 feet
		2,431 approx. acres

Fruit and Poultry Garden 5 acre tracts

Oceana County	2,512
Muskegon County	414
	2,956 tracts, 330 x 660 feet each +/-
	14,780 approx. acres

Total parcels for Muskegon and Oceana counties 45,328
Total acreage for Muskegon and Oceana counties 17,211

The Fruitvale Companies

1913 - The Fruitvale Land and Development Company
- The Fruitvale Light and Water Company
- The Fruitvale Company, a Maine Corp.

1917 - The National Society of Fruitvalers, a Maine Corp.

1919 - The Co-operative Society of America, a common law trust
- The Fruitvale Land Development Company
- The Fruitvale Land, Light and Power Company, a Maine Corp.
- The National Society of Fruitvalers, a common law trust

1923 - The Fruitvale Resort Company, a Michigan Corp.

1952 - Fruitvale Improvement Club

PERSONAL PROPERTY

The following goods and chattels in the greenhouse and garden department of the Fruitvale Ranch in Blue Lake Township, Muskegon County, Michigan:

278 Runs in bench
96 Chrysanthemums - stock plants
336 Myosuthis Victoria 4 1/2"
51 Asparagus Plants 3" pots
35 Asparagus Springfire 4"pots
13 Asparagus plants 5" pots
1 Phalanginm 6" pots
4 Phalanginm 2 1/2 "
1 Latamia Bordorrica
3 Kintia Bilmoreonu
190 Prisnula 4 1/2" pots
68 Faverfam 3"
2 Draena indivsa 7"
14 Draena indivsa 6"
23 Draena indivsa 4 1/2"
50 Plant flats - wood
1 Long-handle shovel
1 Store lamp
2 Round sifts
200 Canna bulbs - small
1 Greenhouse, complete
77 6" Flower pots 10.00M-1.23
315 3" Flower pots 8.00M-2.55
64 6 1/2" Flower pots 29.00M-185
104 Geraniums 3 inch pots
186 Geraniums silver leafed 2 1/2"
35 Geraniums silver leafed 3"
10 Geraniums silver leafed 4"
76 Table ferns 2 1/2" pots
17 Table ferns 4" pots
9 Helitrope stock plant
25 Fuchsia
1 Amaneasia excelia
1 Large Boston Fern
72 Vinia major 4"
35 Salvia 2 1/2"
1 Hanging Fern
1 Gasoline engine 8 horsepower
1 Dble. acting power pump
2 Spades
1 Axe
2 Bracket Lamps
1 Greenhouse water can
50 Gladiolas bulbs
1 Garden house Hot beds and sash, complete

ALSO THE FOLLOWING FARM IMPLEMENTS AT THE SAME PLACE

1 Grub Hoe
1 Sack German millett
1 Sack Alaska peas
1 Sack Gars seed
1 Feed Cutter
I Pig House
18 small pigs
1 Barn, complete with stalls and hayloft
Com Crib
1 Smoke house
1 Set large platform scales (Fairbanks)
1 Pigeon house and pigeons, all fencing around building
11 Boat coushions
44 Life preservers
3 Oars row boats
51 life preservers
3 Side lights
4 Flag poles and flags
1 Mary Parker
1 Buelah Parker
1 Sack timothy seed
1 Sack Morrow peas
1 Sack Beans
2 Pig houses
4 Breed sows
1 Wagon-shed and cow barn
1 Toilet
1 Root cellar
1 Boat house
1 Boat "Diana"
1 Boat "Anita"
1 Boat "Gertrude"
1 Boat freight barge
3 Search lights
2 Rope protectors
16 Long boat cushions
2 Small boat cushions
2 Small desks
1 Office l0 x 12 drop-sided shingle roof, not sealed
2 Desk chairs
1 Large map
250 Surveyor's posts, Surveyor's instruments
1 Wood Stove
4 New wagon skeins
1 1 1/2 globe valve
1 Concrete block machine
300 Feet 2 x 4 B.M. Miscel. finish from hotel
36 Pieces 1 x 10-16 Y.P.D. 4S.
126 Bundles shingles 16" cedar
2 Steel wheelbarrows
1 Tripod
56 Canvas cots
18 Mattresses
2 Folding camp beds
5 Pcs. 4" Galvanized iron pipe 22
160 ft. Lin. 3/4 iron pipe
180 ft. Lin. 1" iron pipe
2 45" Ells cast iron
1 Hand saw
500# White lead
2 Lt. glass 26 x 30
1 Band saw
1 Large wood heater
2 Dozen 3/4 blank bolts 3#
4 Dozen 3/8 x 3" bolts 3# 50 Dynamite fuse
4 Doz. elbows 1/2"
1 Doz. padlocks
1 Doz. window bolts
#4 Lbs staples for matting
arge Dqouza.n tciotyld m cihsics.e lhsa r2d"w are items 1 Toliet stool tank complete
4 Gal. Japan dryer
1 Plumber's gas torch
42 BWihrcithe wpiapseh vbircuessh es ' 2 Plow points
2 16" Stillson wrenches
23 2142"" fSltieilsl son wrenches 21 CCraorpqeunette sre'st Jack planes 1 36" pipe wrench 1 Ice tongs
38 Rolls 3-ply Amazon roofing
1 Hand auger
Chicken woven-wire fenching
2 Rake handles
1 10" steel block
2 8" steel blocks
1 Oak chair
21 Monuments
1 Store room
1 Hollow auger
6 Lengths pipe
1 New 5 panel 3 x 7 door
2 Grind stone
66 pieces 2 x 4 - 16 Yellow Pine
5 ft. 1 x 6 siding, shiplap
600 ft. 1 x 10 Siding, shiplap
1 Stump machine, side roll
1 Stump machine, (small) side roll
4 Wire beds (wood frame)
15 Pillows 5 M. feet 1 x 4 German Adg.
4 Pieces 4" eaves pipe 12
2 Pieces 3" pipe 12
2 Pieces 4" cast iron sewer pipe 1 Hand Jack screw 18" 10 Gal. brown shingle stain 20 Gal. linseed oil boiled
1 Laundry tub
4 Barrels tar
1 Small wood heater
30 Pipe hangers 7/8 2 Doz. door bumpers
2 Doz. closet hooks
3 Doz. tus. 9 Packages toilet paper 3 Doz. unions 1/2" xl" x 38
6 Lantern globes
4 Stove pipe dampers
1 Kitchen sink
1 Steel stencil set
75# French washed ochre.
3 Wire brooms
17 Coils barbed wire 100# 1700
3 Lanterns
1 Pair trimmer's shears
3 Pair pipe cutters 1/2 - 2 1/2"
1 Spring wrench 10"
1 Monkey wrench 1 0"
3 Carpenter's moulding planes
1 Set reed bolt pipe threaders

1 Ice saw
100 Yds. 3-ply screen
260 Yds. 4-ply screen
3 New cow staunches
4 Hoe handles
9 Sq. pt. long-handle shovels, new
7 3 Sq. pt. long-handle shovels, old
10 Axe handles
1 Pick handle
12 Pieces iron pipe
2 1 Gal. linseed oil
3 Boxes glass, 16 x 18
3 Plow points
1 Keg putty 25#
50# Mica axle grease
10# Staples
20 Small cans chloride lime
17 Old axes
1 New box 10 x 12 glass
1 Part box l0 x 12 glass
3 Doz. fruit jars, 1 qt.
1 Cutter point
1 Jug machine oil, 1 gal.
472# Misc. nails
7 Kegs Misc. nails
4 Cans Mica axle grease, 2#

THE FOLLOWING ICE PLANT EQUIPMENT AT THE SAME PLACE.

1 Building 18 x 32 feet, insulated and constructed as an ice-house with slide doors, etc., built properly for same
2 Pairs ice tongs
1 Ice axe
1 Woods' ice plow
2 Pike poles
1 Pitch fork
1 Pair ice tongs (garden house)
1 Iceman's snow scraper

THE FOLLOWING BLACKSMITH SHOP EQUIPMENT AT THE SAME PLACE.

1 Blacksmith Shop
1 Bench vice
1 Horse clipping machine
1 Stationary forge
1 New wagon wheel
1 Boring machine
1 Oil can "brass"
1 Monkey wrench 12"
8 Cold chisels
5 Auger bits
2 Rasps
1 Soldering Iron
1 #63 Easy screw plates and dies
#63 Champion Blower & Forge Co.
1 Lot bolts, horse-shoe nails, flat and round iron
1 Blacksmith's hammer
1 Horseshoeing hammer
3 Wagon wrenches
1 Bipe tongs
1 Hoff knife
1 8# sledge
1 Wagon shed
1 Blacksmith's vice
1 Portable forge
1 Tire binder
7 Whipple trees
7 Double trees
1 Log chain (new)
1 Spring wrench 10"
7 Spring wrench 6" to 12"
2 Flat files
1 Wood mallet
1 Hack saw
1 Hand brace
1 Machine hammer
3 Blacksmith nippers
4 Blacksmith tongs
1 Blacksmith dividers
2 Pokers
1 Colony house 12 x 14; dropsided, tar paper roof
3 Pair scales
3 Pair scales (small)
1 Measure
1 Six-room house with porch and compressed air water supply
1 Coal stove (second hand)
3 Mattresses
1 Small oak table
1 Oak chair
1 Wash stand
1 2-room sealed house, "office"
3 Coops
1 Bucket
1 New kitchen range
3 Single beds-iron
1 Small oak dresser
1 Desk
1 Large wicker chair
2 Canvas chairs
1 23-pen Hall hot water system
1 Brooder house complete, with extra laundry stove boiler, 22 outside wire runs 33 feet long
1 3,000-egg Hall Mammoth incubator, complete
1 Duck House
1 Laying house 14 x20 and shed 20 x 14, complete, with roosts, water, crocks, nests, trappers, dropsided exterior, sealed inside paper roof
2 Laying houses 12 x 14 Portable dropsided tar paper roof
1 16-pen continuous building, complete, fitted with nests, roosts water pans, dry food droppers and 16-70 '0" wire runs outside dropsided exterior, tar paper roof, 1 well complete
1 I5-pen breeding house with alley way extending along entire north side and oats sprouting cellar in center; also 2 wells and pump, complete; each pen complete with roosts, 9 nests, water pan, dry food grit, shell droppers and I5 -70' wire runs outside.
1 13-pen brooding house, complete, fitted with nests, roosts, water pans, dry-food grit and shell droppers, 10-70' wire runs outside.
1 Store room 16 x 36, dropsided exterior, shingle roof unsealed with double floor and galvanized iron between floors.
11 Hall brooders (used one season)
3 Hall brooders (new)
27 Bell's egg cartons
8 Peck measures
372 Complete egg cases - 30 dozen
3 Bundles oil paper
1 Spraying machine
42 Colony houses, portable 6 x 8 feet, with door and window
1 Pump complete
3 Grub hoes, old
3 Posthole diggers
1 Tree wagon
1 Disc plow
1 Closed coupee
1 Old 3-seated buckboard
2 New bus - 3 seated
3 New bus - 2 seated
2 Old bus - 2 seated
1 Farm roller
2 Garden Wheelbarrows
4 Farm horses
2 Manure forks
3 Scoop shovels
1 Set single driving harness
1 Butter chum
8 Cows
1 Barrel cart
3 Saddles
8 Pair old blankets
2 Seeders
1 Lawn mower
2 Sacks grass seed
3 Pitch forks
2 Wooden rakes
2 Red top clover
2 Rolls 3" chicken wire
1/2 Roll 2" chicken wire
1/2 Roll 4" chicken wire
12 12-dozen shipping egg boxes
12 Parcel post boxes
3 Large bundles baby chick boxes
1 Toliet
14 Axes, new
2 Cross cut saws, old
1 Posthole shovel
1 Plow (second hand)
4 Plows
1 Open coupee
1 Bus
1 Single buggy
2 Old 4-seated buggy
2 Slides
7 Farm wagons
1 Hay and straw baler
1 Hay rig
1 Colt

2 Hay forks
3 Sets double farm harness
1 Set double driving harness
1 Cultivator shovel
1 Bull
9 Sets double working harness
4 Sets double driving harness
2 Cultivator horses - 4 new blades
1 Lawn roller
1 Hand cultivator
3 Lawn swings
2 Wire rakes (1 handle broken)
2 Scythes
1 5-gallon crock
2 Long-handle shovels
15 Sacks fertilizer 1500#
43 Bird houses
1 Sack seed com
3 Rd. pointed shovels
150 Labels for garden
1 Bucket arsenic lead
1 Can Paris Green
3 Garden spades
6 Axes
2 2-gallon crocks
2 Lawn Sprinklers
2 2-gallon jars
1 Square spade
2 Com planters
3 Potato planters
1 Pair scales
2 Com cutters
1 Short-handle Pitch Fork

ALSO THE FOLLOWING HOTEL EQUIPMENT AND BUILDINGS LOCATED AT THE SAME PLACE;

1 Hotel complete
41 Tent bungalows
2 Toilets
1 Boat house
1 Club House
5 Cottages
1 Oil House Hotel furnishings.

ALSO THE FOLLOWING MISCELLANEOUS GOODS AND CHATTELS LOCATED AT THE SAME PLACE.

1 General Manager's quarters
1 Frames for water system not connected up; Water system tank, etc., for hotel, barns and houses;
1 Steam gauge and whistle
1 12" file, old
1 Luis, old
1 Small wire stretcher, old
1 Desk
1 Desk chair
1 Typewriter table
1 Rayo lamp
1 Lot office supplies, valued at $25.
1 Superintendent's house (fanns)
1 Triple 3/4 wire cable puller
1 Axe, old
1 Long Howell shovel, old
1 Set counter scales
2 Office Chairs
2 Oak tables
1 Underwood typewriter
Also the following autos at same place:
2 Ford passenger busses
1 Dodge Car

ALSO ALL OF THE OFFICE FURNITURE AND FIXTURES IN THE FRUITVALE OFICES IN THE HEARST BUILDING, CHICAGO, ILLINOIS, AS FOLLOWS:

Private Office: 1 large flat topd desk; 1 table; 3 small desks; 1 typewriter desk; 1 typewriter; 2 swivel desk chairs; 7 office chairs; 1 telephone stand and table; 1 letter filing case; 1 small table; 4 cuspidors; 1. large rug; 3 wicker waste baskets; 1 wall map; 1 safe; 1 large filing cabinet; 1 moving picture machine; 1 electric fan.
Reception Room: 4 tables; 7 office chairs; 1 large rug and linoleum.

Bookkeeping Department: 1 large flat top desk; 1 small flat top desk; 1 typewriter desk; 2 swivel desk chairs; 3 office chairs; 1 hall tree; 1 check protector; 1 adding machine (Sundstrand); 1 adding machine (Wales); 2 desk lights; wicker waste baskets; 1 typewriter; 2 cashier tables; 2 tables; 2 swivel desk chairs; 3 bookkeepers' chairs; 1 desk lamp; 1 card filing case.

Mailing and Supply Room: 1 large flat top desk; 2 small flat top desk; 4 typewriter tables; 4 typewriters; 1 large sorting table; 1 drafting table; 1 stool; 3 swivel chairs; 7 office chairs; 1 large table; 3 letter filing cases; 6 card filing cases; 1 rotary neostyle No. 8F; 1 addressing machine.

Sales Department: 1 flat top desk; 1 table; 4 office chairs; 1 letter file; 1 card index; 1 rug; 1 addressograph; 4 office chairs; 2 typewriters; 1 telephone operator's desk; 3 name cases; 3 small tables; 2 office chairs; 1 large case (with shelves); 1 wall board; 1 filing case; 16 folding chairs.

Miscellaneous: 2 large tables; 1 small table; 8 office chairs; 5 tables (divided 2 sides); 1 wall bulletin board; stationary and literature on hand.

Misc. Records Liber 14M Page 163- 169, Muskegon County Register of Deeds Office, dated 20 November 1917.

West dining hall, Rochdale Inn.

Rochdale Poem

Beside a pond so smooth and still
That reflects back as mirrors will
The trees, the sky, the sun at eve
A happy carefree place to be
Is Rochdale Inn, beside the stream
Nearby the Falls, in which we scream
When feet get itchy in the spring
and all the birds begin to sing,
When the trees leaf out in green
And it's time the house to clean,
Then starts a pilgrimage that ends
At Rochdale, where they gather, Friends
They come by busses, boat and train
Some drive their cars and come in rain
Where joy abounds, and hall with laughter ring
And they all join in the songs and sing,
From early dawn until the eve.
In fact right up until they leave.
The guests are busy having fun
They grieve, It's o'er, ere half begun,
A Family Grand, The working crew.
As a one as I ere knew.
Their father, Dark, with Spanish eyes
That's never bothered by their cries,
Cause he and the Maw of this lively brood
Are not even married, nor e're in the mood.
Their troubles are many, their worries are few
But they are ambitious and all work and do.
Their sons number four, such very fine boys
All grown to an age they've no interest in toys.
Edward, Their eldest, just out of college
A waiter right now, but plum full of knowledge
Will turn his back upon this shack that's been his home for years
To enter in big business, and leave his Maw in tears.
Now Jim, the second son in college keeps quite busy
But during the summer, at the Inn, his rhymes makes one quite dizzy.
He started out as pantry man, but found he'd missed his calling
So now he's waiting table, and the girls for him are falling.
He wins them with his happy smiles, and the wise cracks that he makes
For his big brother Eddie coaches him in what it takes.
Adelbert? our problem child, a tall and fair haired lad,
In summer is a waiter too and doesn't do so bad.
He loves to read, and often with his older sister Jean
Playing in the water or sketching may be seen.
Quite oft' at dusk, when he sits alone
Playing Piano, AH! What tone.
Junior, our fourth son, and baby so cute
Is so entertaining when he plays the flute
He too can wait table, and does it so neat
Our Aunt Gwen, that's with us, thinks he is so sweet.
When we reprimand him, she intercedes
At a spoiling the child she fully succeeds.
She takes him out dancing and keeps him out nites,
When he gets home he's all covered with bites.
Now we have praised both long and loud
Those sons of which we're very proud,
but we have three nice daughters too
and would like to tell you what they do.
Now Margaret the eldest of these three
During the summer head waitress will be
At the Inn, ~he does wonders in that dining room
But they all take it smiling and just love her more,
for she is so sweet they all her adore.
Our Jean is an artist, so tall, dark and clever
Her sketches and paintings the cleverest ever.
But she took to roaming and staying out late
Her folks were so worried as to her fate.
For she with a Muchilo went one night
Tarowing her folks in a terrible fright.
The youngest daughter of the three, by the name of Buckey
Excelled in outdoor games and sports was ever very plucky,
She'd danced and swam, played tennis and ball
It was for her the guest would call,
But they were not alone, for even the crew were heard to yell
"HEH, WHERE IS BUCKEY? WHAT THE HELL."
We lived in the annex above the wash room
That have swinging doors and close with a boom
There's an orchestra too, that plays every night
To have parties far into the dawn they delight.
They swing those doors loudly and laugh and yell
Till Gussie wakes up and tells them "TO HELL"
"come out of there Harold, and stop making noise"
"or I'll come down with a ball bat and quiet you boys."
In case I've neglected about each to say
That they keep so busy all through the day
Each a waiter or waitresses job does so well
And waits on the guests at the GRAND HOTEL.
In our spacious lobby, right at the door
You'll find Gustave Kopp, who welcomes and more
"MAKES EVERYONE HAPPY," that is his aim,
If they're not, then I'm telling you he's not to blame.
He's early to rise and he's willing to please
In fact he enjoys all the girls he can tease.
When the sunshine, he runs all over the place
With his camera in hand, and he snaps every face.
And when the sun sinks, the dew falls and it's night
You'll see him out chasing around with a light.
Searching poor little girls who've ..gone off on a lark,
But they always tell him, "they were lost in the dark."
Behind the desk we find Aunt Drew
Who tells them when and how much is due.
As a very young girl, she a guest came from Gary
She met Raymond Baker, and then they did marry.
So now Uncle Ray keeps a business in town
While she struggles with figures and often will frown.
For running a hotel isn't all Glee!
And often I hear her say "Hell and Oh Gee!"
Shuey is our family Doc. and such a treasured friend
For when the gang is on the fritz, it is for him we send.
He looks us over, grins and tells us we're O.K.
Back he goes to plan his hikes and schedules for the day.
It's Shipe Hunts, houses hunted, ball games and tennis meets.
Treasure hunts, ping pong and cards, and all the guest he meets.
So goes his Daze, but his nights are long -
And he has time to sing a song.
Then he slinks away from the guests on a date
Sometimes early and sometimes late.
Then he and Margaret ride for laundry
And I'm telling you and Little Audrey
That we laugh and laugh ....
Because ... Who wouldn't...?
We have a dancing teacher, a pert and pretty Miss
Before she came to Rochdale she never knew kiss.

Here she went over with a Wow
Because, she has many a night, And How?
She puts on a floor show each Friday night
And comes from behind, to bask in the Lime Light.
Now their's a pantry where the boys work.
None of them have ever been known to shirk.
The glasses and silver they polish each day
And hurriedly all of them all put away.
The sheik of the tavern, the man of the hour
Who started a pot washer, learning to scour.
Reins in the pantry, from early till late,
But each night he's known several girls to date.
He dishes out fruit with gusto and ease
Cereal and coffee cream too if you please.
When he peels peaches he sings with delight
The salads he turns out, a marvelous sight.
A team unexcelled in the pantry play
Sing and laugh as they work all day.
One short and fair, one dark and tall
They wash and wipe the dishes, all.
Muchilos are what we call them; Dubbed so by one Marius,
And educated chef we had, an awful Ornory cuss.
He drew a knife and would have hurt
Our darling pot washer named Burt.
His temper he lost, so enraged he saw red
Picked up a milk pitcher and hit Paul instead.
After consulting the powers that be
He cooled off a bit, and finally could see.
With his bag and baggage he hurried away
And we've ne'er heard a word from him to this day.
So Jeff the Chef ... The cook at the place.
Rolled his dark eyes and made a grim face.
Wrung his large hands, scratched his bald head,
Said "We must find someone to cook in his stead."
They sent out an S.O.S. and on the very morrow
From Chicago came Jim Rogers, Alas and to his sorrow
He fell for a girl, Marcella by name
Who for Hay Fever cure to the Inn came.
Now one may learn of love as sung by a poet,
But boy it really can't compare with those that really know it.
They looked into each other's eyes and found themselves afire.
Their Love Life started in right then, or I'm a cocked eyed liar.
The Rochdale Moon came out at night, and shone for only these two
They get a coke, they'd walk and ride, and neath it bill and coo,
And it's my understanding e're another spring rolls round
They'll be coming back to Rochdale, with their feet upon the ground.
And they'll be very happy and we'll all congratulate
Mr. and Mrs. Rogers," even though a little late.
Now at the Inn the lights are dim
There electric lights have never been,
and though his back is weak and lame
Our father tends lights just the same.
With gas he fills the tanks and pumps the gages high,
When Paw just holds his back, and gripcs, and talks as if he thought though he'd die,
But he is a great old faker, and for himself does well
When the girls would "Go to Town" it is for him they yell.
A Handy Man, a Mr. Fix It, working early; late
So busy everyday and night he never has a date.
Morris Pelton is the name, he has been here for years
And any call of trouble, ' tis he who always hears.
He drives the station wagon, hawls garbage, carries ice
And takes us to beach parties, and wiener roasts so nice.
When the sewer's backing up, it's he who digs the ditches.
Though he storms, and rants, and raves and says, "The Sons 0 Bitches,"
Tommy Trenter a graceful young lad
Who at taking pictures don't do so bad.
Wrestles baggage, light the lamps and hangs the lanterns up
Though the guests and office force complain, "taint soon enough,"
Most anytime of day, you'll hear him round the kitchen door
Yelling "Gee I'm hungry," and always eating more.
Early mornings, late at night, or when he should be sweeping
You'll find him in the lobby, leaning on the counter sleeping.
For he was born with a feeling "Too Tired."
And ambition, so far, he has not acquired.
The man who runs our night club, just across the street
Good looking Bill Jarvis, He just can't be beat.
His smile is a honey, his dimples divine.
Boy can he hand the girls a line,
But Bill was not immune to the romance in the air,
When Winnie came along, he fell, they make a charming pair.
Because of the enchanting atmosphere the place became quite noted.
To have their dinners, to frolic and play, by many clubs was voted.
Hardy's for a picnic, and the Lions dinner late
Exchange Club not to be out done had a double date.
Now after dinner on the eve of the Lions party
We held a beauty contest, which they endorsed right hearty.
'Twas won by a charming little girl, a very lovely guest.
I know you'd ne'er forgive me if I failed to tell the rest.
Again the romance of the place took root and let me tell you
In a short acquaintance, nine days, Eddy Dierks knew what to do.
He up and pops, to Margaret, that most important question.
That to our Eddy she said Yes, I hardly need to mention.
There's many I'd mention if I would tell you all
About a charming chambermaid, and a Fire Chief so tall
Our housekeeper Mr. Stockely and her working crew of maids
Who are very busy people giving many household aids.
There in the welcome shade beside the pond
Public enemies: number one and two so fond.
Jim the pot washer, whom we like right well
Helps Dick who peels taters and vegetables swell.
They laugh and talk as their work they do
Then off they hurry to their igloo.
So I might rave, for hours and hours
About the scenery, birds and flowers,
That adds to the enchantment of the Inn
Accompanying for romances that are, and have been,
But with a warm handclasp, we'll say "Adieu."
And cheerfully sing our "So Long" to you.
Our farewell song, that you'll all hear
We hope we'll be seeing you all here next year.
by Ruth Price- August 23, 1935

CHICKENS AND CHERRIES AT FRUITVALE, MICHIGAN

State Bank of Whitehall, Michigan
March 17, 1917

TO WHOM IT MAY CONCERN:

We have known intimately the officers of the Fruitvale Company for a period covering five years. During that time we have known them to be strictly honorable in all their business transactions.

They have spent thousands of dollars in developing a beautiful tract of land to the northeast of this city.

We have never heard any complaints from any of the people to whom they have sold land. We understand that anybody who buys a piece of land from the Fruitvale Company, who is dissatisfied after seeing it, is given back their money. We know of no more honorable method of doing business, nor any better guarantee of the men back of the enterprise.

To our knowledge, they have spent in cash more than $80,000 for land and buildings and the necessary equipment for conducting so large an enterprise.

Very truly yours,
M. B. Covell - signed
President

WHY NOT MAKE $2,200 A YEAR ON CHICKENS AND CHERRIES AT FRUITVALE

Copyright 1917 - by C. S. Jones

STOP RINGING THE TIME CLOCK

You can easily become the owner of an income producing poultry-orchard-home at Fruitvale, Michigan, live out in the open air, and have friendly helpful neighbors. How different such a life would be from the existence in a big city - the long hours in the store, office or factory, the "domination of the boss," and the slim pay envelope that comes to you every week, which, after paying your actual living expenses, leaves little surplus.

This is a message to those of you, both men and women, who have toiled with hope of big success, but with that success still as distant as the horizon. Sooner or later, you know, that the time is surely coming when some younger man or woman will shoulder you out of your present job. You know that when your best energy is spent, when you are a few years older, you will be merely junk in the whirlpool of the city, unless you manage to save a competence.

You ARE GETTING OLDER EVERY DAY

Can you save a competence out of your present income? With the cost of living going up every day, with the advancing rents, and the additional cost of food, and with the other added demands that call for more money every day, what is going to become of you? With your salary practically controlled as nearly all salaries are, can you look forward to an old age when you will not be a dependant?

Why not prepare now while you have an opportunity? A few dollars saved every month, invested in an income producing poultry-orchard-home at Fruitvale will make you absolutely independent for life.

WHY NOT PREPARE WHEN You HAVE THE OPPORTUNITY

Think what you could do if you had an income. of $2,200 a year. Think what it would mean to you and those dependent upon you, to be able to say, "This home is mine." "No man can take it from me." "In time of peace, or in war, in plenty, or in famine, this home is mine." And saying this, to know that year after year your place in the country will not only make you a better living than you are now getting in the big city, but would give you a nice surplus in addition. You can accomplish all this by saving the little items you now "fritter" away in so-called pleasures.

LET THE UNITED STATES FEDERAL LOAN BANK HELP You

Don't get the idea that very much money is required to secure independence at Fruitvale. If you comply with the law, the U. S. Government Farm Loan Bank stands ready to help you, and the National Society of Fruitvalers, which has helped so many, will help also. You need have but a few dollars. If you have so little as $150-$50 or $25, that is enough to start.

The law says that any group of ten people has the right to obtain from the new Farm Loan Bank the money with which to start farming, to the maximum amount of $20,000 to the group. This money can pay back in small monthly payments, after your poultry-orchard-home begins to make money. The first group is being organized. Be in it.

What a wonderful opportunity this is for you! It is yours if you act before all the choice locations at Fruitvale are snatched up by the people who see the amazing possibilities for a home and a business combined in Fruitvale, - the garden spot of Michigan.

It is possible for you to earn $2,200 on chickens and cherries. That is what we are specializing on at Fruitvale. No experience necessary-either in the chicken business or in orchard culture. Anybody with good sense, a willing hand an honest heart can succeed out here.

You DON'T HAVE TO BE A FARMER TO SUCCEED AT FRUITVALE

Your are guided by experts employed by the National Society of Fruitvalers, to teach you every movement that is to be made; to watch over you and see that you make no mistakes; to see that you are giving proper attention to this and that; that you will feed your chickens at the proper time (the proper feed is supplied you); that you take care of the spraying and pruning of your trees. You are. given special instructions on these points, in fact you are guided in your every movement. The National Society of Fruitvalers wants you to succeed, and your neighbors specialize in the same products, giving you their helpful assistance also. There is little chance for failures if you follow the expert's instructions.

THE FRUITVALE IDEA THIS IS A COMMUNITY OF FRIENDLY, WHOLESOME PEOPLE

In Fruitvale you are a member of a community of fine, friendly, wholesome people. You are an independent owner and an independent farmer, but you have nevertheless, the cooperation of every other member of the community, and the backing of the great National Society of Fruitvalers. Your home can be made ready to be moved into within thirty days. Nothing will be lacking. At Fruitvale you do not have to do the pioneering. Already the central plants are built. People are living there.

Chickens and cherries are the greatest combination ever worked out for people of small means. You can get five acres of ground, four acres of which should be planted in cherries and the other acre for your poultry buildings and garden. You can buy all these buildings and the necessary equipment for care and running your farm from the National Society of Fruitvalers. There are several styles of houses, one to fit each person, according to his or her means, but no more than 10 acres of land will be sold to anyone person.

You DON'T HAVE TO BE RICH TO START

Bear in mind, if you have not a lot of cash, you can start with so little as $150, $50 or $25, and you can pay the balance in a small amount each month.

In the South and in California there are big profits in growing oranges, avocados, olives, grapefruit, lemons, etc. But these are "rich men's crops," farms for people who have a lot of money with which to start.

A person with a small amount of money, with no established outside income, could not afford to wait on the farm until these crops bring in ready cash. Five acres planted in oranges, grapefruit, avocados, etc., the preparation of the soil, fertilizing, the cost of caring for the trees until they are in bearing, would be al most twice as much as it would cost to develop five acres at Fruitvale in cherries and chickens. From chickens and cherries it is possible for you to get almost immediate income, out of which you can pay for your living expenses. If you put as much industry into your business at Fruitvale as any successful business, you should within a short time have an income of $2,200 in addition to the advantage of living out in the country.

The reason why we are specializing in the growth of cherries at Fruitvale is because big cash profits are always made in selling to the "common people," as Lincoln calls them.

If your money is invested, in a successful business, supplying the wants of the masses, you always have a ready cash income, whereas, if your money is invested in supplying luxuries, your income is subject to hard times, bad debts, and everything else. You are always liable, in supplying luxuries, to have your cash income cut off when you need it most. But if your money is invested in the necessities which the common people require, then you are almost sure of always having ready cash.

THERE IS ALWAYS A GOOD MARKET FOR CHERRIES

With the growth of the John R. Thompson chain of restaurants in the United States; the increase in the number of Child's restaurants; and the growth of other cafeterias, which have been springing up in this country during recent years; there is a tremendous demand for sour cherries-sour cherries used in making pies. Small fortunes have already been made, and the demand promises to grow each year. These popular priced restaurants, as you know, are open 365 days in the year. There is a steady cry to the canneries for cherries, and from the canneries to the growers. The price last year went as high as 5 cents a pound.

The big profit in growing cherries is in the growing Richmond and Montmoreney varieties, which thrive so wonderful in the Fruitvale country.

The John R. Thompson chain of restaurants in Chicago make more money, it is reputed, than the fashionable Blackstone Hotel. Comparatively few people can afford to dine at the Blackstone, while nearly everybody can afford to pay 15 cents for a cup of coffee and a piece of cherry pie at Thompson's.

Sears, Roebuck & Company are reputed to make more money than Marshall Field & Company. Everybody can afford to buy at Sears, Roebuck, while a lot of people cannot afford Marshall Field's.

Woolworth's five and ten cent stores are reported as making more money than "Spaulding's" or "Tiffany's."

From these examples you can see that the big cash profits are made from selling to the masses.

In agriculture, as well as in merchandise (for after all, running a farm is like running any other business) the smart man or woman is the one who has his or her money invested in crops for which there is always an eager and waiting market. You know that oranges and avocados are luxuries. The demand is limited. Whereas, eggs, chickens and cherry pies are almost necessities, and there are one hundred million people in this country, nearly all of whom are eating eggs and cherry pies, nearly every day of the year.

$1,296 A YEAR FROM FOUR ACRES OF CHERRIES

Let us give you a few figures on the possibilities in growing cherries and raising chickens-the staples of farm produce.

In the country around Fruitvale, according to Mr. Roach, the canner at Hart, experience has taught that it is best to plant 108 trees to the acre. A tree at maturity should yield 250 pounds. Let us be conservative and say 100 pounds as a mInImum. Last year the canners paid as high as 5 cents a pound. But let us again be conservative, and say 3 cents, which is the minimum price that would be received. That would make $1,296 for four acres of cherries. You do not have to spend any of this money, or waste any time looking for buyers. The canners will be standing at your door, ready to take them when your cherries are ready to be picked. Some of them, according to Mr. Roach, will even be glad to enter into a long time contract at this price, and agree to pay cash the day the cherries are picked.

Inasmuch as it takes 5 years for your cherry tree to come into maturity, you must be provided with a cash income in the meantime. Let us show you how you can get this ready cash income from your chickens.

The National Society of Fruitvalers will build your buildings, furnish you with necessary equipment, such as stoves, feed, baby chicks, everything that is necessary to care for them, and in eight months from the time that you start, they will guarantee to buy your broilers and chickens and eggs from you and pay you for them delivered to the central plant at Fruitvale.

FRUITVALE EGGS SOLD AT 70¢ A DOZEN LAST YEAR

No expense of freight or hauling for you. The National Society of Fruitvalers now has contracts from such institutions as the Midday Club, Kunze's Grocery and the Wesley Hospital, for all of the day old eggs now produced at Fruitvale. So great is the demand of Fruitvale eggs that last year as much as 70 cents a dozen was received for Fruitvale day-old eggs in the Chicago market.

Start on a small scale, which is the proper way in any business. You should get 750 baby chicks, from which you should sell about 300 broilers at a fancy price, leaving you with 300 pullets, which should start to lay in October (we are assuming that you started in Fruitvale either in March or in April). These pullets, estimated according to the U. S. Government average, should lay 144 eggs per year per pullet. The records for laying hens at Fruitvale exceed this average, but it is better to be conservative and use U. S. Government figures. You yourself can figure that, at the price which the National Society of Fruitvalers are now getting, your income from 300 hens should be approximately $1,000 a year. So you can see with chickens and cherries at Fruitvale you can make from $1,000 to $2,200 within a comparatively short time after you start.

You Do NOT HAVE TO WORRY ABOUT A

MARKET FOR YOUR PRODUCE

Take a paper and pencil and figure your present income, with the cost of living in the big city, and compare it with the income that you receive in the country, and add to it the advantages of having your own home, living out in the fresh air, having your own flowers, your own garden, your own fresh milk, and the comforts of the country, such as only the wealthy enjoy in the big city. Bear in mind that you have none of the troubles of marketing your products. This is difficult work and frequently adds to the troubles of farming. But if you live at Fruitvale, your eggs and chickens are disposed of through the National Society of Fruitvalers, the cherries through canneries now established in the vicinity of Fruitvale.

EVERYTHING IN FOOD GROWS WONDERFULLY AT FRUITVALE

While your chickens are growing to laying hens, you will have time for planting your kitchen garden in the crops which grow so magnificently without irrigation in the Fruitvale country-potatoes, cabbage, cauliflower, tomatoes, cucumbers, asparagus, onions, carrots, turnips, strawberries, blackberries, gooseberries and currants. One acre of ground cultivated under the direction of the expert- whose services are free to you (and he will supply you with acclimated and tested plants and seeds at cost) - will produce not only enough for the immediate needs of your family, but you can raise enough to keep you through winter. You can buy fresh milk in the neighborhood. You can buy your groceries at Fruitvale, at Whitehall or in Chicago. Nearly every day some farmer in the vicinity kills a steer, a sheep, a lamb or a ... (pages 11 through 14 are missing).

DON'T DELAY WRITE TODAY

The only way possible to provide for old age with most people is to secure an income producing home out in the country. Read some of the letters on page twenty-one. They are from people who were in your position, but who decided after investigation to invest at Fruitvale. They are good substantial people. You can get all the information you want on the subject of Fruitvale from them, or you can write to the National Society of Fruitvalers.

Every statement made in this book booklet can be verified down to the last point. Now is the time for you to act. Don't delay. Go or write to the Fruitvale office, 516 Hearst Building, today. Let them show you the several different propositions, upon anyone of which you can start in this great enterprise. If you can afford to pay down so little as $25, they can show you a way by which you can ultimately own one of these homes at Fruitvale.

You WILL NEVER MISS THE SMOKY CITY IN THE PURE AIR OF FRUITVALE

Suppose that you had bought a Fruitvale farm five years ago. You probably would never have missed the money that you would have paid for owning it. Think what you would have today-a piece of property to yourself, to say nothing of the possibilities of the life out in the open air, and your time, your own, to do with as you see fit.

Why not look ahead five years. Don't be five years from now what you are today., Why not start today to lay the foundation to future independence. The Fruitvalers are ready to welcome you. Are you ready to welcome Fruitvale opportunities?

Bear in mind that the National Society of Fruitvalers will not only supply you with land, but will build your home and put in all modem improvements on terms suitable to you. You could have cold and hot water, electric lights, anytime you want. You can live in Fruitvale exactly as you do in the city, if you want to.

Any man or woman who will attend to business and follow the advice of the poultry experts at Fruitvale can make good money in the poultry business at Fruitvale. In fact, there is no business which could be made to pay better with so small a capital invested than the poultry business when the marketing problem is taken care of.

LOCATION

To those looking for a location to start in the poultry business, Michigan is without doubt, one of the best states, and especially in the vicinity of Muskegon and Oceana Counties. Fruitvale is located in the center of this section. On the property are the beautiful trout streams Sand Creek, Cleveland Creek and Carleton Creek-and the beautiful White River.

Fruitvale is located only fifteen miles north of the great, prosperous and rapidly growing city of Muskegon. There is probably no' city in the country today whose growth is so rapid and stable, who's manufacturing plants are of such variety that no one kind of business calamity could affect it. Its banks are filled with money-its people are thrifty-and it has one of the best harbors on the lake shore. Fruitvale is five hours from Chicago markets by train-one night by boat from either Chicago or Milwaukee.

SOIL

FRUITVALE IS ONE OF THE HEALTHIEST SPOTS IN MICHIGAN

Soil is of vastly more importance in commercial poultry success than is usually considered. Sanitation is of the utmost importance in handling a large flock, and it is difficult or reasonably simple, according to the character of the soil.

The soil at Fruitvale is of a sandy loam character, normally dry near the surface, still holds moisture. Such a condition is ideal. Its sloping nature keeps it well drained, and, all in all, it is almost perfect for the handling of a large flock of chickens.

CHICKENS

The pure sparkling spring water from its trout streams and the abundance of shade, make it ideal, and in the warm days of early spring the young chicks break the speed limit in their scramble for bugs and grasshoppers along these shady slopes-in the cool nights they rest contented and grow like weeds. The March and April hatched pullets start laying in September and keep it up right through the cold weather.

In summing up the three great essential factors in the raising of poultry, one could hardly find more ideal conditions than at Fruitvale. It is seldom that you get these three important factors in one place. You can find the combination of two in a great many, but to get all three is rare-and Fruitvale has them.

THE FRUITVALE COMPANY'S HOME PLANT IS ONE OF THE LARGEST IN THE U.S.

The Company's home plant is long established, well stocked with blooded fowls and conducted in a manner calculated to make for the success of those who adopt poultry raising on either a large or small scale at Fruitvale. An ideal spirit of co-operation is therefore available at Fruitvale for poulterers. The Great Chicago Market is open to Fruitvale poulterers, with cheap, overnight water transportation at all times. The Chicago Market will probably always take the poultry output from Fruitvale, but should it ever become advisable to enlarge the market, there is Milwaukee just across the lake, and even nearer than Chicago, and Grand Rapids and Detroit right in the same state.

We wish that you could go through the National Society of Fruitvalers' laying houses with us and see the thousands, hardy vigorous fowls they contain and hear the merry song of these wonderful layers and the constant "click" of the trap nests, as each (as it seems) vies with the other to produce better than 200 eggs per year, which will entitle them to a place in the breeding house another season.

The Fruitvale strain is kept up each year. The National Society of Fruitvalers spend hundreds of dollars in injecting new blood into its stock. "Winter layers" is the slogan, and we defy anyone to find a sturdier, healthier flock of a single comb white leghorns in the country.

Let us give you an estimate of the first year in the poultry business at Fruitvale, from past experience:

First, a building 14 x 50, having a capacity of 750 baby chicks.

Buildings complete	$450.00
750 day-old chicks	112.50
3 brooder stoves	48.00
2 tons coal	24.00
Feed for 5 months	150.00
	$784.50

(These figures based on 1916 prices which, as you know, are exceptionally high.)

Y OUR CHICKENS WILL MAKE You INDEPENDENT

At the end of three months, you should have about 300 broilers ready for market. These will weigh about one and one-half pounds each and should bring (conservatively speaking) 30¢ per pound or a total of $135.50.

Let us say you raise 80% of your 750 chicks. These will run 50%, pullets. You will have 300 laying pullets which are worth $1.25 each or $375.00

Although Fruitvale hens are trap nested to lay 200 eggs per year, let us figure you will receive 144 eggs a year per hen. We will figure these eggs worth 30¢ per dozen the year round, although we received 45¢ to 70¢ per dozen last winter; 144 eggs, or 12 dozen, which at 30¢ per dozen would mean $3.60 from each laying hen during the season. We will allow $1.00 per head for feed for the eight months, which leaves us a net of $2.60 per hen for the season.

These pullets will very likely start to moult (or lose their feathers) in August and must then be sold as breeders, as their laying period is over.

Good breeders often bring $1.25 to $1.50 each, but let us play safe and figure these worth 75¢ each, or $225.00 for the 300.

Now, let us review our year's work:

Poultry house, complete		$450.00
3 brooder stoves		48.00
2 tons hard coal		24.00
Feed for 5 months		150.00
Feed for 300 pullets @ 1.00 each		300.00
300 1 1/2 lb. pullets @ 30¢ per lb.		135.50
3,600 doz. eggs @ 30¢ per doz.		1,080.00
300 breeders @ 75¢ each		225.00
		$1,938.50
	Cost	972.00
	Profit	$966.50

Profit in addition to being your own employer and having a home in the country and living among friendly people.

You are only a night's ride from Chicago on the Goodrich boats and five hours' ride on the Pere Marquette.

You can visit your friends whenever you want to, and have them visit you.

Farming wasn't anything new to us when we cast our lot among the colony of Fruitvalers. Big fields of com, oats, wheat, barely, rye and grass, horses, cattle, hogs and sheep-year after year grind of plowing, planting, sowing, cultivating, reaping, stock feeding and crop selling-such were our preconceived notions of farming. What a relief to find conditions so vastly different here at Fruitvale! "On a farm" it was work, work, work, work day in and day out. And here-why it's almost a year-around picnic compared to what we were accustomed to. We always considered chickens as a sort of side issue. They were handy to have around, eat scraps and furnish eggs to trade at the grocery for flour and sugar. Here our chickens are one of our chief sources of income. And what with our chickens, fruit and vegetables we are actually making more clear money on our ten acres than we did on the big farm.

Signed,
Mr. and Mrs. Simon George
R. No.4, Fruitvale, Montague,
Michigan.

It has been my observation that in most sections where fruit growing is a recognized industry, large acreage and a great deal of help are primary essentials for success. Much to my surprise, I found that just the opposite is true here at Fruitvale. Here a 10-acre tract will yield as large a net profit as ten times that large a tract will yield in many so called fruit belts. For here quality is the key note of success. And the wonderful fertility of the soil, together with the steady demand in nearby markets for quality products, insures success.

Signed,
Mr. and Mrs. Chas. Hurrell
R. No.4, Fruitvale, Montague,
Michigan

We can truthfully say that we have never really enjoyed life so much as since coming to Fruitvale and joining the happy, prosperous colony of chicken and fruit raisers here. Our ten-acre tract of land is productive beyond our highest expectations, and, since selling arrangements are all looked after by the National Society of Fruitvalers, we always make a good profit on our products. And thanks, too, to the sound advice and able assistance of the company's poultry expert, we have had wonderful success with our chickens. We're mighty glad we came and here we intend to stay.

D. R. Toney,
R. No.4, Fruitvale, Montague,
Michigan

Will you rest content to follow in the same old routine of the job in the city, as you have been all these years! Or will you decide now to break away and get out to this beautiful country, where friendly neighbors await you. Where you can live on your own little farm under the beautiful skies of Michigan. Make your decisions now.

Will you any longer take the chances of the man in the big city crowd, which is pushing, crowding, hustling, making very competition more difficult every day, or will you go where you are sole owner of the beautiful piece of land which will give you a satisfactory income the year round?

Again we say to you- you need practically no capital. The Farm Loan Bank will help you and the National Society of Fruitvalers will help you. A group of ten is now being formed. Join this ten. Don't delay. Do it now. Today. Either write, or call in person.

If you are not quite ready to move to Fruitvale, secure your land, have the company plant your orchard and take care of it, and in five years from now, when you are ready, you can step into an income producing orchard.

"Let what ere befalls,
The Farmer feeds them all."

ACKNOWLEDGEMENTS

I would like to offer my thanks to the following individuals and organizations for their assistance, for without their help, this book would not have been possible.

The Montague Museum-John Leddick
Everett J. King Jr.
The Mrs. Mickelson collection
Mr,s. Drucilla Baker
White Lake Beacon
Whitehall Public Library
Hackley Public Library
The Muskegon Chronicle,
Oceana County Register of Deeds
Muskegon County Register of Deeds
Muskegon County Treasurer
Grand Rapids City Library
Chicago Area Council Boy Scouts of America
(Sheridan Nunn & Glenn Roberts)
Joseph Duerringer
William Duerringer
Chicago Public Library
Don Sandel Surveying
The Newburry Library
Chiago Area Historical Society
Musakegon County Road Commission
Mrs. Edith F. Axelson
Dr. Bealuh Parker Will
Edwin C. Hansen Real Estate
Mr. Harrison (Buddy) Friend
Michigan Dept. of Natural Resources
Dr. Robert E. Reed Sr.
Jessie B. Hagewood
Mrs. Laura Schultz

REFERENCES

It was my goal during this research, to compile as complete a record as possible on the history of the Fruitvale Land Development and the Rochdale Inn. Thus, all printed materials relating to this subject was copied in it's entirety, as are the ones reprinted in this book. Because of this, no references are given as to were the research material was obtained. Instead, a copy of all published works, taped interviews, maps, photographs, etc., are being donated to the Muskegon County Museum, 430 W. Clay AV, Muskegon, MI 49440, as a single source for further reference by anyone interested in this topic.

William P. Hansen, author

CPSIA information can be obtained at www.ICGtesting.com
Printed in the USA
BVIW12n0314051216
469731BV00069B/725